REMEMBERING THE POOR

REMEMBERING THE POOR

The History of Paul's Collection for Jerusalem

DIETER GEORGI

Abingdon Press
Nashville

REMEMBERING THE POOR:
THE HISTORY OF PAUL'S COLLECTION FOR JERUSALEM

This book is printed on recycled, acid-free paper.

Library of Congress Cataloging-in-Publication Data

Georgi, Dieter.
[Geschichte der Kolleket des Paulus für Jerusalem.] English:
Remembering the poor: the history of Paul's collection for Jerusalem / Dieter Georgi.
p. cm.
Translation of: Geschichte der Kollekt des Paulus für Jerusalem.
Includes bibliographical references.
ISBN 0-687-36117-6 (alk. paper)
1. Bible. N.T. Epistles of Paul—criticism, interpretation, etc. 2. Church finance—History—Early church, ca. 30-600. 3. Jewish Christians—History—Early church, ca. 30-600. 4. Paul, the Apostle, Saint—Journeys. 5. Poor—Biblical teaching. 6. Jerusalem in Christianity. I. Title.
BS2655.C53G46 1991
225.6'7—dc20 91-12720
CIP

MANUFACTURED IN THE UNITED STATES OF AMERICA

PREFACE TO THE ORIGINAL GERMAN EDITION

The following study was accepted as a thesis for qualification as a university teacher, by the Faculty of Theology of the University of Heidelberg, in 1962. It represents the result of a suggestion made by Professor D. Günther Bornkamm, my admired teacher.

My special thanks are due to my friend Professor Dr. Klaus Wegenast for his selfless assistance in promoting the publication of this book.

I must also mention my gratitude to the Deutsche Forschungsgesellschaft for the printing, and to the publisher for the help rendered in the preparation of this volume.

Dieter Georgi
Cambridge, Mass., April, 1965

PREFACE TO THE ENGLISH EDITION

Biblical studies in the United States and Canada, multifarious as they are, have at least three concerns in common: the drama of the text, the drama of the environment, and the drama of hermeneutics.

Structuralist, rhetorical-critical, and literary-critical discussions and those on intertextuality view the text not as something flat and dead but as a textual process, a world full of suspense and fascination. The letters, words, and sentences function as buoys on a deep and moving sea with any number of under- and cross-currents.

The insight relates easily to the other drama, that of the environment of biblical texts. Studies in archaeology, history of religion, and social history explore the interplay between the situation of the text and its audience, their response and reaction. The issues of the texts are not taken in ideological isolation but are related to their historical, cultural, social, and political environment. The faces and voices of others besides the author, insiders and outsiders alike, are looked at as involved in a much larger environment. Possible opposition or modification beyond the author's intention are at least as much issues of inquiry as the interpretative affirmation of the text. The author is but an element, object as well as subject, in the momentum of history understood no longer merely as a religious development but as a cultural, social, and political process as well.

The trend to bring out Christian uniqueness and superiority vis à vis Judaism and paganism, fortunately, is the goal of fewer and fewer biblical scholars, at least on the American side of the Atlantic. Together with this the tendency to harmonize biblical plurality or to select and single out what is doctrinally true and pure has lessened. There is an increasing acknowledgment of the fact that into the last decades of the first century C.E. the various branches of the Jesus movement represented an internal migration within Judaism, a very pluralistic religion in the first century C.E. anyhow. The History of Religion School's claim that transparency existed between the early church and paganism has also found confirmation.

When I came to the United States in 1964 biblical hermeneutics had become fashionable. But the civil rights movement, black power and black consciousness, liberation theology, the women's movement, and feminist theology, and many other related phenomena showed very quickly that Old World hermeneutics were still navel gazing, affirming the dominant social and political forces. The movements mentioned brought about a new, critical hermeneutics that showed not only the emancipatory trends of the Bible but also its oppressive sides. The fact that the Bible has shaped our present society and culture calls for a critical view of this contribution, ugly as this sometimes may be.

But the discovery of the oppressive nature of the Bible's function in much of our culture and society is also a process of emancipation of the Bible and the praxis behind it. The issues that moved the people of old are suddenly heard again in all their strangeness, frequently functioning as exercises in subversion. They have been covered up, accommodated, and domesticated. These discoveries challenge and question common contemporary presuppositions, bring about new paradigms, and create a new map that thoroughly upsets the old one.

In 1964 biblical studies in the United States and Canada did not have any of these dramatic dimensions. A comparison of the programs of the annual meetings of the Society of Biblical Literature in 1964 in New York and 1990 in New Orleans can easily prove this. The social changes taking place in the world in general and in academic education in particular slowly caught on also in the world of biblical scholarship. While in Cambridge, Massachusetts in 1965 I finished my German book on the collection, during my first year of teaching in the States, the start of nearly twenty years of training students on both coasts of the continent. The book on the collection contained the methodological, historical, and theological charter of my subsequent teaching in the United States. Much of it has been picked up, furthered, and spread by my students and others. I am happy that I could contribute to the changes mentioned above. I have been able to add to this contribution through further teaching visits after my return to my home country in 1984.

But, unlike my book on the opponents of Paul in II Corinthians, this book on the collection has received little discussion beyond the circles of my students at the Graduate Theological Union in Berkeley and at Harvard Divinity School. The book's less-than-off-Broadway existence was due to the marginal place of its German publishing house. Adding to this problem was the format chosen by the publisher, in which the footnotes, often rather long, could be read only with a magnifying glass.

Immediately after the appearance of the German version, Krister Stendahl urged its translation into English, and he has continued to do so. I was prevented from following this suggestion by many factors, not the least my heavy involvement in the practical affairs of teaching on the new continent and now again on the old.

I have revised the old book at many points. But most of the text has remained, for although the changes in biblical scholarship in North America seem to have made a repetition of some of my points unnecessary, there are still observations that need stressing. The issue of the collection has found little interest as yet despite the elaborate treatment Paul devotes to it and its importance for his biography and the organization of his congregations. Only two monographs have appeared on the matter, one by Keith Nickle and the other by Hans Dieter Betz, the latter of which is limited to II Corinthians 8 and 9. Nickle pursues the subject-matter under a more limited scope than I do. Betz has made the two collection chapters a foil for a very interesting exercise in rhetorical criticism. Little else has been done on the collection (see the bibliography). Arguments raised against my own interpretation have led me to some clarifications in this present English translation.

Economy and money have found even less attention in New Testament scholarship despite the increasing interest in social history and social criticism (although the ancient economy or the role of money in it still await intensive description and discussion). The same is true of the Pauline attempt to elaborate on the concept of spiritual worship, and this in the context of the flow of money. The importance of the collection for Paul's vision of the church and his communal organization have remained basically unnoticed. Scholarly discussion has overlooked the close relationship between Paul's concepts of Christology and justification and the collection. I have reflected on the impact of these issues in a meditation I have added as an afterword to this translation.

There is a further point I need to make. As a student I had turned down Professor Günther Bornkamm's suggestion of writing a paper on II Corinthians 9, one of the two collection chapters, for his seminar on "Confession in the New Testament" at Heidelberg in 1949, because the collection theme appeared to me insufficiently theological. When I planned my second dissertation, required at German universities for teaching credentials, political and ecclesial experience had begun to convince me that praxis instigates and informs theory. The combined listening to the praxis of the immediate contemporary situation and to the praxis of the Pauline churches had made me politically and ecclesially conscious. This had given the critical scholarly and ministerial perception new dimensions. The issue of confession had changed into a very lively one. What had turned away the student of 1949, the down to earth side of Paul's discussion of confession, had come to life for the theologian of the late fifties. The restoration of the German state and church alike, the peace issue, and, connected with both, the economy had also become items of the agenda of ecclesial and theological criticism.

Running away from one's own history would not have been the truly critical route. The scholar needs particularly to take a critical stand from within. I have continued to do so. I have remained consciously a theologian and a church person, an ordained minister. My most recent experience of heavy involvement in politics and the administration of a large state university in a major economic center, nicknamed Bankfurt, have confirmed this conviction. The theological disciplines must maintain their identity and integrity in order to remain a form of scholarly discourse of equal value and standing with the other sciences; and this is respected. The ordained minister working as scholar is looked at as anything but a pious harmonizer. Therefore, my book retains this theological and ecclesial dimension. It fits together easily with the critical dimensions of social history and economics.

There are some major differences between this English edition and the German edition. The first version of the book contained a discussion of I Thessalonians 2:14-16. I left it out this time after Birger Pearson decisively changed my mind regarding its authenticity.

There are some linguistic changes, including the use of inclusive language throughout. In my book on the opponents of Paul in II Corinthians, I have argued that there is no historical reason for using the terms *Christian* and *Christianity* as denotations for phenomena of the first century. I have replaced them by such terms as *Jesus believers, Jesus* or *Christ community,* and *Jesus movement.* While these terms are clumsy, we cannot imitate the practice of the early church using terms like *holy ones, elect ones,* and *just ones.* Given our socio-religious situation today, such terminology would only create confusion.

This book would not have come about without some very active help from other persons. My thanks go to the translator, Ingrid Racz, as well as to the three persons whose criticisms and suggestions greatly furthered content and style of the afterword: Dr. Kelly Del Tredici, and my two sons, Karsten and Martin Georgi. Lukas Bormann, Nicol Kramer, Jenny Elisabeth Pauly, and Angela Standhartinger also gave excellent assistance. Dr. Rex Matthews at Abingdon Press, his predecessor, Dr. Davis Perkins, and the Abingdon staff deserve praise for their patient and constructive encouragement, accompaniment, and conclusion of the productive process.

I dedicate this book to Ernst Käsemann and Krister Stendahl because both have constantly challenged my theological presuppositions, particularly with respect to the topic of justification, each in his own inimitable way. Without them I would not have said what I say now. But neither of the two can be held accountable for the results the reader holds in his or her hands.

Frankfurt/Main, September 1990
Dieter Georgi

CONTENTS

INTRODUCTION

The story of Paul's collection for the church of Jerusalem is full of dramatic development. This book has been written to trace that development in its historical context.

As the collection was a constant concern of Paul's from the days of the convention at Jerusalem until his last journey to that city, its story can be viewed truly as a mirror of the apostle's missionary effort as a whole. Hence, depicting the occurrences linked to the collection must inevitably entail a step-by-step study of Paul's mission itself. The difficulties and risks involved in this kind of historical and chronological evaluation are obvious; it must be of a hypothetical nature by necessity. But hypotheses are the daily bread of scholarship; there can be no scientific endeavor without them. Yet, the possible dangers of overhypothesizing are of lesser importance than the other dangerous temptations to which the scholar must be careful not to succumb: those of relativism and extreme historicism. And yet, despite these possible traps, there is no way of dodging the question of historicity when it comes to appreciating the missionary and theological endeavors undertaken within the early church. Once this is recognized as factual, it will become apparent that there is history hidden in the stories the Bible tells us—a circumstance, of course, not entirely unfamiliar to the theologian.

Until the nineteenth century biblical exegetes saw no problem in conjunction with Paul's collecting funds for Jerusalem. The corresponding texts only seemed to show that the members of the early church lived together in harmony and cared for one another, thus standing out as an example to be followed by later generations. It was only in the nineteenth century that a group of theologians at the German University of Tübingen (the so-called Tübingen School) detected a direct link between Paul's collection and the disputes exegetical research had found existing between Jewish and Gentile Jesus believers: the battle between the Judaizers (i.e., intentionally Torah-linked agitators among the Jewish Jesus believers) and Paul. In the light of this discovery, Paul's statement that the collection was based on an agreement reached between himself and the church leadership in Jerusalem (Gal. 2:10) created problems. At first glance Paul's statement seemed to point to his willingness to go along with the demands made on him by the Jesus congregation in Jerusalem, thus yielding to them. This appeared to contradict the fundamental doctrinal opposition the Tübingen School had discovered between Paul and both the leaders of the church in Jerusalem and their Judaizing fellow travelers in the Diaspora. The people at Tübingen had detected that notion of a basic conflict in that very epistle (Galatians).

One could, of course, deny the historicity and authenticity of Galatians 2:10 (as scholars like Steck, Weisse, Michelsen, Baljon, and van Manen had done). Indeed, Paul's mention in Romans 15:30 of his apprehension of possible difficulties arising at the moment the collected funds would be handed over to the congregation at Jerusalem seemed to fit better the hypothesis put forth by the Tübingen School. Ferdinand Christian Baur's denial of the authenticity of the fifteenth chapter of Romans did not meet general acceptance.

At first, attempts were made by the Tübingen people to solve the problem of Galatians 2:10 by ascribing both the initiating and the carrying out of the collection to Paul personally; the entire project and its realization were both seen as Paul's own doing and considered a demonstration of his own theological intentions. The goal and the outgrowth of Galatians 2:10 were read as confession of faith and as testimony to the self-sacrificing love on the part of Paul's non-Jewish Jesus believers meant to convince the still Torah-bound Jewish Jesus-believing congregations by means of material evidence: The congregation at Jerusalem and those who went along with them were to realize that God stood behind Paul's missionary work. The collection was to herald by material means the still missing unity of faith of all Jesus believers. Carl Holsten, for instance, held the opinion that Paul was hoping to check Judaizing opposition, particularly in Jerusalem, to ensure the continuation of his mission both in the West and in the East.[1] On the basis of this consideration the collection for Jerusalem had suddenly acquired a clearly historical profile.

However, such reading of scriptures contained an element of inconsistency in the otherwise consistent exegesis typical of the Tübingen School. But it was probably this contradiction to the otherwise (allegedly) overly consistent, and therefore disliked, view of the Tübingers about the early church that gave their idea of the collection undisputed acceptance throughout the nineteenth and part of the twentieth centuries.

Only when Karl Holl published his famous article on Paul's concept of the church was the missing link in this traditional exegesis finally found. According to Holl, the collection sharply reflects the fundamental difference between Paul's own notion of what the church should be and the position adopted by the early Jesus believers in Jerusalem. Holl was the first to attempt a just evaluation of the actual part played by the Jesus believers in Jerusalem in planning the collection and to determine this part with the greatest possible accuracy. For him the collection was a tax demanded by the leaders of the Jerusalem church corresponding to the traditional Jewish temple tax. Paul, on the other hand, tried to instill an entirely different meaning for the collection—one that he derived from his pneumatic and charismatic concept of the church, a concept closely bound up with the idea of *ἀγάπη*.

By the time Karl Holl wrote his article, it had, of course, become increasingly clear to biblical scholars that there existed a close interdependence between the concept of the collection and the principles according to which the early church was to be run—and Holl decided to make this interdependence the very focal point of his inquiry. He was the first to realize that it had been the eschatological expectation that prompted the Jesus believers in Jerusalem to participate actively in promoting the collection plan; when addressing the Jesus believers of Jerusalem as the "poor" or the "saints," Paul was only pointing to their own eschatological self-understanding. Starting from there, Holl drew attention to the possibility that the demand for a collection might have had something to do with the highly eschatologically oriented Jerusalem ideology of that time and that this ideology must have had a bearing on the thinking of the Jesus community in Jerusalem. Holl felt that the Jesus believers must have been guided by that ideology in establishing their concept of "church" itself, just as they were guided by it when calling for a collection.

Various other scholars have also stressed that the special role within salvation history traditionally ascribed to Jerusalem as the privileged locale predestined for the eschatological event, on the one hand, and to the Jesus congregation in that city, on the other, must be taken into account in seeking to arrive at a correct understanding of what the collection represented at the time.[2]

Today Holl's idea that the collection had originally been a centrally oriented tax has lost much of its momentum. Only Ethelbert Stauffer has defended it and has done so even more radically than its originator.[3] But the theory that Paul's collection and the church-constituting principles adhered to by the early Jesus community were intimately related to each other has found general acceptance.

On the other hand, the true objective pursued by Jerusalem when agreeing on a collection is no longer investigated. Hardly anyone seems to be interested now in Holl's other—and basically correct—findings; namely, that the descriptions given of the collection in the various New Testament documents do not always attest to the same outlook on the matter. Holl had stressed the absolute need for keeping in mind that the collection and the concept of "church" must not be viewed as two separate issues. He insisted that the collection was meant to highlight the soterological principle behind the founding of the Jesus community as a whole and the political dependency, historically speaking, on Jerusalem by all individual Jesus groups elsewhere—that is, the dominant role performed by Jerusalem as the very heart of all Jesus-related life.[4] Thus, while shedding sufficient light on the commonly accepted view of the church in early Jesus thinking, he was able to maintain in the foreground of his analysis Paul's true intentions by placing his strongest focus on the practical (indeed pedagogical!) objectives that guided the apostle when starting the collection. Such a focus acknowledged the historic character of the church and Jerusalem as its place of origin, although without any juridical prerogatives attached to that position (see Rom. 15:26-33). It also protected the Gentile church from drifting off into a series of disconnected "mysteries" groups, devoid of all historic frame of reference.[5]

It was primarily Johannes Munck who demonstrated the close relationship between the collection, its establishment, and its organizational structure, on the one hand, with Paul's missionary thinking and strategy on the other. Munck focused his investigation on the soteriological motifs guiding Paul's activities, stressing both their eschatological and demonstrative edifying aspects. Unfortunately, Munck's work fell short of its own objective—namely, the laying bare of the apostle's missionary and theological pragmatism. This is due to Munck's failure to differentiate between eschatological hope and Apocalyptic speculation, as well as to his determination to view the latter as an exclusively historical criterion. This, of course, meant forcing the texts.

W. Franklin's monographical study on the collection (the only one of its kind) offers, in spite of its inherent methodological insufficiencies, enough material for recognizing Paul's collection for Jerusalem as having evolved within a framework of historical and circumstantial determination.[6] For Franklin, the collection sprang from the existential situation of the early church, especially as regards the financial neediness of the Jesus community at Jerusalem. But Paul shifted the emphasis to that of solidarity and participation by everyone in all faith related activities. This solidarity was to provide a firm basis for the lasting interrelatedness and unity of all Jesus-believing congregations. Paul aimed to check both the danger of isolation, which threatened the Jesus believers at Jerusalem, and the risk of a schismatic separation on the part of the Gentile Jesus believers. According to Franklin, the collection represented the living, tangible evidence not only of the universal orientation of all Jesus-believing congregations, but also of their rootedness in history and, thus, of their mutual relatedness through tradition.

The present study is intended to draw a picture of the ups and downs involved in the history of Paul's collection for Jerusalem.

All questions raised in exegetical scholarship in conjunction with these vissicitudes will be taken into account. In so doing, light will be shed not only on the historic character of Pauline theological reflection, but also on the theological component of the historical act.

CHAPTER 1

THE CONVENTION AT JERUSALEM (48 C.E.)[1]

+I+
+I+

A. THE DEVELOPMENTS LEADING UP TO THE CONVENTION

No less than thirteen years after his calling as "apostle to the nations,"[2] Paul, together with Barnabas, traveled to Jerusalem to enter into negotiations with the leaders of the local Jesus congregation.[3] Given the successful missionary work of the church of Antioch, as well as Paul's (and Barnabas's) probable active participation in it, the meeting in Jerusalem could have constituted the crowning of Paul's (and Barnabas's) past endeavors, had it not marked the beginning of a far more important development. As it happened, following this meeting Paul found himself with a completely new missionary task, bearing much more of his personal stamp than his work before and destined to become the very foundation of his later fame.

A first look at the special constellation of events surrounding this so-called Council of the Apostles shows the following: Modern research (especially that of Martin Dibelius[4] and Ernst Haenchen[5]) has demonstrated that the description of this synodical convention given in Acts 15 cannot be considered a trustworthy account of the event. The only dependable reference we possess is Paul's own report in Galatians 2:1-10. Yet, even this document has met with strong skepticism on the part of numerous scholars, who justify their doubts by pointing to the apparently adversarial style of the Epistle to the Galatians as a whole.[6] One cannot doubt that after 1:6 Galatians is highly polemical or that the passages describing the incidents that occurred during the Jerusalem convention are clearly meant to reject the accusations made against the apostle by the later Galatian opponents.[7] Certainly, Paul gives only an extremely succinct picture of what happened in Jerusalem, occasionally shifting the emphasis as he sees fit. But he does so on account of the new situation that had unfolded following the meeting.[8] When Paul wrote the Epistle to the Galatians, he no longer acted as a delegate of the Jesus congregation at Antioch. His connection with that congregation had, generally, become very loose. In fact, the very contact with Barnabas, his co-delegate to Jerusalem, had now been broken off.[9] Even from a purely objective point of view, Paul had meanwhile developed into the most outstanding missionary among pagans, so much so that—since the time of the convention at Jerusalem—the mission to the Gentiles had become very much identified with his work and person (even though this identification might not be entirely historically accurate). Similarly, since the year 48 C.E., through his own missionary activities, Simon Peter had acquired a position that clearly set him apart from other leading figures in Jerusalem.[10]

All these changes are reflected in Galatians 2, but it would be erroneous to view the narrative here as a tendentious distortion of facts. Three considerations speak against this hypothesis:

1. The convention and the events connected with it still held great importance for Paul when he wrote Galatians. Paul would have to presuppose that his opponents, who were apparently knowledgeable about affairs in the conservative Jewish Jesus community, would be critical co-readers of his presentation in Galatians as well.

2. Paul's report clearly mirrors the tensions existing between his desire to give a historically correct description of what happened and his urge to actualize the related events. The syntactical unevenness well testifies to that.[11] It is precisely this balancing intention behind the narrative that warrants its authenticity.

3. There is no proof that Paul deliberately suppressed essential information or that he had (wittingly or unwittingly) forgotten anything. All this is equally valid for the issue of the collection itself.

A superficial reading of the report leaves one with the impression that Paul and Barnabas had been prompted by divine revelation to speak to the congregation in Jerusalem as if it were a superior, authoritative body, and to receive from it a declaration of unobjectionability or license.[12] Had this been the case, however, the convention would have been overshadowed from beginning to end by the idea of dependency on the part of the Antiochenes and their delegation on the Jerusalem authorities as their decision-making church government. Logically, the agreement to set up the collection would have to consider this governing authority of the Jerusalem church, in particular that of the "Pillars." This impression must be strongest for those who consider the picture drawn in Acts of the relationship between Jerusalem and other Jesus congregations as historically correct, particularly when one accepts as plausible the designation of Barnabas as "Syrian nuncio" of the congregation at Antioch.[13]

However, a close study of the text of Galatians 2 reveals that the Jerusalem convention had come about as a summit meeting evolving as a result of and response to some widespread and complex intrigue within the church itself. This intrigue, which probably originated among Torah-bound Jesus believers within the Aramaic-speaking church in Jerusalem's sphere of influence (perhaps even in Jerusalem itself), was already undermining the communities of the Gentile Jesus believers, even as far as Antioch.[14] It is indeed only in describing the negotiations on the collection that Paul refers to the "false brothers and sisters, stealthily brought in" who "had come to spy on us and to see what freedom we enjoyed in Christ Jesus, so that they might enslave us" (Gal. 2:4).[15] The very content of this declaration, as well as its position in the immediate context of the epistle, shows that the delegates from Antioch had for some time been familiar with such people and thus had good reason to be on their guard against them.[16] Further, the aggressive wording of Galatians 2:4 seems to indicate that Paul and Barnabas were confronted with those brothers and sisters again, not only in Jerusalem itself, but also in other congregations, where they had to fight similar opponents at a later date.[17]

It appears that those "false brothers and sisters"—who must have been Judaizing zealots—had penetrated Gentile Jesus-believing communities and "spied" there.[18] The very choice of terminology seems to indicate that those "false brothers and sisters" had nosily pried into the Gentile Jesus community's freedom from the Law to find out its actual character and the resulting practice. Obviously their intentions had not been of a friendly nature, or they would not have given the impression of "spying," nor been reproached as planning to put Paul and his friends "in chains." It seems reasonable to conclude, therefore, that these Judaizers were not only collecting incriminating data, but that they also meant to put their findings to practical use. The use they must have had in mind was to produce evidence for the benefit of the Torah-abiding Jewish Jesus believers in Palestine (and in Jerusalem in particular) to the effect that the Gentile Jesus people's teaching and practice of freedom from the Law was incompatible with and dangerous for the Jesus faith. The material gathered was probably intended to compel the Jewish Jesus believers either to order the Gentile congregations to submit to circumcision and the Law in general, or, failing this, to cancel all relations with them.[19]

Logically, the church in Antioch felt that something had to be done about a threat such as this. Should they allow it to develop further and unhampered, they risked the danger of seeing the entire community of Jewish Jesus people eventually swayed by these plotters, opening up the danger that the Gentile Jesus believers would be threatened with a choice between either their freedom from the Law or the disintegration of the larger church community as such. It was precisely this danger that caused the Antiochenes to send Paul and Barnabas as their delegates to Jerusalem.[20]

None of this contradicts Paul's statement that they had decided to come to the city of Jerusalem following a "revelation." He does not specify where or in what way the revelation had occurred, but from what we know of him and the general custom of the early church, we may assume that the revelation in question was the outcome of an assembly of the congregation at Antioch, with the final decision understood as a breakthrough of prophetic authority.[21]

Furthermore, Paul had chosen Titus, a Greek member of the Antiochene congregation, to come along with them to the convention. The provocative aspect of this gesture was obvious: it is hardly possible that Paul—with his former zeal for the Law—had not foreseen the powerful effect the presence of the young Greek would have on the Law-abiding Jewish Jesus believers in Jerusalem.[22] Seen from this angle, Titus's accompaniment of Paul and Barnabas establishes circumcision and obedience to the Law as major issues for calling the convention. Paul's decision concerning Titus—indeed, the fact that he went to Jerusalem at all—testifies to the true objective pursued by Antioch: to seek complete clarification on all constitutional problems in question, and to do so openly and publicly. In the person of the non-circumcised Titus the entire non-circumcised Gentile church was symbolically attending the meeting. The attitude taken toward Titus must instantly reveal what the Torah-abiding part of the church intended to decide on the crucial issue of communion with non-circumcised Gentile Jesus people—a decision that would, in its turn, mirror the position they were willing to adopt to the type of preaching this brand of the church had been developing.

B. THE NEGOTIATIONS

In Jerusalem, Titus became the living illustration of what the freedom of Gentile believers was all about.[23] Apparently, someone did demand his circumcision.[24] We can no longer find out exactly who made the request and on what grounds they did so. The request could have come either as an ultimatum or as a proposal of compromise. In any case, we know that Paul and Barnabas remained adamantly opposed to the proposition.[25] They must have done so because they understood the requested circumcision obviously not as an *adiaphoron* (a matter of indifference) but as an act that symbolized submission under the Law as a necessary requirement for ecclesial communion and full partnership in the church.[26]

One can conclude from all this that the participants at the convention dealt with one another as partners, not as superiors and subordinates or as decision-making authorities, on the one hand, and decision-accepting subjects on the other. The situation was one of a joint struggle for a reasoned solution to a conflict, not one where a report was submitted by one party in the expectation of hearing a ruling by another party acting as an authoritative board. That the Antiochenes had journeyed to Jerusalem and not delegates of Jerusalem to Antioch should not surprise us, since the clarification was in the interest of Antioch. This interest was not merely juridical; on a very basic level this issue was seen as threatening the ecumenical nature of the church, and should, therefore, be discussed and decided on an equal level by the entities concerned. Because the congregation in Antioch was under attack, and because they were more immediately concerned about a resolution of the differences, they took the initiative. Thus it would be a mistake to view the coming of their delegates to Jerusalem as an expression of their recognition of the superior juridical and doctrinal authority of the Jerusalem church or its leaders.[27]

Nothing in Paul's epistle points to the leaders of the Jerusalem church as fulfilling the functions of a centrally organized administration of the early church at large. Had this been the case, Paul and Barnabas would have been summoned for a hearing or negotiations or, at best, granted an audience. There is no hint that the Antiochenes had requested such, nor had they been subpoenaed or ordered to appear.[28]

Although Luke never tires of stressing the superiority of the "Twelve"—the allegedly original, or "true," apostles—not even Acts refers to any real administrative or governing functions of the Twelve that could be viewed as central ecumenical governance. Certainly, Luke has the Twelve send delegates (*nuncios*) into the world on a missionary tour, Paul being one of them. Luke also mentions occasional reports made to Jerusalem by such delegates. But all this cannot be interpreted as a sign of "Jerusalem" standing for "government" in the sense of a governing authority over other churches.

So Luke proves that Paul's silence about a governing function of either Peter or James or the Twelve or the "Pillars" cannot be ascribed to any tendentiousness on the part of the author of Galatians. For Luke, the Twelve were some sort of impartial, superior board, untouched by the frictions or little squabbles inevitable in the everyday life of any group. He saw the agency of the Twelve as both representing the Jesus community to the outside world and as a board of appeal and of arbitration within the church. This concept corresponds to the image a person living in the eastern provinces of the Roman Empire held about the character and function of the caesar's establishment in Rome around 100 C.E.

Heinrich Schlier holds that Paul's journey to Jerusalem was to bring about an "exchange of views between the new and extraordinary apostle Paul and the old and regular apostles."[29] This, however, would amount to judging the apostles of the early church in terms of modern-day career patterns applicable to public servants of both the church and state bureaucracies. Such exegesis is not borne out by I Corinthians 15. But, most important, at the time of the Jerusalem summit, Paul had already been active as an apostle for thirteen years; it would be incongruous, therefore, to argue in terms of "old" and "new" apostleship. Finally, how could an interpretation like this be concordant with Barnabas's functions and the situation prevailing in the Antiochene congregation as a whole?

But there is also Paul's statement: "I presented to them the Gospel I had been preaching to the Gentiles and I turned especially to the esteemed ones (with the question) whether my running was or is in vain" (Gal. 2:2). Must we conclude that this desire to fetch an opinion was necessarily synonymous with his acknowledgment of the juridical superiority of the Jerusalem ecclesiastic nobility?[30] The original Greek wording calls for no such reading. Expert opinions can also be given by equals. Neither was Paul seeking an arbitrator's certification on the correctness or incorrectness of his preaching or theological position, and even less so did he come to Jerusalem fearing he might perhaps fail his theological exam.[31] Quite to the contrary, the Antiochenes had come to Jerusalem in order to confront the congregation there as directly as possible with their case—that is, to ask straight out whether the message promulgated in and by Antioch was not, in fact, conducive to constructing and safeguarding the church.

Paul uses the term *running* elsewhere to refer to successful preaching—namely, the founding and maintaining of a congregation full of stamina and life.[32] But successful preaching for him was not merely in the interest of Gentile believers but of the Christ community as a whole. For Paul, one could not exist without the other; there was only one church community, however scattered it was geographically.[33] Hence, the solidarity and communion among all the various Christ communities constituted the very prerequisite for Paul's work. This is the basic meaning also behind Galatians 2:2, even though the passage appears to address first of all the Gentile church.

Paul tells us nothing about whether his (or, better, the delegation's) report in Jerusalem met with success or not. He simply continues by saying that not even Titus was asked to undergo circumcision (v. 3). No doubt, Paul is rather purposely uninformative. Could it be that he meant to pass over in silence a doctrinal and/or juridical decision taken against the Antiochene report by the leadership of Jerusalem? Does he remain silent here to forego even the slightest suspicion about any statutory dependency in which he might have found himself in respect to the Jerusalem authorities?

Various considerations indicate that this was not the case:

Paul could not have manipulated his report to this degree and with such imposterous intent in the face of his assertion in verse 1:20: "What I am writing to you about, by God, I am not lying."

Such deliberate passing over in silence of vital information would have been extremely poor tactics, since any formal resolution on the correctness of his preaching the gospel unfettered by the Law would have equipped him with a powerful weapon against the Galatian opponents.

The special mention that not even Titus had been asked to submit to circumcision indicates that a general discussion must have preceded on the necessity of circumcision for Gentiles—a discussion focusing in particular and in an exemplary way on the person of Titus.[34] But such a debate—including the controversy over Titus's circumcision—would have been pointless had there been a prior doctrinal or juridical resolution on the acceptability of the Law-free gospel as preached at Antioch.

Consequently, the transition from verse 2 to verse 3 should be read as a tacit reference to what could be paraphrased as follows: "I did so in order to inquire whether my way of preaching the gospel had not, after all, proven effective in setting up a congregation instilled with true life. Yes, indeed it had, answered most of them; and even during the subsequent discussions on the lawful requirement of circumcision for Gentiles, our point of view had such persuasive force that not even the call for circumcision (at least on the part of Titus) could carry the day."

The further development of the negotiations also shows that no juridical or doctrinal resolution had been adopted following the Antiochene report; there was no ruling on the correctness of the preaching performed in Antioch itself or the areas of mission adjacent to it. Such a resolution would have shown forcibly in the final results of the entire convention, specifically in regard to the agreement on the collection. In fact, all I can conclude from the texts themselves is that, on the basis of the report submitted by Paul and Barnabas, the "Pillars" were satisfied to take note of the spiritual and theological independence of Antioch.[35] They had "seen" (v. 7) and "acknowledged" (v. 9). This can only mean one thing: The results and the content of the agreement arrived at in Jerusalem had been worked out by equal partners. It is precisely this agreement that defines the "esteemed ones" of the Jerusalem congregation and the delegates from Antioch as peers in the discussion. The "esteemed ones" or the "Pillars" did not understand themselves as a superior body.

Further, verse 6 could, at first glance, indicate that the leaders of the Jerusalem congregation held special rights: "And from the esteemed ones—whatever people they were, does not make any difference to me; for God does not pay attention to the appearance of an individual—they namely did not enjoin anything in particular." This statement seems to warrant the conclusion that the leaders in Jerusalem had the power "to add" something, but that they had foregone their rights in this particular case. Understood in this sense, the statement would mean that the Jerusalem church dignitaries were indeed a superior body. The syntactical inconsistency of the sentence could then be understood as an indication that Paul had started to give a more elaborate historical report, but then resolved to suppress this information, fearing that such specification might strengthen the idea of special privileges of the Jerusalem authorities, and thus prove prejudicial to himself in his disputes with the Galatian opponents.

But this means that Paul had found it difficult to give an exact description of the events because the truth about them would have been bad press for him in the actual situation of the letter.

Such politics would have been a poor defense and an even poorer offensive strategy in the face of people who—being familiar with the situation themselves—would immediately have seen the weakness of the argument. Hence, for greater accuracy the Greek must be rendered thus: "The esteemed ones did not impose anything further on me"—the implication being that Paul alludes here to the so-called Decree of the Apostles (Acts 15:24-29). As soon as one accepts this reading, it follows that Paul wanted to say that there had been a special condition added later to what had previously been negotiated and decided in Jerusalem, but that this new burden had come later and without his consent.[36]

This implication presupposes that the tactics pursued by Simon Peter and other Jewish Jesus believers in connection with the Antioch incident (Gal. 2:11-21) had not only resulted in a break-up with Paul personally but had also brought about a compromise solution between Jewish and Gentile Jesus believers, following which circumcised Jews and non-circumcised Gentiles would be able to co-exist in mixed Jesus congregations (the resolution laid down in the so-called Decree of the Apostles).[37] The leaders of the church in Jerusalem might even have had the final say in the drafting of that Decree.[38] But, no matter when exactly it had been passed, the stipulations contained in that Decree had broadened the original Jerusalem agreement and altered it drastically.

Assuming that Paul was aware of the Decree and its stipulations, the wording of this particular passage in the epistle would prove that he wished to distance himself from the Decree and, in so doing, show that he was the only one from the former Antiochene congregation to continue to hold to the initial terms of the Jerusalem agreement. This might also be the implication behind the emphasis on the "to me" in Galatians 2:6.

The parenthesis in Galatians 2:6 is best understood as a polemical rectification Paul felt had become indispensable after the mention of "the esteemed ones"—a rectification to the position of his opponents concerning these Jerusalem dignitaries.[39] And when he writes that it makes no difference to him what kind of people these esteemed ones were, he clearly means to stress that whatever their former merits or qualities were, he could not consider such merits the basis of their "esteemed" status. For Paul, they were esteemed because God had resolved to elect and to call them—just as God had called Paul himself (Gal. 1:15-16).[40] I fully agree with Heinrich Schlier,[41] who also reads this passage as a refusal on Paul's part to bequeath to the Jerusalem authorities leadership and superior status on the grounds that they had formerly been connected with the historical Jesus,[42] and because they were of Palestinian Jewish origin.

Such reading accords well with the overall polemical tone of the Epistle to the Galatians, especially in chapters 1 and 2.[43] Paul must simply have felt that he had to polemicize here in order to introduce a necessary correction. Once the correction had been made, he resumed his narrative by marking a new start stylistically. The adjustment Paul had undertaken was meaningful also in terms of the correct understanding of the negotiations as such: It was to establish once and for all that neither then nor now did the leaders of the Jerusalem church hold superior status.[44]

C. THE AGREEMENT

1. Mutual Acknowledgment of Independence

The convention in Jerusalem resulted in a contractual accord reached by the representatives of both the Jewish and the Gentile Jesus-believing congregations. As Paul puts it: "James and Peter and John, esteemed as the Pillars of the church, gave us the right hand of fellowship" (Gal. 2:9).

It was Heinrich Schlier who succeeded in showing that the handshake mentioned here stood for the conclusion of a contract, the formal and official sealing of joint trusteeship or executorship.[45] It cannot be made out today whether Paul gives the wording of the contract or merely reports on the essential points listed therein or provides an actualized allusion. The detailed reference to the names of the partners to the agreement, as well as the use of an unwieldy phrasing characteristic for contracts, leads one to believe at first that the entire text of the contract is to follow. But the succinctness and vagueness of the ensuing text contradict this. On the other hand, the meticulous introduction, with its legal figures of speech, clearly does not agree with the idea of an insinuated up-dating of the agreement. The most likely interpretation would, therefore, be that Galatians 2:9*b* and 10*a* represent a listing of the most important key words of the agreement.[46]

The key words of the first article of the contract are: "We to the Gentiles, they to the circumcision." This elliptical expression hardly suggests a separation of the Mediterranean world into two areas of mission, or that a rift was intended between the Jewish and Gentile addressees of the preaching of the church and its missionaries. Such a connotation would hardly agree with the facts of the historical situation.[47]

As Paul and Barnabas were the delegates from Antioch and empowered to conclude an agreement in its name, in the same way the "Pillars" acted as representatives of the congregation in Jerusalem. The "we," therefore, can logically be substituted by the expression "congregation of Antioch," and the "they" by "the congregation of Jerusalem." Consequently, the εἰς cannot, of course, be meant directionally. As a matter of fact, the entire argument presented above speaks against this. In the face of the absence of similar elliptical expressions, it still seems justified to assume that εἰς (as often in Koine Greek and in Paul) stands here in the sense of "for the sake of" or "in the interest of."[48] Such a reading implies an emphasis on the responsibility held by the congregation concerned and could be paraphrased as follows: "That the congregation of Antioch should be responsible for the Gentile Jesus believers, and the congregation in Jerusalem for the Jewish Jesus believers, respectively."

Read in this way, the passage points to a very broad spectrum of possibilities, and the emphasis is to be understood as being more on the obligations than on the rights of each congregation which it had to exercise with respect to the Gentiles or, as the case may be, to the Jews. In short, stress would be on the responsibilities of either community.[49] The focus of interest in this sentence would definitely be on the work to be accomplished by each community, not on the limitations to its freedom of action.

This reading does not exclude an overlapping of operations and operatives. On the contrary, it concedes the existence of different theologies, organizations, life-styles, and missionary activities. Understood in this way, the text presents fewer difficulties as regards the prevailing historical possibilities.

Unfortunately, the textual evidence is not unequivocal enough. Thus the reading proposed lacks final proof. Yet, no matter which way the passage is translated, there always remains the fact that much more is hinted at here than a mere division of labor or a series of mutual concessions. Paul's report clearly shows that there was a mutual acknowledgment of independence.

2. Demonstration of Partnership Through Honoring the Special Position of the Jerusalem Congregation[50]

As has been argued thus far, the communality of ecclesial responsibility was to be pursued by both Antioch and Jerusalem on the basis of mutual recognition of full independence for either congregation. The communion of the church was thus to be ensured by means of a certain separation. This outcome of the convention in itself constituted a decision full of risks for the future. But these risks were the background for the second part of the negotiations—namely, as Paul stated, "only the poor—that we should remember [them]" (Gal. 2:10*a*). The position of "the poor" at the beginning of the phrase indicates that the emphasis is on them.

This does not mean, however, that in this passage I find the one issue in which Jerusalem's negotiators prevailed in pushing their privileged authority: an enforced tax or some compromise solution that disguised the recognition of Jerusalem privileges with allegedly charitable activity. Such reading would stand in contradiction to all we have seen so far. It seems much more plausible that the reason for which the emphasis is put on "the poor" here is rooted in the content of the preceding subordinate clause, which runs parallel to this statement. As it were, this subordinate clause does refer to separation. The emphasis on "the poor" (achieved through its position at the beginning of the sentence), therefore, highlights the second half of the parallelism, which can be interpreted as meaning that the second final clause simply refers to the only visible link between the Gentiles and the Jews in the church.

Being "the poor" appears to be the essential dignity held by the congregation in Jerusalem, to be granted and respected by all other Jesus congregations. The absolute use of this appellation in Galatians 2:10 and the fact that it does not need any explanation show that it must have been a title commonly bestowed upon that congregation.[51]

This titulary usage was modeled after other, previously existing onomatic examples in the Jewish Bible. In it, and especially in the Psalms, the name "the poor" is used in very specific contexts and is further elaborated in later periods of early Judaism, until eventually it is used synonymously with such designations as "pious" and "just."[52] Since the Maccabean wars the denomination "the poor" had been used as self-designation by a variety of Jewish groups, all of whom meant to express that they alone were the true devotees, the true Israel, the "Holy Remnant."[53]

As time went by, the eschatological aspect of the name had become increasingly dominant. "The poor" saw themselves as the hidden, oppressed, and persecuted repository of the covenant, the future co-rulers of God; though as yet harassed by the old aeon, they nevertheless constituted the true representatives of God's chosen, eschatological people.[54]

The prestige inherent in this proud self-appellation often went together with certain attitudes, behavior, and actions that led more or less involuntarily to actual material neediness. But in the case of the community at Qumran, the parallelism of economic poverty and the religious claim of being (God's) poor ones, and thus the eschatologically chosen, was consciously realized and incorporated into the entire way of communal life.[55] The Qumran community had gone to dwell in the desert to demonstrate the perfect purity of the truly eschatological people of God through stripping themselves of ordinary means of individual livelihood and common comfort. Besides many other things, they had let go of money and personal property to show that they were cleansed of all the evils of this world (Dam. VI., 15-16). All their personal belongings had been handed over to the Order, thus establishing their life according to the principles of joint property. This state was thought of as evidencing through actual individual poverty the holiness of the member and, hence, as showing that he was one of the "chosen few," one of the "called."

On the other hand, archaeological excavations have brought to light the fact that the Order as such was not meant to survive exclusively on the assets and the property brought in by the novices; it also acted as administrator of those assets and estates and worked with them. The Order constituted a well-organized economic system and was not itself poor.

The case of the early Aramaic-speaking Jesus congregation was quite different: this community[56] also claimed to be "the Poor," the "Chosen," the "Called," and the "Saints,"[57] and lived together holding property jointly.[58] But their economic situation, as a group, appeared to be rather deficient. They were not at home in Jerusalem, and were thus without established resources. Neither were their inner conditions conducive to establishing themselves there economically. The economic interests of neither the community as a whole nor the individual members were sufficiently taken care of.

The claim of the Jesus congregation at Jerusalem to be the eschatological people of God was made right in the middle of the holy city. That claim carried the implication that the Jesus believers thought of themselves as the only true devotees. All the self-designations they chose were meant to express that idea.[59] Hence, they must encourage opposition on the part of the Jews, and eventually provoke hostilities.[60] "The poor" in turn understood these persecutions as the external confirmation of the propriety of their claim.

Certainly, it was initially (and for different reasons) only the group of Greek-speaking Jewish Jesus believers[61] whose lives and physical survival were imperiled and who had to suffer expulsion from the city.[62] But soon the Aramaic-speaking branch of the Jesus congregation at Jerusalem was persecuted as well. These harassments certainly increased the economic neediness of those Jesus people who, contrary to the Essenes and the Jesus circle that had established itself around Stephen, persisted in Jerusalem in the very face of their predicament.[63] Standing firm in this way bore witness to their extraordinary capacity to endure—a capacity that must, essentially, have resulted from their self-image. It lay in the nature of this self-image not to try to avoid poverty but, rather, to take it as a matter of course accompanying intent and action. Material neediness was probably bound up with their beginnings as a Jesus community, the initial eschatological expectation that, in turn, entailed the practice of joint property.

There seems reason to believe that the disciples had reacted to

Jesus' arrest with a headlong flight, and that this flight had brought most of them back to their homeland, Galilee.[64] The post-resurrection appearances of Jesus in Galilee, however, prompted them to form communities, and one of them, around Peter and the Twelve, had returned to Jerusalem. This second anabasis to the Holy City where Jesus' crucifixion had occurred in the meantime can only be explained by the new christological certainty and eschatological awareness they had gained. In this expectation Jerusalem must have received an important place—an importance that city had never been credited with by Jesus himself. This shift in understanding explains why Peter, the Twelve, and those around them went back to Jerusalem and remained there in spite of the extreme hardships and pressures they had to face, adversities that were undoubtedly intensified further by the dangerous claim of representing the chosen people of God in possession of the promise of the impending eschatological completion.[65]

Within the biblical and Jewish expectation of the eschatological events, Jerusalem and Mount Zion as geographical entities were often merged as the predestined location for the imminent occurrence of the Last Things. The eschatological event itself had often been understood as Yahweh's own coming (occasionally this coming was also viewed as the joint appearance of Yahweh and the Messiah) on Mount Zion, and as the glorification of the city of Jerusalem in the Last Days.[66] Jerusalem was to receive the entire people of God, including those of its members who had so far been scattered around the lands.[67] Mount Zion and God's City were considered the goal of the forthcoming eschatological pilgrimage not only of the Jews but also of the nations of the world.[68] The heathen peoples would come there and bring all the riches of the Earth to Jerusalem to pay homage to Yahweh and his people, and to serve them.[69]

Occasionally the pious hopes voiced in conjunction with Jerusalem and Mount Zion were explicitly linked to the expectations of the economically poor. Isaiah 14:30 and 32, for instance, state:

> The first-born of the lowly shall be afforded sanctuary in my pasture and the poor shall lie down in peace. . . . And what will the messengers of the heathens say? "The Lord has founded Jerusalem and the poor of his people will find refuge within her walls."

Also Zephaniah (3:9 and 12) ends with:

> At that time I will change the peoples so that their lips will be cleansed and they all call on Yahweh's name and serve him in one mind. From beyond the rivers of Ethiopia they will bring the sweet-smelling incense offering of the community of all my dispersed devotees in worship to me. That day you will no longer need to be ashamed of all the actions by which you sinned against me. Then I will remove all the proud and arrogant men from among you, there will be no more pride and haughtiness on my holy mountain. I will maintain in your midst a poor and lowly people as the remnant who will take refuge in the name of the Lord; these will be the Holy Remnant of Israel. They will commit no more sins and will speak no more lies; there will not be one single deceitful tongue to be found in their mouths. It is they who will find pasture and live undisturbed in peace.

It is important for our discussion that in the present composition of the Zephaniah book an eschatological Zion-psalm follows this text.[70]

The eschatological expectation of the Aramaic-speaking Jewish Jesus believers in Jerusalem must have developed on the basis of this biblical and subsequent Jewish theology of Last Days hope, with the difference, however, that, in the view of the Jesus community, the crucified and ascended Jesus had been the very eschatological prophet or, as the case may be, the Son of Man to come, and they themselves now constituted the Holy Remnant of Israel.

Passionately carried forward by this belief, it seemed only natural for them to feel that they must not leave the Holy City in the hands of the unbelieving Jews but, rather, that they were called upon to occupy the place of the divine parousia and to take on the task of the eschatological forepost, God's avant garde as the watchmen upon the battlements of that city (Isa. 52:8), and that, therefore, it was incumbent upon them to make known to the world and all the dispersed members of God's people the imminent approach of the celestial monarch in the fullness of time. They were prepared to take on this difficult office vicariously for all those who shared their faith and hopes. So when the convention in Jerusalem was called, it went without saying that they felt entitled to suggest that they be "not forgotten."

The connotation inherent in the kind of "remembering" referred to in Galatians 2:10 is certainly a positive one. *Μνημονεύω*[2] (with the genitive) occurs only twice more in New Testament documents and always in contexts similar, it would seem, to that of Galatians 2:10. Both in I Thessalonians 1:3 and Hebrews 13:7, the term refers to a calling to memory and to a keeping in mind of people whose accomplishments are worthy of recognition. The verb applies in both cases because someone is to be remembered in recognition of personal merits. Particularly in Hebrews 13:7, this recognition also implies an inner engagement toward persons who have excelled through exemplary achievements, and the corresponding obligations specifically incumbent upon those who have benefited from these persons.[71] It is precisely this connotation of remembering on which Galatians 2:10 primarily focuses. On the other hand, the connotation of "caring for materially" is not really substantiated for the verb *μνημονεύω* by literary evidence. The only example advanced in this connection is the one cited by Walter Bauer: I Maccabees 12:11. But there the expression is not used in the sense of remembering through means of economic care; it merely implies a remembering through prayers and ritual sacrifice or through ritualistic intercession by means of prayer.

It would seem, therefore, that the agreement reached in Jerusalem simply stipulated that the Gentile Jesus believers were to give recognition to the exemplary performance on the part of their fellow believers in Jerusalem. In other words, the agreement was about the recognition of the Jerusalem congregation's ongoing and self-forgetful eschatological effort. In this it was also about the eschatological expectation as displayed by the entire Jesus movement, as such. It must basically have been this very eschatological expectation as something very concrete, which in the contract constituted the unifying link of all Jesus believing congregations.

Ferdinand Hahn, however, objects that the self-understanding of the Jesus congregation in Jerusalem as regards their eschatological outpost position was hardly what the Hellenistic-Jewish Jesus believers—considering their blatantly critical attitude toward the Temple and the cult pertaining to it—could have been willing to acknowledge unobjectionally.[72] For Hahn it was only "the priority of Israel in the history of salvation" that had been accepted as the basic criterion for the negotiations and that had warranted the arrangements concerning the collection. But this objection does not hold for the simple reason that Hahn's argument is based on an imprecise alternative, and also because his interpretation is not factually supported by the original wording of the text.[73]

A correct exegetical analysis of Galatians 2:10 above all requires a satisfactory explanation as to why the Jesus believers of Jerusalem were acknowledged as "the poor" and on what grounds a collection was agreed upon for the Jerusalem congregation.[74] All I can say with certainty is that the Antiochenes accepted this claim for recognition and that they gave their approval to the agreement.

We know that one of their delegates was Paul; and, as will be shown, the vision of the pilgrimage of the nations to Jerusalem—a motif closely linked with the Zion tradition—is what was to influence Paul's future theology and the scope in which he was to develop his concept of the collection—although in Paul's thought and action this idea turned into a rather modified version of the earlier eschatological concept.[75] The second Antiochene delegate was Barnabas, who in the context of the conflict between Jerusalem and Antioch finally took the side of the group of people sent by James from Jerusalem.

Thus both Antiochene delegates would understand the request, for did it not lend theological importance to the concept of the ἐκκλησία as an eschatological community, and would it not—from the point of view of church polity—because of the particular position of the Jerusalem congregation, grant also to the other congregations abroad their own particular life and a certain independent juridical status accompanying it?

We do not know of a critique of the Temple and of its cult by Paul, nor do the texts indicate any such criticism on the part of Barnabas, nor is there anything in the texts pointing to a critical attitude toward the Temple by Antioch. In fact, the Antiochene incident makes such criticism highly improbable.[76] It would be even less justified to speak of such an attitude of critical opposition to the Temple cult among Hellenistic-Jewish Jesus believers as a whole, mainly because the Hellenistic-Jewish section of converts never constituted a homogeneous entity.[77] As a matter of fact, widespread criticism of the Temple cannot be found within the Hellenistic-Jewish part of the church.[78] Among Hellenistic Jews criticism of the Temple was not common—not to mention the fact that such criticism would not have automatically amounted to questioning the central importance attributed to Jerusalem itself, as the writings of Luke clearly show.

Naturally, the fact that the Gentile Jesus believers acknowledged the congregation at Jerusalem as being of special significance further enhanced the interconnectedness and the feeling of solidarity between the different groups. It also assisted the Jerusalem church in the conviction that they were not fighting a losing battle. It would, therefore, have been out of step with the recognition granted Jerusalem had this acknowledgment not also carried with it genuine engagement in intercession for Jerusalem—a notion also inherent in the Greek verb *μνημονεύω*. However, the readiness to endure displayed by the Jerusalem congregation implied not only inner but also economic problems; therefore, the readiness of the Antiochenes to subscribe to a relationship based on solidarity and engagement also comprised a willingness to offer material aid.

Indeed, the congregation at Jerusalem could never have gone through with their exemplary task on behalf of the entire Jesus movement and would have had to abandon its eschatological outpost had it been denied financial support. Still, such economic assistance was only secondary to the clearly theological principle entailed in "remembering." The conclusion most commentators tend to draw from Galatians 2:10 as a matter of course—namely, that it refers directly and entirely to a collection of money for Jerusalem—is to be refuted in the light of the contextual position and the textual formulation chosen by Paul.

Besides, the above reading of the verb *remember* is upheld by the grammatical form in which the term is used here. Paul chose the present tense subjunctive *μνημονεύωμεν*, not the aorist. This indicates that he meant to refer to continued action. But neither in this nor in any other passage dealing with the actual economics of conducting the collection is there proof that the Gentile Jesus congregations were to pay a regular levy or tax to Jerusalem. In all his congregations Paul carried out but one collection.

Now one could argue that since Paul later made the collection an integral part of his personal concept of mission and church his unique gathering of funds within his own congregations constituted a subsequent and unilateral amendment made to the agreement by Paul himself. Had Paul reshaped the concept and execution of the collection in such a way, then this could have covered what originally had been agreed upon in Jerusalem—namely, a tax.

Had such been the case it would have been a measure of surprising extremity on Paul's part. But the decisive objection to this interpretation is contained in an *argumentum e silentio,* to be added to all the above-listed observations on the overall nature of the negotiations and the agreement. There can be no doubt about the fact that Luke integrated into his Acts some material distinctly stemming from Antiochene traditions.[79] If that material had contained any indication whatsoever of a tax levied on Antioch, Luke would certainly not have missed the opportunity to report on it, because such data would have fit in perfectly with his idea of what the early church had been.

It is impossible to imagine that the Antiochenes had drawn back from a previously stipulated tax, particularly not since they had decided shortly after the convention—and against Paul's veto!—to strengthen their ties with the Jerusalem church. In short, the Antiochene source material used by Luke contained no reference to a tax levied there, because such a tax had never been stipulated, nor was it ever levied.[80] By contrast, the Antiochene tradition seems to have known about a collection carried out there for the church in Jerusalem.

But I want to take up once more the question of the verbal mood in Galatians 2:10*a*. As has been shown before, the continued remembering of the "poor" cannot mean a tax to be paid to them. Hence, the primary meaning of the expression "to remember" was not one of financial assistance to be given to the Jerusalem congregation. Such succor was certainly implied as well, but something more comprehensive was in view: the situation the congregation at Jerusalem found itself in. Its significance and achievements were to be brought into memory to the Antiochene and Gentile churches continuously. In other words, the "remembering" meant primarily an inner attitude—an attitude that was to be expressed through recognition, gratefulness, intercession by prayers, and, finally, financial aid as well. And even as in later years when Paul had—in the light of entirely different circumstances—attributed much greater importance to the collection and given its organization demonstrative significance, did the economic implication of "remembering the poor" retain merely secondary importance.

As the congregation of Jerusalem probably upheld its claim to represent the eschatological temple of God,[81] it could be that in conjunction with the second part of the agreement, and especially as regards agreements on material assistance, the participants had in the back of their minds also certain biblical reports on voluntary contributions made for the construction of the Temple.[82] Of course, such parallel vision of the Temple's construction and the necessary financial donations would have been seen now from an exclusively eschatological perspective. At the same time, they must have reflected back on the old motif of the nations' pilgrimage, as this theme was traditionally viewed as part of the eschatological expectation, on the one hand, and bound up with the vision of the heathens bringing the riches of the world to the holy city on the other.

But, most probably, there was no extra time at the convention in Jerusalem for elaborate reflections on the applicability of the motifs of the pilgrimage of the nations and the return of Israel to Jerusalem to the actual situation, or on the impact these eschatological occurrences presently might have on the missionary effort undertaken among both the Jews and the Gentiles. As to how far Paul himself conformed or differed with the Jerusalem church may be an interesting question, but a difficult one to answer. All I can assert is that Paul did not, at that point, integrate the organizational aspects of the economic assistance into the formation of his missionary work. The way he eventually went about developing this integrational objective can be seen from his later epistles.

For the time being, the agreement on the necessity to "remember the poor"—that is to say, to honor the demonstrative eschatological status of the congregation at Jerusalem and to assist that congregation both morally and economically—constituted a confession of unity of the community of Jesus Christ grounded in the hope of Christ's impending return. It did not imply the recognition of any kind of judicial authority held by the Jerusalem congregation or its leaders.

CHAPTER 2

THE FATE OF THE JERUSALEM CONVENTION (48–53 C.E.)

A. START AND TEMPORARY CESSATION OF THE COLLECTION

The only document informing us about what happened to the remembrance for the poor in Jerusalem between the time of the ratification of the agreement and the moment the collection was actually started within the genuine Pauline congregations is Paul's simple remark in Galatians 2:10: "I was eager to do just that." Nothing in this sentence hints at a collection that might have been organized prior to the convention or was delivered in Jerusalem at the time of the convention itself.[1] Obviously, Paul here refers only to his zealous efforts undertaken to see the second point of the agreement fulfilled after the convention had come to an end.

It must not be overlooked, however, that Paul refers to his zeal as if it were a thing of the past—notwithstanding the fact that at the time the Epistle to the Galatians was written, the great gathering of funds within the Pauline congregations was still to come. Moreover, there is nothing in Galatians 2:10 to infer that the fund raising had already been started in Galatia at the time. Neither does Paul mention any such development in any other section of the epistle. So when he states in I Corinthians 16:1: "As to the collection for the Saints, do as I instructed the congregations in Galatia to do!" he is evidently referring to directions he gave subsequent to having written to the Galatian congregations. As far as Corinth was concerned, the general impression is that nothing had been collected there, either, when I Corinthians 16:1 was drafted—in fact, it seems as though the entire campaign was still in its very beginnings. On the other hand, our sources tell us nothing about how the Antiochenes reacted to the convention, especially as regards the second agreement.

The texts do not report on the immediate reaction of the Antiochene church. Are we to assume, therefore, that they had started to step back from the agreements negotiated by their delegates immediately after the summit? Hardly. Quite to the contrary, the Antiochene congregation was so large and probably so wealthy that it must have been only natural to expect it to come forth with an appropriate donation for Jerusalem.

In Acts 11:27-30 Luke reports on a collection organized by Antioch, but he dates that collection back to a time prior to the convention. For Luke it was the prediction about a world-wide famine made by Agabus, an itinerant preacher from Jerusalem, that had prompted this collection; Luke names Paul and Barnabas as having been charged with delivering it. As mentioned earlier, this report is certainly not historically correct.[2] Ernst Haenchen assumes that Luke had used, among others, source material on Paul's journey to Jerusalem to deliver the (historical) collection, but that those documents were of such poor drafting or of such imprecision that he had misunderstood them. But, had this been the case, why was Antioch mentioned in those texts? Referring the problem back to the tradition attached to Agabus does not suffice to explain Luke's error either. Nor does the interpretation given by Haenchen explain why Paul and Barnabas are the conveyors of that collection.

It seems much more plausible that, however veiled or hidden, the entire passage in Acts where this point is dealt with contains the (spoiled) report on a (historical) collection effort undertaken in Antioch after and in accordance with the Jerusalem agreement. When Luke wrote his text, however, the motivation behind it and the exact date of the collection had simply been forgotten. As for the Lukan error that Paul had gone to Jerusalem together with Barnabas to hand over this collection, one can assume that in the memory of the Antiochenes both these names had traditionally been linked to the collection—not, however, originally in conjunction with its conveyance to Jerusalem, but because Paul and Barnabas had both been instrumental in the development of the agreement and because they had also most probably subsequently initiated and controlled the fund-raising campaign at Antioch, their names were later associated with that particular conveyance as well.[3]

The conflict between Paul and Peter at Antioch (Gal. 2:11-21) seems to have arisen shortly after these events—a disagreement resulting in Paul's separation from Barnabas and his estrangement from the Antiochene congregation.[4] From that time onward, Paul pursued his missionary work alone.[5] First he traveled to Galatia, where he set up a number of congregations. From there his itinerary led him to Greece, where he journeyed as far as Corinth.

We possess a document reflecting the ideas guiding Paul during that period of his life—namely, the first Epistle to the Thessalonians, written shortly after Paul had arrived in Achaia (written from Corinth?).[6] Although the congregation at Thessalonica had been founded only a few months previously, it had at the time the epistle was composed already developed considerable vitality and acquired a character very much its own—so much so that its existence must immediately have constituted a weighty influence on the world around it (I Thess. 1:7-9). Yet, Paul's letter to the Thessalonians contains no indication that the congregation had been informed about the agreement of Jerusalem or, for that matter, that they had been induced—or were to be induced—to proceed with a collection themselves.

Thus this epistle confirms the implication of the aorist of the phrase *ἐσπούδασα . . . ποιῆσαι* in Galatians 2:10; that particular wording refers to Paul's eagerness to help fulfill the second point of the agreement of Jerusalem as a past effort, long behind him, when he wrote the epistle to the Galatians (from Ephesus or some place nearby). Also the Galatian congregations had already existed for some time before the epistle to the Galatians was written. Paul had even returned in the meantime to pay them a visit[7]—and yet, nothing at all is said about a collection being organized, or to be organized, in these congregations—not even when he reports on the collection at the Jerusalem summit. Indeed, had a collection been started in those Galatian congregations, Paul would at least have referred to it by writing something like, "As you know. . . ."

Why then, must I ask, had Paul's initial zeal to keep the agreement slackened? Why had he not persisted in his efforts to organize economic assistance schemes for the benefit of Jerusalem in his own newly founded and already very vigorous congregations? The answer to this question seems to be obvious, although it cannot be given with absolute certainty: Paul's interest had probably declined in the wake of the frictions within the Antiochene congregation, his separation from Barnabas, and, possibly, his temporary break-up with Antioch as a whole.

The Antioch incident had disrupted the bond of trust previously revived at Jerusalem. Paul himself blames his Jewish fellow believers in Antioch for the estrangement. The reproach that Jewish Jesus believers had broken the agreement can be read between the lines of Galatians 2:11-21. The alienation must have been a blow to Paul. Although the convening of the meeting at Jerusalem had, of course, not been the apostle's own doing only, he had certainly been one of its most fervent promoters. By attending the convention and by subsequently displaying such zeal in implementing the decisions taken there, Paul had clearly shown how important the unity of the larger Jesus-believing community was to him. His report on the disturbances at Antioch gives telling evidence of the disappointment he felt over the incident.

Conversely, Paul's Jewish fellow believers must also have been perplexed at his behavior during and after the meeting in Antioch. His attitude there, his separation from Antioch, the beginning of his independent mission, and the new situation resulting from his discretionary establishment of his own missionary territory—all this stood in their minds in puzzling contradiction to the organizational and theological premises underlying the treaty negotiated at Jerusalem.

If not already at an earlier stage, it must have been at that time at the latest that Paul became suspect of doctrinal and organizational privateering. There was no guarantee now that the collection stemming from his congregations would be received gratefully by Jerusalem—indeed, just as the premises for the agreement had been abandoned, so also the decisions taken with respect to it would necessarily be nullified. Characteristically, Paul never again refers to the agreement when initiating a collection in any of his subsequent congregations or when explaining why and for what purpose it was launched.

B. THE UNIFYING BOND WITH THE ESCHATOLOGICAL PEOPLE OF GOD

In his dispute with the Galatian opponents Paul went so far as to identify the geographical city of Jerusalem with the slave Hagar, and to call it a place of servitude (Gal. 4:22-31; esp. v. 25), which amounted to attributing to the celestial Jerusalem (the Jerusalem "above") a nature totally opposite to that of the earthly one. In this concept, the heavenly city of Jerusalem is viewed as a totally transcendent entity. The best parallel examples for such stark antithetical thinking are found in Gnostic writings.[8] Could it be that Paul had finally made up his mind in favor of Gnosticism's dehistoricizing (often even ahistorical) tendencies and its interest in the individual and the small group, and pronounced himself against a historically minded church community held together by the same eschatological expectation?

As pointed out correctly by Walter Schmithals, one must not forget that the Galatian opponents were themselves pneumatics.[9] But we must not, as Schmithals does, isolate the polemics in chapters 1, 2, 5, and 6 from those contained in chapters 3 and 4 (esp. 3). The pneumatics' thinking was law-oriented; they were "Judaizers," exactly like the opposing teachers referred to in the Epistle to the Philippians.[10] As such, they were forerunners of a type of Torah-related Gnosticism that would subsequently be attacked in the Epistle to the Colossians[11] and in the Ignatian letters.[12] The Galatian opponents had turned the Law into a speculative wisdom teaching, comprising both a cosmological and a soteriological aspect.[13] All Jesus-related thoughts were incorporated into a doctrine, giving the last finishing touch to a certain Jewish syncretism that had by then become heavily enriched by a variety of pagan themes.[14] Their goal was pneumatic perfection.[15] In order to reach that goal they used nomistic practices together with certain sacraments, like circumcision and baptism, that were considered true mysteries.[16] In this context Jerusalem was probably regarded as the holy hub of these mysteries, with the Jesus disciples in Jerusalem as their guardians (principal mystagogues).[17]

Under these circumstances the Jesus-believing community was in serious danger of being turned into an esoteric sect—indeed, into a mystery club. As to Paul's own Gnostically tainted statements, they were meant to illustrate to the Galatian opponents that the mystical sublimation of history and the Law would not lead to the greatly desired freedom but, rather, to enslavement and chaos. Nothing but the good news of the gospel was bound to bring freedom; it alone was capable of creating a true community—not, however, within the framework of some relatively esoteric tradition, but within that of communal participation in the gospel alone.[18]

Paul appears much more interested in the community of the church than his opponents do. His goal was twofold: history brought about by the living interaction between God and humans, and history experienced as a living unfolding in the occurrences between all persons sharing the faith in Jesus Christ. Paul wanted to show that the speculation and the methods put to use by the alleged "orthodoxy" the Galatians were being seduced by was merely a seeming orthodoxy that in reality amounted to no more than syncretistic mysticism.[19] But above all else he wished to hold up against the opponents the eschatological character not only of a Jesus-oriented life but of the church of Christ as such.[20] In Paul's eyes, the Jesus-believing community is the eschatological people of God; it had been by this conviction that the representatives of Jewish and Gentile Jesus believers had essentially been bound together also in Jerusalem during the convention.

When Paul wrote the Epistle to the Galatians, he was still holding on to that conviction, as evidenced by a remark toward the end of the epistle (6:15-16) and also in 4:31, where he advances ideas to the same effect. Obviously, the Epistle to the Galatians was still based on the spirit of the Jerusalem convention.

Further, the first Epistle to the Corinthians proves that, at the time, Paul was still positively inclined toward the leading figures in Jerusalem, in particular Simon Peter; even Barnabas is not spoken of negatively.[21] From Acts 18:22-23 we know that Paul had returned once more to Antioch between his first major campaign around the Aegean Sea and the return there.[22] The former good rapport had certainly not been regained by this visit, but Paul was enabled again to draw attention to the great interest he had in the church community as a whole.

CHAPTER 3

THE COLLECTION: A NEW START AND, ONCE AGAIN, ITS IMPENDING END (53 and 54 C.E.)

A. THE GALATIAN AND CORINTHIAN OPPOSITION AND THE NEW START OF THE COLLECTION

From what has been shown so far, one can hardly say that Paul had decided to revise his principles thoroughly when he began to organize the collection again shortly after having written to the Galatians. And yet this new beginning comes somewhat as a surprise. We have no reason to assume that the resumption had been triggered by any particular person, group, or place outside the Pauline mission territory. This second time around the collection clearly constituted a purely Pauline initiative within the apostle's own congregations only, and must, therefore, have evolved out of the situation prevailing in these congregations. What is surprising, however, is that at the time Paul started once more collecting funds for Jerusalem, he was beset by ever-increasing worries about his congregations. Would it not have been more appropriate, under the circumstances, to concentrate entirely on his own work? Yet, it was precisely in Galatia that he began to organize the collection again.[1]

It certainly may be assumed that the Galatians—brought somewhat back to earth by the admonitions made in Paul's epistle—had succeeded in disentangling themselves from the influences of the opponents. But was that sufficient basis to ask of these people, who had only just regained reasoned independence, to commit themselves to something that, by necessity, must plunge them right back into the ideological whirlpool that swirled around the issue of Jerusalem? Further, in Corinth the appeal for the resumption of the collection was made at a time when the congregation found itself in a state of increasing inner turmoil. Were these not inauspicious times for a collection that benefited a congregation like Jerusalem, which, besides all else, was so far away?

Paul did so nevertheless because he intended to establish a connection in principle between his concern for the troublesome situation caused by false teaching in his congregations and his interest in the well-being of the church in Jerusalem, hoping to find, in the renewal of the commitment, something like a pedagogical instrument for straightening out the confused minds of his converts.

The Pauline congregations in Galatia had been penetrated by another Jesus-oriented teaching that—in the disguise of tradition-minded and Law-abiding orthodoxy—was threatening to disintegrate the zestful Jesus community that had developed in the area and to suffocate true history under a blanket of spiritual speculation and mysticism, to dissolve living order into artificial constructions falsely called "law." Even worse, whereas the Galatian opponents pretended to fight anarchy with orthodoxy (all the while creating chaos behind the screen of correct teaching), the opposition in Corinth made disorder their very program.[2]

Tradition, of course, had not been abandoned in Corinth completely; the traditions of baptism, the Last Supper, and the death and the resurrection of Jesus were all scrupulously upheld and considered of paramount necessity.[3] The sacraments were so highly cherished, in fact, that they were viewed as a sure panacea, capable of providing immortality here and now.[4] Mystical ecstasy, together with the twin practices of libertinism and asceticism, was seen as proof that the Christ-bound pneumatics had reached a heavenly mode of being already in the present.[5] The entire congregation was in danger of breaking up into mystery clans or mystic circles of various kinds. More often than not the unity of the individual congregation—indeed, of the entire community of Jesus believers—was utterly neglected. Yet, as can be seen from the address section of the epistle, it was precisely this unity that Paul emphasized the most strongly: "To the congregation of God which is in Corinth, [to] the Holy Ones in Christ Jesus, [to] those called

Saints and [to] all those who call the name of our Lord Jesus Christ, wherever they may be, [to] their and our [congregations]."[6]

That this "catholic" introduction should constitute a mere marginal gloss seems highly doubtful. I would rather argue that what we have here is a comment made by Paul himself, meant to clearly state the very *leitmotif* of I Corinthians. That the purpose of this epistle lay in the formulation of the universal character of the church is also evidenced in chapters 1, 3, 12, and 14.

Chapter 15, on the other hand, is intended to prove to the Corinthians that they had really not understood their tradition at all—their conviction that they had made tradition practically an integral part of themselves notwithstanding.[7] They were not aware that the first witnesses to the appearances of the resurrected Jesus had not been overpowered by some mystical experience of self-identification with the Lord, but rather had met him as a paramount counterpart who had taken them into service. The Corinthians would not see that this Lord always remained a counterpart both in his word and in his sacraments. Moreover, they proved utterly unwilling to accept that this Lord would, through his own fellowship, remain the authority in the future as well.

It was probably on the grounds of the symbolic interpretation they had made of Jesus' resurrection, and the tradition to which it gave rise, that the Corinthians denied the resurrection of the body. For them the specifically Christ-related existence was gained here and now—with its completion in the experience of mystical union with Christ.[8] Such identification amounted to the total obliteration of any sense of time, or the possibility of any encounter with those who are "other-than-myself."

The Corinthians were unwilling to accept the fact that the testimony of Jesus' resurrection from the dead referred to a Lord who had opened the gates toward a newly created area of responsibility, whose limits were set by him alone. This is why Paul was speaking of a resurrection of the body! In Pauline theology, the term *body* implies the idea of a historic encounter. The concept presupposes the "body" of Christ as the one factor that determines all else, not the other way around.[9] This explains why I Corinthians 15 is not concerned with the fate of the individual but with the destiny of the community of Jesus Christ as a whole.[10] The testimony of Jesus' resurrection represents no less than the preaching on which the church is founded.

Paul also used this argument to explain to the Corinthians that faith also encompasses the past; faith is not made up only of something that comes "after"; it also comprises that which comes "before." The soteriological event, the testimony of the appearances of the resurrected Jesus, and the fact that other people also believe in Jesus' resurrection from the dead are all faith—the implication being that the Corinthians must be thankful to all those who preceded them in the faith in Jesus Christ.

First Corinthians 15 is meant to instill the idea of historic indebtedness on the part of later Jesus-believing congregations to the first witnesses. As far as those first witnesses themselves are concerned, it is not possible to refer to them without remembering the first Jesus-believing community as well (this being for Paul the community in Jerusalem). The emergence of a Jesus community in that city bore witness to the power inherent in the testimony of the appearances of the resurrected Jesus, a power capable of calling into existence the church. That primitive community was foremost in the development and the continuance of that preaching which constituted the church. At the time Paul wrote this epistle that community probably still harbored a majority of the first witnesses to the Easter appearances of Jesus. Hence, the Jerusalem community acted as a constant reminder to every Jesus believer and to all Jesus-believing communities of their common origin: the resurrection of Jesus from the dead.

According to this perspective, the direct link Paul draws between the collection (I Cor. 16:1-4) and the radical attack on the Corinthian misunderstanding of the eschatological expectation (chap. 15) does not appear quite so coincidental. Paul may well have been quite deliberate about choosing to refer to the collection directly after these attacks in chapters 8 and 10–15. Turning their attention back to the unity of the community of all believers—a community born both of the firsthand testimonies concerning the resurrection and the history common to all Jesus believers—might assist in jolting the readers out of their mystical introversion.

There is reason to assume, therefore, that Paul had brought up the issue of the collection as part of his effort to counter the disintegration into mystery cliques and esoteric circles that threatened his congregations. The events at Corinth had shown only too clearly that such a danger really existed. Those events may have triggered the resumption of the collection. Paul must have sensed that under these circumstances the collection could be instrumental in giving expression to the joint will toward unity as something perfectly in tune with the original spirit of the Jerusalem agreements.

Similarly, the collection launched in Galatia can be seen as a demonstration against a Judaizing ideology propounded in a community that had succeeded only recently in its reconciliation with Paul. Seen this way, the collection was meant to show that the Jesus-believing community represented a new creation with its roots in the resurrection of Christ, and to stress that this community was neither the prolongation of nor an addition to the old world order.

But let us consider I Corinthians 16:1-4 itself, in which the terminology used here for the collection is especially interesting.[11] In verse 1 the collection is called *λογεία*, and in verse 3 *χάρις*. Surely, Paul was not thinking of a "tax" when employing the term *λογεία*; he was not thinking of a permanent institution, only of a one-time measure, even though intended to take some time. This collection was to be raised in various private gatherings every Sunday (v. 2). *Λογεία* in this context means a collection of funds, nothing else.[12] The expression "the saints," used here in the same absolute sense as "the poor" in Galatians 2:10, refers to the Jesus congregation at Jerusalem. As Karl Holl said, *οἱ ἅγιοι* constitutes—just as does "the poor"—a self-designation of that congregation.[13] By calling themselves "the saints," the early church had found one more way of voicing their claim to being the representatives of the genuine eschatological people of God. Contrary to the title "the poor," however, "the saints" was later used to designate Jesus converts in general.

Since Jerusalem was a temple city, Greek readers would believe that the expression "collection for the saints" referred to a measure destined to reward the congregation at Jerusalem for the accomplishments it had achieved in the area of cultic practice and to provide it with the material assets it required to continue to fulfill its ritual tasks.[14] There was no implication that the Jerusalem congregation held hierarchical privilege—at least not to Paul's understanding. This is evidenced by *χάρις*, the second term designating the collection, which—contrary to *λογεία*, was also used by Paul in later texts (II Cor. 8:4, 6, 7, 19). In the light of all this, one might be inclined to understand *χάρις* as a gift to thank the brothers and sisters in Jerusalem for the gifts the Spirit received from them in the past. However, this meaning is reserved for thank offerings made to God.[15] The term must, therefore, be understood as referring to a token of favor.[16] Generally, a favor is granted out of a certain feeling of obligation toward the recipient of the gift. However, it is especially granted to oblige the favored party and to ensure close association with the other party with a view to further benefits for oneself.[17] The idea of a contract is not far away from this kind of thinking. In a still broader sense, *χάρις* can stand for a "legal guarantee"[18] given either to equals or by superiors to their inferiors. When Paul speaks of a *χάρις* to be bestowed on Jerusalem by Corinth, he does not consider either of the two parties concerned as superior to the other, but rather sees both as equals—the essential point being, however, that the collection is described here as a desire for true partnership. At this stage of the argument (I Cor. 16) there is no indication as yet, however, of the kind of return the Corinthians were to expect from the partnership.

B. PAUL'S PLANS TO ENSURE THE SUCCESS OF THE COLLECTION

From the wording of I Corinthians 16:1-4 it appears that Paul must have informed the Corinthian congregation briefly at a previous date as to the need and purpose of the collection, and that he must have been asked questions about its practical organization. These verses provide the answer to those questions.

Obviously, the practical side of the organization of the collection had to be looked into systematically. Verse 2 tells us that on the first day of each week,[19] every member of the congregation was urged to put away privately as much money as he or she could spare.[20] It is interesting to note that—although Paul says that such private gathering is to be done on Sunday—nothing is said about any money being collected during the actual church service. We must conclude, therefore, that the sums set aside privately by every member were to be pooled by the congregation only shortly before being conveyed to Jerusalem. This, however, seems to have been a point of only secondary importance to Paul. He was much more interested in drawing attention to the necessity of personal initiative and the active role to be assumed by the congregation in its entirety (but only as regards the actual transfer of the money to Jerusalem). The emphasis on individual initiative reads like an anticipation of II Corinthians 8 and 9, where voluntariness and readiness are stressed.[21]

Verse 3 shows that Paul expected to find the full amount ready for transfer the day of his arrival in Corinth. He also expected the congregation to already have selected those of its members thought worthy and capable of carrying the collection to Jerusalem (if need be without Paul).[22] Paul clearly wishes to point out the importance of independent decision making on the part of the congregation. This fits very well with the attack the apostle had previously launched against the individualism prevailing in Corinth. The passage also testifies to Paul's desire not to travel alone but rather to be accompanied by the envoys of the congregation, should he decide to go to Jerusalem personally (v. 4). Only then would the collection be welcomed as a true gift from the entire Corinthian congregation and as a sign that it was interested in maintaining a living bond with the early church at Jerusalem. At the same time Corinth would give greater emphasis to its willingness to uphold its connection with the history and the fate of the "one church" of all Jesus believers.

On the other hand, Paul also wanted to make sure he was present at Corinth before the collection was sent off to Jerusalem, because he wished to have the opportunity to send letters to Jerusalem through the Corinthian delegation. After all, Corinth was his congregation, and it had organized a collection (as the Galatian congregations had done also). Paul was eager to show that his mission had resulted, not in the establishment of some disintegrated clubs, but in genuine communities willing to remember in gratitude their origin and, hence, were bound to the church as an ecumenical body. As such these congregations did not shrink away from giving material proof of their individual responsibility.

Should the result of the collection be worthwhile, Paul would join the delegation on its journey to Jerusalem. It is not said whether the amount of money collected would be what made it "worthwhile" for him to come along; the general impression is rather that Paul's personal participation in the transfer of the funds would depend on the true inner commitment the Corinthians were prepared to come up with in the affair. In the light of what has been shown already, this interpretation of the text would surely agree not only with the decisive role Paul attributed to the congregation, but also with the course the events finally took, as well as with the explanations given by Paul himself about those events.

When writing the first Epistle to the Corinthians, Paul was not counting on a speedy settling of the matter. Why else would he have suggested that the individual members of the congregation privately set aside every Sunday whatever sums they could, to be put together only at the end? Paul must have had in mind a period of several months. Judging from I Corinthians 16:5-11, he was probably planning on the time between spring and summer, provided, of course, that the epistle was written in the spring.[23]

In case Paul should travel personally to Jerusalem, the conveyance of the money would be delayed until far into the spring, as he was adamant about spending the winter in Corinth (vv. 6-7). Paul did not plan to go to Corinth directly from Ephesus (where the epistle was written), but rather to travel by land through Macedonia (v. 5). It is not clear whether he was also at that time envisaging a collection in Macedonia. From II Corinthians 8 and 9, one can gather that such a collection was begun when Paul visited the area, but that it was initiated by the congregations themselves. Should Paul have envisaged such a collection at a previous date, the subsequent events prevented him from doing anything about it.

After dispatching the first Epistle to the Corinthians, Paul changed his mind. Instead of leaving it up to the Corinthians to do whatever was necessary about the collection before his arrival, as he had planned, he decided to send Titus and another man, whose name we do not know, to Corinth to launch the collection. This is what II Corinthians 12:18; 8:6, 10; and 9:2 refer to.

One may wonder why Paul suddenly decided to go against his suggestion in I Corinthians 16:1-4 and chose to dispatch something like a commissioner to Corinth in order to press for the collection. One might at first be led to assume that Paul had learned that the Corinthians had rejected his letter in general and the request to organize a collection in particular, and that he felt he must take drastic measures. Yet, as demonstrated in I Corinthians 16, Paul did not consider the collection a project to be carried out speedily. Furthermore, Titus's first visit to Corinth is not, in any of the relevant passages, linked to his task of straightening out things in that congregation. This assignment existed only in conjunction with his second visit to Corinth. His first visit had certainly occurred in an atmosphere of peace and harmony. This is evidenced even by the "Philippica" (II Cor. 10–13), where Paul mentions that Titus and the second (unnamed) individual were remembered positively in Corinth for their collection activities there (12:18). Second Corinthians 9:2 tells that the Corinthians were so cooperative during Titus's visit that Paul was subsequently able to inform the Macedonian congregations about the high degree of readiness of the congregations in Achaia. Hence, Titus and his companion had probably visited Corinth because of the favorable reaction to the first epistle; Paul must have succeeded in silencing the opposition in Corinth entirely.

It is not possible today to determine whether Timothy or the first Epistle to the Corinthians—or both—brought on that victory, and whether Timothy had brought the good news from Corinth himself, although it seems highly probable that he did. At any rate, both Timothy's visit and the first epistle were certainly not wasted.[24] The overall readiness on the part of the Corinthian congregation to comply with Paul's wishes apparently resulted in a distinct urge at Corinth to ensure the speedy and thorough realization of the project. However, nothing was started prior to Titus's arrival. We know from II Corinthians 8:6 that the beginning of the collection and Titus's coming coincided in time.

Here the question might arise whether—the Corinthians' willingness to comply notwithstanding—the congregation proved incapable of carrying out Paul's instructions regarding the different steps necessary for the proper organization of the collection (I Cor. 16:1-4), or if they had perhaps realized their incapacity themselves and informed the apostle about it. But why should they have been unable to organize the collection? Equally far-fetched seems the assumption that the Corinthians had criticized Paul's instructions and demanded better coordination from the very beginning. But since II Corinthians 8 and 9 clearly indicate the Corinthians' willingness to comply, one must look for a solution elsewhere.

It seems that the first Epistle to the Corinthians had kindled in the congregation a desire to keep in direct contact with Paul throughout the venture of the collection in order to make him a witness and a helper to their zeal and to view such closeness as a guarantee of undelayed success. Nothing could have been more in keeping with their eagerness to show how interested they were in true church communion. But Paul was unable to free himself directly from his current commitments in Asia Minor. He solved the problem by sending Titus and another as his representatives, at the same time changing his schedule. Instead of traveling to Corinth through Macedonia (as he had said he would in his first letter), he now anticipated coming to Corinth directly from Ephesus and visiting Macedonia afterwards—before returning once more to Corinth. He would thus be visiting Corinth twice within a relatively short period of time (II Cor. 1:15-16). The Corinthians were very interested in Paul's implementation of that revised plan. The strength of their interest shows in their subsequent deep disappointment about his further change of plan. They held this alteration against him even after a second reconciliation with him (II Cor. 1:13-22).

It is impossible to say with certainty whether Paul intended to organize the collection in Macedonia the first time he rescheduled his traveling route, but one can assume that he did. Much more important is the fact that, contrary to the rescheduling of the itinerary described in I Corinthians 16, Paul now also intended to travel to Jerusalem from Corinth himself; suddenly it had become worthwhile for him to come along personally (I Cor. 16:4) and to intertwine his own interests and his personal fate with that of the collection.

What might have triggered this decision? One of the reasons lay in the Corinthians' apparent readiness to commit themselves fully to the collection, engaging in the venture with all their zeal but also demonstrating through their involvement their solidarity with Paul. Later, in II Corinthians 8 and 9, Paul still refers to that readiness. It must have impressed him. Another reason for the change in Paul's plans might have been a worsening in his relationship with Jerusalem or a fear on his part that the Jerusalem congregation had meanwhile formed a negative image of him and his congregations.

It is also possible that the church in Jerusalem had heard about Paul's disputes with the Judaizers in Galatia and about the various statements on the Jewish Law and similar issues he had made during those disputes. Equally conceivable is the possibility that news had spread to Jerusalem about the liberality Paul's other congregations enjoyed with regard to the Jewish Law (especially in Corinth). One must further remember that Paul had consistently been carrying out his work in or near Jewish Diaspora settlements, and that there was constant interchange between these communities and Jerusalem. Individual Jews might have given personal accounts in the city of their experiences with Paul. All these things taken together could have deepened the already existing hatred on the part of orthodox Jewry for the Jesus believers—including those of Jewish stock—and hence further endangered the survival of the early church in Jerusalem.

Ernst Haenchen employs this idea to explain why Paul showed such concern in Romans 15:31.[25] But this concern may have been of much longer standing—or Paul may simply have felt that there were good reasons for such concern to develop. This can explain Paul's motivation to make a personal appearance in Jerusalem to clear away all possible misgivings or to give his own version of the events in the hope of countering any existing distrust as best he could and preventing a looming schism.

Paul had certainly long ago decided to expand his missionary work to the western parts of the Roman Empire beyond Greece after his visit to Jerusalem, as II Corinthians 10:16 expressly points out. Resolving complications with the congregation at Jerusalem could only be conducive to that plan.

Judging from II Corinthians 9:2, Titus's energetic involvement in the fund-raising campaign in Achaia had already produced considerable results. But Titus did not carry the collection through to its conclusion. It is impossible to say why that dynamic enterprise was not completed. This cessation had certainly not resulted from the new opposition. The recriminations against Paul discussed in II Corinthians 12:16-18 in connection with the collection, although they definitely testify to a renewed upsurge of enmity in Corinth, were nonetheless in very different tone from what is said about the Corinthians' opinion regarding Titus's visit. But it was precisely this discrepancy that enabled Paul to play one opinion against the other to his own advantage.

C. NEW DIFFICULTIES

1. New Opposition in Corinth

A new development in Corinth that thwarted Paul's entire program must have begun shortly after Titus's visit to the congregation. This development had come as a sudden obstruction to the apostle's plan to wind up his work in one final gesture of all-encompassing magnitude: the voyage from Ephesus to Corinth, from Corinth to Macedonia and back to Corinth, and, eventually, from there to Jerusalem. All the reasons for which Paul had changed his schedule of I Corinthians 16:4-9 evaporated when a new opposition erupted against him in Corinth. This opposition resulted from the arrival of Jewish Jesus-believing missionaries in the congregation during Paul's absence, people who started to agitate the Corinthians with sharp anti-Pauline propaganda.

In view of the zeal displayed only recently for Paul and his cause, the apostle must have been stunned to see this congregation turn against him once again, more viciously than ever before. Hence, instead of visiting Corinth directly as planned, he wrote a letter in an attempt to bring the vacillating minds of the Corinthians back to his side.[26] That letter, still fragmentarily preserved in II Corinthians 2:14–7:4 (with the exception of the unauthentic material in 6:14–7:1), was intended to justify Paul's legitimacy. But it was to no avail. Paul had no choice, therefore, but to travel to Corinth after all (the so-called "intermediate visit"), this time, however, in a spirit differing widely from that which had prompted the initial decision to make a short stop-over on his way to Macedonia.[27] Under these circumstances the issue of the collection had, of course, become less than secondary. Understandably, this visit turned out to be extremely unpleasant for Paul.[28]

Arriving in Corinth, Paul could only acknowledge that the congregation had already fallen victim to his rivals. The impression one gets when reading Paul's report on the incident is that he had to face massive insults. Who exactly insulted the apostle, or what the insults consisted of, is unknown. All we are certain of is that Paul was unable to reverse the situation and that the visit was a failure.

Back at Ephesus, Paul wrote a letter "out of much sorrow and heartache" and "in many tears" (II Cor. 2:3-4, 9). A large fragment of that letter (the so-called "Letter of Tears") was preserved and has come down to us in chapters 10–13 of the second Epistle to the Corinthians. Those passages inform us that the collection for Jerusalem had also figured among the points earning Paul reproaches and suspicious accusations. The context of II Corinthians 12:16-18 substantiates the assumption that in this dispute a connection was established between the collection and the financial support for pneumatics. Paul may himself have been partly responsible for that mix-up by linking (albeit indirectly) his own achievements as a missionary with the collection.

Hence, upon arriving at Corinth, he was probably reproached not only with lovelessness for his alleged refusal to accept the remuneration for pneumatics,[29] but also (and in direct conjunction with this accusation) with "swindling" in the matter of the collection. This latter reproach is hinted at in Paul's statement: "Possibly, I have not caused you hardship, but perhaps I am a smart fellow who took you in with trickery."[30] This remark is followed by Paul's attempt to show the absurdity of the accusations leveled against him by elaborating on the true circumstances of the collection and, above all, by drawing attention to the positive example set by Titus, which, he was sure, the Corinthians had not yet forgotten.

Why was Paul accused of impostrous manipulations in regard to the collection? He was certainly not charged with embezzlement or similar fraudulent measures; had that been the case, verse 16 would have been worded differently. In view of the events leading up to the collection and Paul's own attitude regarding the financial retributions to be given to pneumatics, another reproach appears more probable—namely, that he had deceived the Corinthians about his true purpose behind the collection. I assume that he was accused on the one hand of refusing to have recognized pneumatic achievements by means of remuneration (and bragging about this refusal), while on the other trying to obtain recognition for his personal accomplishments through such indirect means as organizing a collection for Jerusalem. In other words, Paul was denounced for (mis)using the concept of the collection to gain tangible approval for his own person while ostensibly promoting the unity of the church.

2. Ephesian Captivity

Thus, after only a short period of ease and hopefulness, Paul was faced with new disappointment in Corinth as his relationship with that congregation turned into one of unprecedented hopelessness. Indeed, shortly after having sent his "letter of tears," Paul's entire work seems to have been on the brink of termination. Later, looking back on those difficult times, Paul wrote the following in a letter still available to us as a fragment preserved in the second Epistle to the Corinthians: "We do not wish you to remain uninformed, brothers and sisters, about the affliction come over us in Asia; a burden beyond all measure—indeed, beyond all strength, was laid upon us there, so heavy we had to despair even of life; in fact, within ourselves we had pronounced our own death sentence, (so much so that) we did not any longer put any trust in ourselves, but only in God who resurrects the dead."[31] The affliction referred to here was not just a mere momentary difficulty, but rather one of such duration and magnitude that it had become a question of life and death.

Paul can hardly have meant a deadly illness or a dangerous voyage by land or sea.[32] Both the mentioning of an unbearable burden and the anticipation of a death sentence render such a reading impossible, all the more as the death sentence in question clearly points to a judgment pronounced by a legal court.[33] Not even a simple unrest could be meant here, even if it had been more dangerous in nature than the one described in Acts 19:23-40. The most probable reading would, therefore, be that Paul is referring to actual imprisonment following an unrest or persecution, an imprisonment during which the apostle and those persons who may have been accompanying him were awaiting a court sentence that they must have felt at times would be a death sentence.[34] Nothing of all this is mentioned as yet in the long catalogue of circumstances in II Corinthians 11:23-33; only the so-called letter of reconciliation informs us about such dangers. On the other hand, there is reason to believe that the fragments of the canonical Epistle to the Philippians were written in a prison at Ephesus. Philippians 1:19-26 and 2:12-30 bear witness to the fact that Paul was indeed expecting a death sentence while in captivity in that city.

D. PAUL'S RESPONSE TO THE PHILIPPIAN COLLECTION (THE COLLECTION AND THE DOCTRINE OF JUSTIFICATION)

When it seemed that Paul's work was drawing to its end and that all his achievements appeared to disintegrate (at least as far as Corinth was concerned), the Jesus congregation at Philippi gave solace to the apostle. Having heard of his situation, the Philippians succeeded in organizing a collection, which they handed over to Epaphroditus, their delegate, to take to Ephesus (Phil. 4:14, 18). Paul calls Epaphroditus an "apostle" (Phil. 2:25) in the same way he later used this term to refer to the delegates of the congregations who were entrusted with the conveyance of the collection to Jerusalem (II Cor. 8:23).

We do not know whether the Philippian congregation was aware yet of the collection envisaged for Jerusalem. But in the fragmentary letter of thanks preserved in Philippians 4:10-23 Paul expresses ideas identical to those voiced in conjunction with the collection intended for Jerusalem.[35] In Philippians 4:15, for instance, he declares that the Philippian congregation and he were bound to each other by "a mutual settlement of accounts."[36] This was just one way of expressing the concept advocated in Hellenistic syncretism of the necessity of providing financial support for pneumatics—a formula commended also in Corinth, where Paul opposed it, although he also used the concept to justify his collection for Jerusalem (Rom. 15:27).[37] The difference between the principle of financial remuneration to pneumatics and the collection is that the first stands for repeated aid (Phil. 4:15), while the latter is a one-time donation.

Paul's attempt to divert attention away from the material aspect of the Philippian donation and onto its spiritual content is particularly striking and remarkable. The phraseology he uses for this purpose is full of contradictions and suspense. It has been observed that he makes no mention of his gratitude to the Philippians for their gift; rather, he expresses joy over the opportunity given the congregation to demonstrate their caring concern (v. 10).[38] Paul even adds somewhat harshly that he does not really need such help. To the modern reader this statement, bordering on impoliteness (v. 11),[39] is all the more stunning, as it had certainly not been easy for the congregation to come up with such assistance. But Paul claims that he has learned to be fully self-reliant (v. 11),[40] still stressing the spiritual aspect—he says that he is happy to note the ability of the Philippians to demonstrate their active concern for his personal difficulties (v. 14).[41]

The thoughtfulness of the Philippians stands in agreement with their previous attitude. But Paul resists the temptation to refer to this thoughtfulness with sentiment or edifying intent, switching to sober, indeed business-like, formulations (vv. 15-16).[42] But since such style could give rise to the impression that the gift had come in handy after all, he immediately objects that this is not what counts; what counts is that by their gift the congregation had earned itself a reward (v. 17).[43] Only after making this clear does Paul take up the material aspect of the matter, and he does so through a succinct and matter-of-fact formula customary in antiquity for receipts in business transactions (v. 18).[44] At any rate, the sum sent him is more than he needs.[45] Most important, however—and this is the climax of the entire train of thought—in the final analysis the gift is not something that is given to him, but to God; it is "a sweet-smelling fragrance of offering, a pleasing sacrifice agreeable to God" (v. 18).

This passage stands out remarkably not only because of the usage of highly spiritualized language of cultic piety, but also because such language is applied here to a gift of money. This well demonstrates Paul's attitude to his own Jewish tradition, a circumstance significant enough to be looked into more closely. The metaphor of sweet-smelling fragrance rising up from the sacrificial offering on the altar is biblical imagery.[46] In Jewish theology, especially the wisdom-oriented schools, the metaphor was used in an increasingly figurative sense; it served to show that "man is not offering a sacrifice to God, but you (my) God have made this offering to yourself through me," to quote from the Jewish Abraham Apocalypse.[47] Such traditional cultic imagery takes on its most weighty meaning where the metaphor of sweet-smelling sacrifice is applied figuratively to human activity.

The earliest example of such metaphorical transfer is found in Sirach 38:13-14.[48] That text, probably written under the influence of Persian literature,[49] is meant to describe something like the charisma inherent in the life of the pious and just person.[50] This corresponds to the tendency detectable in Jewish wisdom teachings (particularly those stemming from the Hellenistic-Jewish context) where the life of the just and wise person is defined as being of a charismatic nature. The principle on which such charisma is founded is mostly seen in "wisdom" or in the "divine spirit," the latter being more or less identical with the former.[51] The same idea is expressed in Apocalyptic texts, although perhaps with lesser force.[52]

Second Baruch 67:7 uses the image of a divine "sweet smell" in conjunction with this charismatic principle: "The balm-like fragrance of justice flowing from the Law has died (away) in Zion."

Such transfer of metaphoric symbolism had become possible because, in the Jewish wisdom movement and in Judaism as a whole, law and wisdom became synonymous, even identical.

On the whole, with the increasing sophistication of wisdom-oriented thought patterns as developed in Jewish Gnostic wisdom, externals such as concrete historic action were increasingly left outside the spectrum of subjects worthy of theological consideration.[53] Ever greater emphasis was on the inner attitude of the person, which was thought to result from an infusion of grace (*gratia infusa*) from above.[54] In this development the idea of sacrifice was shifted and increasingly bound up with the prayer of thanks. This tended to become more mystical and turned finally into silent prayer without content.[55] Gradually, the concept of sacrifice became a popular metaphor in mystical language and thought.[56] But this trend was not really toward spirituality—at least not in terms of what spirituality stands for in modern thinking. As a matter of fact, the concepts and means of expression put to work in connection with such mysticism were being imbued with ever greater realism.[57] What happened was a turning away from history-oriented reasoning and language toward the mythical, thus putting the strongest possible emphasis on revelation and spiritual gifts, at the expense of history and the historic.

As in many other instances of Pauline writings, in Philippians 4:18 the apostle expresses himself in patterns of speech typical of syncretistic Judaism—more precisely, of Jewish wisdom—thus affording himself the opportunity to sublimate the material aspect of the offering by laying bare its true value and intrinsic meaning, and implicitly pointing to its true origin. But there is a difference between Paul's tendency in the use of such language and what one finds in Jewish wisdom literature; the apostle chooses this terminology, borrowed from cultic language and now imbued with mystical significance, in order to describe an external, and not a mystical, reality: a collection of money! For Paul it is God's own Spirit that is at work in all practical dealings between people—in fact, he felt that the spiritual character of the human experience of faith can demonstrate itself only by those tangible dealings.

By drawing the attention of the Philippians to the very ground and purpose of their giving, Paul was moving the emphasis away from his own person and placing it more visibly on the true subject and object of the process of giving as such. It is as though Paul had said, "I accept your gift as if it were a gift offered by God, before God, and to God." It was precisely the spiritual richness inherent in the act of giving that so overwhelmed Paul. This is why verse 19 contains the significant promise that the act of giving performed by the Philippian congregation will itself result in God's ("my God's") fulfillment of all their needs.[58] And it will be an abundant and glorious return, as always happens when God confers gifts: God will give to them "in Jesus Christ."

Through this logic Paul intends to heighten the congregation's awareness of a certain effectual mutuality, a circular movement that starts out in God and returns to him, but through the medium of humans dealing with other humans. In this theology the issue is not about a process of "destiny," or about a rationally transparent "necessity"; on the contrary, the circular movement described here is wholly contained in that "space" that is moved and determined exclusively by Christ Jesus, God's eschatological commissioner of salvation.[59] And since that "space" is synonymous with the community of Jesus Christ, Paul's liturgical language in this context is not accidental.

Already in verses 19 and (particularly) 20 he writes: "Glory to God and our Father from eternity to eternity"—a wording distinctly reminiscent of the doxological opening of the Epistle to the Galatians (1:3-5), where he said: "Jesus Christ, who, as willed by God and our Father, gave himself for our sins in order to snatch us from the current evil eon; glory to him through all the ages of eternity. Amen." In this passage it is clearly the salvation brought about by Jesus Christ that determines the "space" of the congregation of the redeemed—a salvation itself grounded in God's sovereignty.

The Epistle to the Galatians is an exposition of this theological concept.[60] Paul interprets salvation as the justification of the godless. This theme is the topic covertly dealt with also in Philippians 4:10-20, where it is applied and explained in highly original terms.

I understand the theological argumentation on which Paul elaborates in Philippians 4:10-20 as an exegetical model for the further interpretation of all Pauline literature pertaining to the collection. The letter of thanks to the Philippians and the texts about the collection for Jerusalem were written at about the same time, and the issues discussed were more or less the same.

Moreover, the letter of thanks has numerous similarities in style, terminology, content, and religio-historical detail with the Pauline collection texts; what is but touched upon in one is elaborated on in the other. Whether Paul produced these similarities wittingly or not need not concern us; we need only state that they exist.

How important the Jesus congregation at Philippi proved for Paul during his Ephesian captivity is further evidenced by another epistolary fragment preserved within the Philippian correspondence: Philippians 1:1–3:1 and 4:4-7. In that epistle, which has survived almost in its entirety, still nothing is said of the collection for Jerusalem. It must have been shortly after dispatching that letter that Paul learned that even this, his most faithful congregation, was threatened with being undermined by approaching adversaries, although the opposing missionaries had apparently not yet established themselves firmly. In an attempt to avoid the worst, Paul sent a letter of warning to the Philippians. Fragments of this letter are preserved in Philippians 3:2–4:3 and 4:8-9.[61] Here, the opponents against whom Paul is warning the Philippians have much in common with the Galatian adversaries,[62] although it would be a mistake to identify one group with the other,[63] as there is no indication of an earlier clash between Paul and these individuals.

As Paul does not say that he plans to visit the congregation in the near future, we may assume that this letter of warning was also written while the apostle was still in prison. The tone of this epistle makes it read almost like a last will. This is particularly true of 3:15–4:1. The general impression is that Paul believed this epistle to be perhaps the last thing he would ever write to the congregation. As to the warning itself, it is first formulated in concrete and precise terms, before it becomes (after an interjected self-description of Paul as the very opposite of the false preachers) more general in character.[64]

Yet, Paul was released from prison once more. One can have no certainty about the duration of his imprisonment. When he drafted Philippians 2:19-30, he must have been detained for several weeks at least. During that time Epaphroditus had fallen ill and become well again. We know that the congregation at Philippi had heard about the illness and had probably had time to send an answer back to Paul about it. After these occurrences, more time, probably several weeks, must have elapsed before Paul was released. Paul left Ephesus shortly after his release.[65]

CHAPTER 4

THE COLLECTION IS RESUMED FOR A SECOND TIME (SPRING AND SUMMER 55 C.E.)

A. THE VISIT TO THE MACEDONIAN CONGREGATIONS

Paul began his journey with a trip to Troas (II Cor. 2:12). We do not know whether or not it was his intent to travel through Macedonia hurriedly to reach Corinth as quickly as possible. All we can gather from II Corinthians 2:12 is that such a plan would not have hindered him from doing fruitful work also at Troas, had the circumstances afforded him the possibility to do so. He was prevented from engaging in such work by his longing for Titus's return from Corinth—a return he must have been looking forward to for a long time. Paul must have known that Titus would be traveling by land (II Cor. 2:13). It seems that Titus, having returned from Corinth, was due also to visit the Pauline congregations in northern Greece and Macedonia. But Paul must have left Ephesus under the assumption that Titus had almost completed his tour. Why else should he have hoped to meet Titus at Troas? Hence, Titus must have set out for Corinth to pacify the congregation there in fulfillment of Paul's request while the apostle was still in prison.

I assume that Titus had departed for Greece before Paul was

thrown into jail, as the Corinthians had heard only vague rumors about the predicament their apostle had fallen into (II Cor. 1:8-11). Had Titus been sent to Corinth by Paul while the latter was still in captivity, they would no doubt have known more. Further, Paul would certainly have used his detention as a defense of his change of schedule.

The mission for which Titus had proceeded to Corinth was difficult enough. Still, as one can see from II Corinthians 7:5-16, he finally succeeded in putting things right again. It is not known whether Titus had arrived at Corinth in time to meet and to engage in controversy with the foreign agitators. At any rate, they were no longer in evidence toward the end of his stay.

No further mention is made of those people in the letter of reconciliation Paul had written on the basis of Titus's report. The success of Titus's handling of the situation was such that the Corinthians spoke about him and their affection for him in terms bordering on exuberance (II Cor. 7:5-16; contrast this to 2:5-13). From these texts we can gather that the collection itself had not as yet been one of the issues. All we can say is that Titus's successful mission in Corinth had taken up much time. How much time exactly is uncertain—neither do we know how long he stayed in Corinth, nor how much time he had set aside for his visits to the remainder of the congregations in Greece afterwards. In any case, for Paul, Titus's journey was becoming overly long. He eventually met up with Titus only in Macedonia. The texts yield nothing as to the precise place of the encounter. Could it have been Philippi?

Titus met Paul at a time when the apostle was beset by great hardship.[1] Not only was he worried about Corinth and uncertain about Titus, but he was also in great anguish about the Macedonian congregations, which had, in fact, been his most reliable ones so far. Referring to these tribulations, Paul even speaks of "battles" (II Cor. 7:5). But these "battles" never stand for persecutions; in all Pauline texts where the term is not used in a military sense, it is always synonymous with "contentions" and "quarrels."[2] Hence, Paul must have had in mind his fights with the opponents who had infiltrated Philippi and against whom he had voiced warnings in Philippians 3:2–4:3.[3] As Paul is speaking of the Macedonian congregations in their entirety, it seems plausible that all of them had been contaminated by this adversarial agitation.

The blow to Paul must have been enormous! Whereas his release had looked like an opportunity to round out his work in all the congregations located around the Aegean Sea, demonstrate in Jerusalem the success of his mission, and set out for a mission in the western half of the empire, he now had to worry about the survival of his congregations. Not only was he not fully informed about how things really stood at Corinth, but he was also faced with the possibility of seeing his most devoted congregations slip through his fingers.

So when he met up with Titus and heard his report, it was like a liberation. Remembering that moment, he wrote: "But God who cheers the humble, cheered us by the arrival of Titus" (II Cor. 7:6). Corinth had been won back. In other respects as well the situation was soon to change for the better. In II Corinthians 8:1-5 we read:

> We want to tell you, brothers and sisters, of God's grace given to the congregations in Macedonia; through heavy probation in affliction, their exuberant joy and their deep poverty flowed over into a wealth of humble goodness. Indeed, according to their ability and, I testify to that, even beyond their ability, and out of their own free will, they besought us with much entreaty to be admitted to the work of grace and to the participation in the service to the Saints; and not only as we had hoped, but they gave themselves above all to the Lord and (then also) to us through the will of God.

From the parallel reference to "affliction" in 7:5 and 8:2 (*θλιβόμενοι* and *θλῖψις* respectively) we may conclude that the "affliction" mentioned in II Corinthians 7:5 had also befallen the Macedonians.[4] But nothing is said in that text about the congregation's having taken up an encouraging position. By contrast, in 8:2 and the surrounding narrative Paul is nearly carried away with joy about the positive attitude shown by those congregations. A reversal of attitude must, therefore, be assumed, not only in Paul, but also on the part of the Macedonian believers. Consequently, Paul can hardly have meant a period of persecutions during which the congregations concerned had stood their test, but rather that they had held firm against opponents, perhaps after some initial vacillations. This reading would substantiate the above-mentioned assumptions about the general situation in the Macedonian territories.

That the Macedonians had finally resisted what Paul considered to be false teaching is evidenced by the active "upsurge of joy" mentioned in II Corinthians 8:2. For Paul, "joy" is not just a happy mood; it is a saving gift from God, part of the new creation, and brought on through the Holy Spirit (Rom. 14:7; I Thess. 1:6). It is already present; joy is not an inner felicity wholly directed toward the beyond, or simply the delight in being a believer. Essentially, "joy" refers to that special delight taken in the presence of other fellow believers, in their doings and in the community with them. This meaning of joy is best gathered from II Corinthians 7:13, Philippians 2:2, and I Thessalonians 3:9. In some cases, this type of joy can even be identified with certain persons or with an entire congregation (Phil. 4:1; I Thess. 2:19-20). The Pauline concept of "joy," therefore, points to a soteriological gift whose eschatological character becomes manifest in the pursuit of true community among believers.

Since the Macedonians had found again their fellowship with Paul, there was reason for "joy" indeed. And it was a joy that brought forth fruit; it was the gateway to simplicity, the exact opposite of the perfection offered by Hellenistic-Jewish Gnostic wisdom. The one text elucidating this is Philippians 3:15, where Paul speaks of the conceit of the Judaizers, who deemed themselves perfect. The Macedonians' simplicity contained a readiness for giving; not only were they delighted in the renewal of the community, but they also were prepared to strengthen and to ratify this community through giving. This readiness had become a visible reality in the plea to be allowed to participate in the collection for Jerusalem—a plea even surprising to Paul. In all this, the emphasis is on the voluntary character of the resolve to participate, while the participation itself is depicted as an unreserved giving of oneself, not just to the brothers and sisters in Jerusalem, but to God himself and to the founder of the congregations, Paul (v. 5).

In this passage we have yet another example of the fact that it was the attitude and action of those congregations themselves—negative and positive as well—that caused Paul to become increasingly synonymous with the collection. Paul had no illusions about the amount to expect from the Macedonian congregations. In verse 2 he mentions the extreme poverty of these people. The reason for this poverty, the overall economic situation in the province, was no temporary emergency in the congregations, as, for instance, a persecution would have been. Paul avails himself of the reality of this neediness on the part of the Macedonians to insist on the importance, not of the material value of the gift, but of the readiness to give of oneself, for the good of the community. Even stylistically Paul is very impressive about this; the subject in the sentence is not only the joy of the Macedonians but also their poverty, which amounts to saying that both are at the root of their readiness "to give themselves."[5]

Paul drafted II Corinthians 8:1-5 as if he were but a spectator to the event. The event itself is unfolding without his personal intervention; everything is happening as if it were a gesture of grace performed by God for the sake of the Macedonians (8:1). It is no coincidence, therefore, that χάρις becomes the very *leitmotif* of chapters 8 and 9 of the second Epistle to the Corinthians. Certainly, Paul had called the collection a χάρις already in I Corinthians 16:3, but only in the sense that the Corinthians were doing the congregation at Jerusalem a favor. That the collection originated in and was performed by the grace of God was not expressed as clearly in that instance as in II Corinthians 8 and 9, although Paul would not have contradicted this interpretation at that time.[6] The situation had now changed; things had to be formulated in a new and different way. This was warranted by the course of events involved. When the collection was first started, there had been much hope; then everything had seemingly come to a halt. The influences opposing Paul's work had threatened to destroy his congregations, thus appearing to deliver the *coup de grâce* to the collection—even though the collection had been meant as a medicine against the agitation of the adversaries and as a means to root the individual congregations firmly in the church at large as one pluralistic body. But eventually, against all odds, the project had started moving again and now seemed to be running as if by itself. This is why Paul suddenly felt deprived of his founder rights and transformed into a mere spectator.

B. A DELEGATION IS SENT TO CORINTH

In view of the newly won freedom from the pressures of adversaries—a freedom so impressively displayed by the Corinthians to Titus—it seemed only appropriate for the congregation to allow their readiness to team up with Paul once more to translate this reconciliation into a renewed participation in the collection.[7] So Paul asked Titus, given this young man's renewed good relationship with the Corinthian congregation, to return to Corinth and to carry through to its end the collection he had launched there about a year earlier. In fact, Titus was himself eager to return to Corinth, in order to resume the venture, as Paul, correcting himself, points out in verse 17.[8] Here we have a typically Pauline twist in depicting a given situation in which the apostle skillfully describes a particular state of affairs as a combination of being willing to act and being moved to do so.

So Titus went to Corinth, but not alone. Two more persons, whose names are unknown, went with him.[9] Their names must have been in the text originally, and it is not clear why they were deleted in the later edition of the present epistle. It is unlikely that the first of those unnamed companions had already been to Corinth with Titus in connection with the collection at an earlier stage, or that he was the unnamed person mentioned in II Corinthians 12:18.[10] Had he been the same, Paul would certainly have said so in II Corinthians 8.

One of the now anonymous persons mentioned in II Corinthians 8:18-21 was a spokesman elected by democratic vote; the expression *χειροτονηθείς* in verse 19 is the customary technical term used in Hellenistic times for the process and result of a democratic election.[11] The text does not say by which congregations this deputy was elected. They need not necessarily have been Macedonian congregations; one should not exclude the possibility that it was Ephesus or some congregation in Galatia.[12] In that case the Macedonian congregations would certainly have confirmed him.

The one feature to be stressed in regard to this deputy is that he was not simply ordered to travel to Corinth; rather, he had been chosen to accompany Paul officially on his journey to Jerusalem (in conjunction with the conveyance of the collection). He had been appointed because he had gained the esteem of the congregations for his qualities as a preacher (v. 18). His reputation as a trustworthy propounder of the gospel had spread among the congregations.[13] Obviously the assignment had not so much been given to a man with organizational talents, as it was given to a capable preacher and theologian; he was to explain to those who might want to know about the considerable and steadily growing amount of money Paul was carrying on his collection tour and to fend off any hint of irregularities or other criticisms directed against the apostle.[14] Swindle and embezzlement were not the only possible issues; Paul might also be compared to a money-greedy manipulator, or even simply derided for traveling around with money instead of the gospel.[15] Contingencies such as these had to be dealt with, particularly since the collection was bound to move increasingly into the foreground as time went by.

Another possible explanation for the presence of this traveling companion could be seen in the expression "bountiful return" (v. 20), which could be a reference to past accusations mouthed by the Corinthians that Paul was swindling them with the collection (II Cor. 12:16). Similar denunciations might also have been made by other congregations. In such cases, this companion would be called upon to testify not only that the collection had been gathered in an orderly fashion, but also—and above all!—that the congregations had agreed to it for reasons of the gospel and that the economic aspect of the affair was only secondary.

This reading would agree with the overall concept behind the collection, as explained several times above. No change had been made to the earlier scheme of sending delegates entrusted with the transport of the collection to Jerusalem (I Cor. 16:3-4), only now the first of these delegates was given much broader responsibilities. By appointing such a delegate, the congregations not only demonstrated their active involvement in the entire venture of the collection, but they also testified to their own importance and their newly found influence. On the other hand, it would be wrong to presume that this first delegate had been set over Paul as a watchdog or supervisor; the apostle was free to send him along any time he wanted—something he could not have done with Titus.[16]

The second unnamed person had already proven his worthiness in accompanying the apostle in the past (v. 22), but he too must be seen as a true apostolic envoy of the congregations (v. 23).[17] We know nothing of his specific assignment. Verse 23 starts out as if to inform the reader of the different functions Titus and his two companions were charged with for their journey to Corinth. Titus is initially set ahead and apart: "As to Titus, he is my comrade and partner for your sake." After this opening one would expect Paul to go on to say something like, "As to our brothers, they are apostolic envoys of the churches." But he reshuffles the sentence to add a further qualification, which—parallel to the statement about Titus—factually ascribes much higher rank and more prestige to those communal apostles: "As to our brothers, the apostles of the congregations, they are Christ's own reflection"—that is, they are the very representatives of the heavenly splendor of Christ! By ascribing to these two envoys a dignity higher even than the apostle's fellow worker, Titus, Paul clearly points to the immense importance he assigns the congregations.

Here the issue is no longer the loving respect paid to Jerusalem in virtue of its position of honor; the issue is the love and respect paid—through willing participation in the collection—to Jesus Christ as represented by the envoys, no matter from which congregation they had come. "Show the proof of our praise for you to them (as well as) in the presence of the congregations," Paul urges in verse 24. He does not even mention Jerusalem, although the gift of love would eventually be received there. In other words, the focus is no longer on any one congregation taken separately; the issue now becomes one of ecumenical publicity. What one community is prepared to carry out for the sake of another constitutes the concern of the entire ecumenical community of Christ, and the actions resulting from this commitment are carried out responsibly, in full view of this universal partnership, in the justified hope that all of the individual congregations will benefit equally by those actions. This public forum of the church at large is represented by the delegates mentioned.

C. A BRIEF EXCURSUS ON THE LITERARY-CRITICAL PROBLEMS INHERENT IN II CORINTHIANS 8 AND 9[18]

Second Corinthians 8 is meant as a recommendation for the envoys mentioned. But was this laudation part of a larger whole as the present epistolary arrangement pretends, or was it a separate letter of recommendation? If the latter, did it include also chapter 9?

As mentioned earlier, there exists a contradiction between II Corinthians 7:5 and 8:1-2. These two passages clearly describe two different points in time with a lapse in between. During that intervening period a reversal must have occurred in the situation prevailing in the Macedonian congregations. This alone would be reason enough to question whether both passages (i.e., II Cor. 7:5-16 and 8) had originally been part of one and the same document. In case II Corinthians 8 had initially belonged to the letter of reconciliation, the entire epistle must have been a letter of recommendation for Titus and his companions. In this hypothesis, however, there remains the disturbing fact that no mention is made of Titus or his assignment at the beginning of the letter of recommendation in the form available to us today, which starts with II Corinthians 1:1. Equally incomprehensible in this hypothesis is the fact that in none of the passages of chapter 7 mentioning Titus is the least allusion made to Titus's willingness to return to Corinth. On the other hand, nothing is said in chapter 8 about Titus having only just come back from there. Moreover, had these chapters really been part of the letter of recommendation, one would reasonably expect more outspoken reference to the recent reconciliation than what is found in II Corinthians 8:8 or 8:20. Paul could easily have written something like, "Now, that you have come forth with such clear evidence of your love, give that love and affection material proof by bringing the collection to completion!" Instead, he refers to the example of the Macedonians. This, now in direct connection with II Corinthians 7:5, does not make a persuasive impression.

All these observations more or less also apply to chapter 9 and its relation to the letter of recommendation—the only difference being that the general impression is that, here, the envoys had been on their way for some time and, hence, that there must have elapsed even more time between this event and those described in II Corinthians 7:5. Therefore, it seems reasonable to conclude at least that both chapters 8 and 9, whose main subject-matter is the collection, did not belong to the letter of recommendation.

All in all, however, not even chapters 8 and 9 (as they stand now) seem to belong together. The discrepancies detectable between these two chapters have been noted repeatedly in past biblical research.[19] In II Corinthians 9:1, for instance, Paul starts out by saying, "Indeed, there is no need for me to mention to you the help to be given to the Saints." This is not the approach one would normally have expected in connection with something that had been dealt with earlier at such length. Why should it have become unnecessary, suddenly, not to mention it? Only if we assume that Paul is introducing a new subject at this point does this formulation make sense.[20]

In II Corinthians 8:1-6, Paul cites the example set by the Macedonians and calls on the Corinthians to follow suit. In II Corinthians 9:1-2, he campaigns for the donation of the addressees (the Corinthians? the Achaians?) by stressing that he had always praised them to the Macedonians in pointing especially to their year-old readiness for the collection. We learn that the Macedonians had been spurred on by the addressees' initiative—though perhaps not by all of them, as Paul cautiously admits, but only the majority. So, II Corinthians 9 is written as an incentive for the addressees; they are urged to proceed with the collection diligently and quickly—but why? To avoid leaving the apostle shamefaced in the eyes of the Macedonians! Paul now even refers to his intention to take some Macedonians along with him to Achaia—a reference made exclusively, it would seem, to give more force to his plea not to be shamed by the congregation(s) addressed. The sending of the envoys is described as a measure preparing Paul's own visit (II Cor. 9:4). That this preparatory step is described now as another measure intended to prevent all possible embarrassments in front of the Macedonians is also at variance with chapter 8. We see that the discrepancies between chapters 8 and 9 of II Corinthians are many.[21]

On the other hand, both chapters also have many points in common. Both contain references to the sending of the envoys; both insist on the *προθυμία* required on the part of the readers. The importance of the inner attitude of people and the causal nature of the activity of divine grace is given special emphasis in both chapters. Second Corinthians 9:8-14 bears great resemblance to 8:13-14.[22]

The differences and parallels existing in both chapters are probably best explained on the premise that we are dealing here with two separate letters written shortly one after the other. The beginning and the end of both these letters must be considered lost. Chapter 9 was most probably written and dispatched subsequent to chapter 8, since (as Windisch saw correctly) in chapter 9 Paul is pressing for the completion of the collection, whereas in chapter 8 he is still encouraging his readers to resume it. As to the "brothers" mentioned in chapter 9, whose names must have been deleted (as in the case of chapter 8) by the final redactor, they must have been known to the addressees. That chapter 9 was drafted after chapter 8 can be followed also from the observation that in chapter 9 Paul announces his forthcoming arrival in Achaia, but does not do so in chapter 8. Windisch was probably right in assuming that II Corinthians 9 originally constituted a circular letter to the congregations in Achaia, as the province is mentioned only here. Windisch points out that all the exegetical problems at hand (i.e., the repetitions, the complementary data, the contradictions, as well as the simultaneity of the events described) can be more easily explained by this hypothesis. Indeed, using this logic, the discrepancies between II Corinthians 9:2 and 8:7 can be (with Windisch) considered as resulting from the fact that by the time chapter 9 was composed, more had been done to further the collection in the Achaian congregations outside of Corinth than in Corinth itself.

Nevertheless, even Windisch admits that also in this interpretation many of the literary difficulties found in these texts remain unsolved.[23] He suggests that the expression "of all the Saints that are in Achaia" (II Cor. 1:1) was added by the redactor in the light of the opening of the circular letter in II Corinthians 9. This is possible, but not absolutely necessary. The results of the opponents' interference, as well as those flowing from the reconciliation, had certainly been felt, too, in the congregations around Corinth, although, perhaps, not to the same extent. Besides, as pointed out earlier, II Corinthians 8 ought to be seen as separate from the letter of reconciliation.[24]

But there is yet another possible reading; this would be not to identify the "brothers" referred to in II Corinthians 9 with Titus and his companions. In which case, Paul would have conceived, in addition, this second letter on the collection also as a letter of recommendation for the envoys sent off to visit congregations in Achaia other than those mentioned in II Corinthians 8 (perhaps even brothers and sisters), not including Corinth. Against this reading stands the fact that there is nothing in the text recommending those "brothers (and sisters?)" in particular, nor any reference to another, earlier delegation.

It looks as if Paul is aware that the envoys of chapter 8 are still on tour, as he writes II Corinthians 9, but that he expects them to be back in Achaia before his epistle had arrived at Corinth. Hence, if II Corinthians 8 was written in Philippi, we must assume approximately three weeks for the letter to reach Corinth. As one of the envoys was the "brother" delegated by the churches, that person may have made it a point to spend more than one night in each congregation visited on the way, because of the importance of his mission; after all, he was acting as official representative of all the congregations in each of the congregational assemblies convened on his arrival (II Cor. 8:18-20, 24). Consequently, the journey must have taken much longer than the usual three weeks. During that time Paul could have left Philippi, gone as far as Thessalonica, and written II Corinthians 9 from there. This change of whereabouts would certainly explain some of the incongruities between chapters 8 and 9. It would also imply a second opportunity for Paul to send a letter to the south quite some time after the first one, and that he had done so, in order to revive the interest of the entire province of Achaia for the collection.[25]

CHAPTER 5

THE LETTER OF RECOMMENDATION FOR TITUS AND HIS COMPANIONS (II COR. 8)

A. THE INNER PARTICIPATION OF THE CONGREGATIONS AND GOD'S WORK

On what grounds did Paul assert the need for a collection in his letter of recommendation for Titus and the other envoys? Biblical scholarship has noted repeatedly that he does not employ a uniform terminology to describe the collection.[1] This is, of course, no accident. But what do the various names given to the venture have in common? What does the collection really stand for? A first reading of the texts shows that the answer is not easily found; the common denominator we are looking for is hidden between the lines of a strangely encapsulated, abruptly changing, and sometimes highly ornate narrative.[2] From a literary point of view, this narrative in II Corinthians 8 (rather similar to the formal style in chap. 9) is particularly striking. According to Hans Windisch, both texts constitute business letters.[3] Yet, in a business letter one would expect clear and succinct writing, while the opposite is the case here.

I have already spoken of the opening verses of chapter 8. Still, some complementary observations are called for here. Verse 2 notes that the external unfolding of the collection had somehow receded into the background in the light of the emphasis put on the motivation for it.[4] Verses 3 through 6 explain the preceding assertion that the opportunity to participate in something like the collection amounted to nothing less than an act of grace granted from above. This rationale is expressed, however, in the form of a syntactical inconsistency.[5] While the reader would have expected a statement to the effect that the Macedonians had collected money according to and even beyond their means, Paul interjects that they had themselves—and by their own free will—requested permission to participate. More important, the argument in this sentence is essentially about offering oneself, not for the congregation at Jerusalem, but for God and Paul. The mental leap inherent in the text at this point is forcefully stressed by the opening words: "And not as we had hoped, but . . ."—a particularly harsh remark.[6]

The reference to God-willed offering on the part of the Macedonians harkens back to the statement made at the beginning, which claimed that the activity was a demonstration of divine grace. The true subject matter under debate here is the inner involvement of the Macedonian congregation and the foundation of their involvement in God's own action.

Paul's use of the expression *κοινωμία τῆς διακονίας* to designate the collection in verse 4 supports this interpretation. I have already attempted to show that the translation "(rendering) service" falls short of the full meaning of the Greek term *διακονία*, just as "servant" is not fully satisfactory for *διάκονος*, or "to serve" for *διακονεῖν*.[7] The early church associated all these terms with the idea of mission, of an individual being sent to perform a particular function for the one who sends. This individual fully represents the sender, acting out his or her mission as an ordained, fully legitimated task. This concept also implies that the sender, the envoy, and the receiving party are bound together in one single act.

The idea of rendering service is also certainly present in this terminological pattern, but in most cases it is of secondary importance. However, the case in II Corinthians 8 and 9 is somewhat different. Here *διακονία* and *διακονεῖν* denote first and foremost service, but service in terms of stewardship and ministry. There is still a sender who commissions and is represented by those who serve. The notion that sender, envoy, and recipient are bound together, united in one and the same fateful mission, is not lost. The principles of representation, vicarious action, reciprocity, and shared destiny are tightly connected to the concept of a collection for Jerusalem and its conveyance.[8]

As noted earlier, in II Corinthians Paul wants to convey the idea that the preparatory phase of the collection has its roots in an action of grace given to the Macedonians, which manifested itself again and again in a process that was finally to touch the Corinthians as well. This idea is particularly clear in the transition that takes place in verses 5 and 6.[9] The immediate impression one receives from verse 7 is that Paul means to draw a simple comparison.[10] He writes: "In the same way as you are rich in everything, in faith, in speech, in knowledge, in all kinds of zeal and the love that originated in us and (which) is dwelling among you (now)." Here, one would expect him to continue by saying, "So you will also receive abundant riches from this work of grace." But the second part of the comparison does not come. The sentence is reshuffled syntactically. By introducing a subordinate consecutive clause, Paul replaces the expected second part of the opening comparison and writes: "In order that you, too, be abundant in this work of grace!"

In the popular Greek parlance of the time it was certainly not out of the ordinary to wrap an imperative in a consecutive clause,[11] but to connect an imperative phrase with a comparison, as in II Corinthians 8:7, was extremely unusual and, therefore, striking. Paul must have opted for this literary tour de force to make the Corinthians see that participation in the collection was the consequence of all the gifts of grace (*charismata*) they had previously been granted.

The uncanny phrasing of the statement "the love that originated in us and (which) is dwelling among you (now)" bears witness to Paul's conviction that charismatic gifts are by nature active, and that they press for a specific realization, in this case participation in the collection for the sisters and brothers in Jerusalem. Consequently, in this context *χάρις* means the work of grace.[12]

Since Paul constantly speaks of the urgent and pervasive nature of the collection, he cannot—nor must he!—write about it as if he were giving orders (v. 8).[13] All he can do is stress the enthusiasm of the Macedonian congregation, knowing that this comparison would put Corinth to the test and probe the authenticity of their love. Doubtless, Paul had said that the love granted the Corinthians as a charismatic gift had originated in him. But he could not be the basis or cause of their love.[14] Verse 9 speaks of that proper basis and cause: "(For) you know the gift of grace (*χάρις*) of our Lord Jesus Christ: he became poor for your sake, although he was rich, in order that by his poverty you would become rich."

As in cases where another text is cited (and here we have a formula from the theological tradition of the early church), this quotation is not woven seamlessly into the surrounding text.[15] This christological formula is not quoted for purposes of edification; rather, it is to give the reason for the restraint displayed in verse 8 and for Paul's trust in the Corinthian congregation. The principle behind all that has been said thus far is stated in this confessional reference. The *χάρις* referred to here is interrelated with everything called *χάρις* elsewhere in chapters 8 and 9 that refers to the collection. The quote highlights Paul's interest in the concept of *χάρις*, its shades of meaning and their relevance for the enterprise in question.

In this christological formula, being "poor" and being "rich" define the respective states of heavenly and earthly existence, not the availability or non-availability of human possessions. The issue is not about Jesus of Nazareth's renunciation of worldly riches; it is about that event in which the heavenly dimension of life became human.[16] Jesus did this for the sake of humans, to enable them by being human like them to partake in heavenly life. Whereas the transitional formula clearly uses "you" with a view to all believers, here Paul applies it directly to the Corinthians.

It would be a mistake to consider this formula a model for a devout life—an example for ascetics to follow by means of economic or other material sacrifice.[17] Even in this context, where the model is specifically applied to the congregation of Corinth, this is certainly not the implication. The Corinthians are not urged "to do as Christ did." Paul simply wishes to make a universal pronouncement on God's saving action in the world. The application of the sentence is given by its very content. As it is a pronouncement of principle, it carries its own terms of application. They have their basis in the events referred to. The one who becomes human brings heaven into the concrete, historical life of the community. Because God's grace has manifested itself in this way, Paul can wait; he need not be impatient. On the basis of this conviction he can speak in an almost off-hand manner; he can be noncommittal, pointing the Corinthians to the dynamic momentum entailed in the matter of the collection (v. 10).[18] This is why he feels free to remind them that they had not only been contributing their share to the collection for quite some time now, but they had also shared in its benefits. The whole affair has truly become their business and must also necessarily result in a return for them. This is exactly what Paul had told the Philippians about the significance of their donation (Phil. 4).

All these points, perhaps somewhat confusing at first, are expressed in II Corinthians 8:10, where Paul writes: "For this [i.e., the collection] will prove fruitful to you—to you, who have started not only the doing but also the wanting to do for as long as a year." In the awareness of all this the Corinthians ought to draw the necessary conclusions and carry through their action to its completion (v. 11). Here Paul's use of the imperative mood well reflects the speediness with which he wished the business to be concluded.[19]

Verses 11-13 are a little difficult due to the inconsistency of the thoughts presented. Paul expresses himself in hints and innuendos, as if he were counting on the bearers of the epistle (who were familiar with his thinking and the true nature of the cause at stake, and who would also be attentive to the reaction on the part of the readers) to elucidate the passage—including verses 14 and 15—as best they saw fit. But since the modern reader must do without such oral elucidation, the text remains cryptic, particularly verses 11 and 12. One must resist the temptation to manipulate the passage; it would be too risky to make it yield any clear information on the measures Paul might have suggested to ensure the successful conclusion of the undertaking. By contrast, verses 13 and 14 are not as veiled; from them we can more easily discover Paul's thoughts about the collection.

B. THE MOTIVATION AND THEOLOGICAL MEANING OF THE COLLECTION

The striking feature of II Corinthians 8:13-14[20] is the double occurrence of the word *ἰσότης*—otherwise absent from Pauline texts.[21] Ἰσότης ("equity"; "equality") was one of the basic notions in both Greek and Hellenistic thought.[22] It denotes primarily the legal equality of all citizens, realized in the democratic order of Greek cities. At the same time, *ἰσότης* is also the source of righteous activity in a general sense, not just of that of the judge.[23] The term is closely linked to *δικαιοσύνη*. The dominant role of the concept of equity/equality in the overall cultural context of the time had led to the personification of *ἰσότης* as early as the classical Greek era. As such it is seen even as a divine power bringing about salvation.[24]

Philo, for instance, ascribed great importance to *ἰσότης*.[25] The great treatise on *ἰσότης* in Quis Rerum Divinarum Heres 141-206 (hereafter referred to by its abbreviated title, Rer. Div. Her.) belongs to a larger section of sapiential tradition in 129-236. Here the terms *logos, wisdom,* and *spirit* (*νοῦς*) are interlocked in an expanded metaphysical speculation. This particular combination of terms by itself firmly locates the tract within the wisdom tradition. Other details also provide links with Jewish wisdom, but an analysis of these would lead us far beyond the scope of the present study. The relation between Philo and the Wisdom of Solomon (including the various traditions it presupposes) have long been noted by numerous scholars; in fact, to the parallels firmly established so far, supplementary ones could be added. That this leads to far-reaching consequences in terms of the history of religion has not, until now, been sufficiently realized.

The term *νοῦς* itself occurs in the tradition of Jewish wisdom employed by Philo for the first time in this treatise. But this was simply an expansion of relations with the general culture, which Hellenistic-Jewish wisdom had already established. The Jewish Gnosis presupposed in Philo's thought, particularly its Alexandrian component, had opened itself to syncretism even more than in its earlier stages, including that of the Wisdom of Solomon. The gist of this expression of wisdom thought did coincide with certain speculative tendencies that evolved through a more cosmic and transcendental understanding of *νοῦς*.

In Appendix 2 of this book the reader will find an illustrative survey of the traditional piece incorporated in Rer. Div. Her. At this stage of our study it will suffice to give a summary of the basic points of interest in the tradition with which Philo was working:

1. *ἰσότης* constitutes a divine force. In accordance with a tendency in the Hellenistic tradition toward a personified conception of *ἰσότης*, the Hellenistic-Jewish tradition identified this concept with God himself.

2. As had been the case in the Hellenistic tradition, *ἰσότης* is instilled with a cosmic nature. Cosmological speculations of this type touch upon an essential concern of Jewish wisdom.[26]

3. In accordance with the Greek and Hellenistic traditions, *ἰσότης* is seen in close conjunction with *δικαιοσύνη*, with the difference, however, that *δικαιοσύνη* is not understood as either inferior or equal to *ἰσότης*, but rather superior to it. This corresponds to the meaning *δικαιοσύνη* had in Jewish wisdom tradition.[27]

4. The cosmic meaning of *ἰσότης* is bound up with a mystical component. This combination corresponds to certain trends in the wisdom tradition concerning *δικαιοσύνη* and *δίκαιος*. This kind of combination is particular to Hellenistic-Jewish Gnostic wisdom, and can be gathered already from texts in the Wisdom of Solomon.[28]

5. As in the Wisdom of Solomon, the mystical component is associated with a charismatic one,[29] but *ἰσότης* now turns into an identification for grace granted from above. Philo employs in his argument Exodus 16:18, the same text to which Paul also referred in connection with *ἰσότης*.[30]

6. The idea of community, the most intrinsic connotation of *ἰσότης* in Greek thinking, loses all its weight in this wisdom tradition. This development logically follows from the tendency in Hellenistic-Jewish Gnostic wisdom to suppress as much as possible—indeed, to eliminate entirely—all consideration for history and, hence, for the concept of a historically based community.[31]

It was Hans Windisch who suggested the possibility that Paul and Philo had borrowed from a tradition common to both—a tradition that had established a connection between Exodus 16:18 and the term *ἰσότης*.[32] This is now certain. As pointed out earlier, Philo was working out of a particular wisdom tradition. Paul's peculiar terminology in II Corinthians 8, which clashes not only with the context but also with his usual theological language, suggests that he was drawing from a particular tradition. That this tradition was not entirely foreign to Paul's thinking can be seen from the fact that—as mentioned earlier in connection with the motif of sweet fragrance and the idea of spiritual sacrifice—

Paul was involved with the wisdom tradition and, specifically, also with Gnostic wisdom. We encounter elsewhere in the Pauline texts concepts and motifs similar to those used by Philo. It must be stressed, however, that the tradition from which Paul borrowed in II Corinthians 8:13-15 was not identical to the tradition that stands behind Philo in Rer. Div. Her., although each is definitely related to the other, having grown from the same root.

In the following we shall utilize the motif of ἰσότης ("equity") as it appears in Philo's tradition as a means to explain the difficulties pertaining to II Corinthians 8:13-15. Verse 13 starts out with a soothing statement: "For not as a relief for others, for you a burden." Usually this pledge is viewed as an attempt made by Paul to cool down overly enthusiastic zeal or perhaps even anger.[33] Hence, the reader expects a reference to a true and reasonable compensatory equilibrium—that is, the application of the motif of "equity" in the original Greek sense; something like, "For this is not meant as a relief for others, and for you as a burden, but it is meant as a measure of equity." And indeed Paul writes at the end of verse 14: "so that there be equity" (ὅπως γένηται ἰσότης).

It is not surprising, therefore, that commentators always insert for ἰσότης in verse 13*b* the original Greek sense of the term. But here Paul does not write "so that there might be equity"; he writes "ἀλλ᾿ ἐξ ἰσότης" ("but out of equity"). Clearly, this unexpected wording gives special emphasis to the motif of "equity"/"equality," but this alone does not explain the striking usage of the preposition ἐκ. After the preceding text, the reader expects a statement concerning the goal and purpose of the giving, not the ground on which it is to be performed. Added to these considerations is the fact that the sentence is incomplete; thus the unexpected preposition ἐκ makes it appear even more open-ended.

Usually this exegetical difficulty is circumvented by avoiding the logical, yet more difficult, translation of ἐκ as "from" or "out of." Hans Lietzmann, for instance, translates it as "according to the measure of equity" ("nach Maßgabe von Gleichheit").[34] Others solve the problem by carrying the incomplete sentence over into the next phrase. But all this is to no avail. Such semantic manipulations only leave verse 13 even more crippled in its own meaning, and verse 14 gains no clarity by the merger. On the contrary, it becomes unwieldy and muddled—not to mention that by this strategy *ἰσότης* appears twice in the same sentence. This repetition—combined with the suggested translation of "according to the measure of equity" for *ἐξ ἰσότητος*—is not acceptable linguistically, because the double usage of *ἰσότης* confers almost the same meaning to the term in both cases. First it stands for "measure," then for "purpose." It follows, therefore, that any exegesis that wants to streamline the syntactical leap in verse 13 fails to assist one in understanding the verse. It is precisely this confusing leap in style that must be explained, and, contrary to verses 11 and 12, such an explanation can be found.

Instead of entering upon the expected argument over the "measure" and the "purpose" of the collection, Paul refers back to its ground. On the basis of the Greek understanding of "equity"/"equality," the ideological foundation of the collection would be legal and juridical equity/equality. In other words, it must spring from *ἰσότης* in the true Greek sense.

One might ask whether two such different approaches can be considered in conjunction with each other at all. Certainly not. Consequently, the intended contradiction in the text would have to be understood as an expression of Paul's objection that the essential nature of giving and receiving is not properly understood as long as it is carried out in a calculating, grasping fashion. But it seems hardly plausible either that Paul meant to recommend some kind of legal equity as ground and premise for the collection alone; this kind of mere formalism would hardly correspond to Paul's usual argument, and it would not provide an answer to the function of the phrase within its context.

The picture changes, however, and a dialectical point consonant with Paul's custom shows up when one suggests the Hellenistic-Jewish variety of the notion of *ἰσότης* as the basis for understanding the verse. When *ἰσότης* is seen as a divine force and can be used for paraphrasing even God himself, and when it is endowed not only with cosmic but also with charismatic-mystical connotations, an affirmation stating the causative effectiveness of the concept becomes understandable. The aforementioned parallels to Jewish wisdom render possible a reading that gives *ἰσότης* causative meaning. Given this background it appears to me that the expression *ἐξ ἰσότητος* is practically interchangeable with ἐκ θεοῦ. On this premise, Paul's objection suddenly makes sense. Given the workings of the divine principle of ἰσότης as the actual source of giving and receiving, the principles of performance and achievement fall aside, and with them all comparing, measuring, and judging.

Thus ἰσότης is brought closer to the understanding of χάρις, which occurs in this context and elsewhere in Paul. In verse 13 Paul could have written ἐκ χάριτος. In using ἰσότης he can—on the basis of the religio-historical tradition on which he has been drawing—emphasize more strongly the extent of the source of the enterprise of giving and receiving. He can assert that what moves the inner person also forms the universe, and vice-versa. It does so evenly.

But I would add a note of caution here. It is clear to me that Paul wants to allude to the associations the term ἰσότης has within the Hellenistic-Jewish tradition. Apart from its being equated with God himself and the charismatic element, there is also the concommitant link to δικαιοσύνη as causative basis of ἰσότης. It was precisely this multi-dimensionality that prompted Paul to use ἰσότης in this particular context. But it must not be overlooked that the text employs allusions only; all the different shades of meaning appear only between the lines.

The main point Paul clearly wishes to make is that the constant and all-encompassing movement of grace, which is and makes both righteous and equal, dwells permanently within its divine origin. By pointing to this principle and relating it to a concrete historic phenomenon of a personal (as well as transpersonal) communal nature, Paul is able to introduce fundamental aspects of his doctrine of justification and to use them as a corrective and as a means of critique. In so doing he holds at bay the dehistoricizing aspects of the cosmic and mystical dimensions of the Gnostic understanding of ἰσότης, which might have been on the reader's mind.

In using the ἰσότης in this way, Paul allows this sentence in verse 13 to remain incomplete. Instead of finishing the sentence, Paul starts another one without directly bridging the gap: "At this point in time your abundance is added to their shortage, so that their abundance might be added to your shortage, so that there might be equity; as it is written: 'Who had much, did not have more, and who had little, did not have less.' "[35] Verse 14 opens with a strikingly elaborate indication of time: ἐν τῷ νῦν καιρῷ[36] The emphasis is syntactically heightened by the absence of any kind of particle of transition. Although this emphasizing effect has not gone unnoticed, most translators complete the second half of the sentence by adding a "then"—just as if there had been a simple νῦν at its beginning and as though this sentence had been intended to explain what preceded. The missing "then" after the emphatic definition of time in the beginning is astonishing and hardly without reason. Paul does not want to draw attention to the preceding material by establishing a syntactical link but rather by creating a breach. What does he intend to say with this?

The expression ἐν τῷ νῦν καιρῷ is used thrice more by Paul, all three instances coming in the Epistle to the Romans, written only several months after II Corinthians 8. We read them in Romans 3:26, 8:18, and 11:5. There the phrase refers to the present as qualified by the act of grace performed on the cross—a present set against both the past (Rom. 3:26; 11:5) and the future (Rom. 8:18). All three instances refer to a period of time; more especially, to time literally understood as something spatial. This is different in character from the simple νῦν, which, in its theological use, always stands for eschatological time, as continuous present and as continuous future.

I do not share Hans Joachim Schoeps's opinion that the concept of an interim messianic rule was as central to Paul's theology as the two-aeons doctrine of Jewish Apocalypticism was.[37] Paul's notion of time is much too complex to be forced into such labels as "two-aeons-doctrine" or "pre-dating of the messianic interim rule." Still, II Corinthians 8:14 contains traces of the idea of the messianic interval. This is substantiated not only by the ἐν τῷ νῦν καιρῷ, which clearly refers to a period of time, even with a spatial connotation. The mention of the "manna" miracle points to the messianic interval too. According to the concept of "hope" as defined in the Jewish Apocalyptic tradition, the repetition of the "manna" miracle belongs to the messianic interim, as one can clearly see in II Baruch 29:8.[38] Paul must have decided to make use of this concept in II Corinthians 8:14 in order to combat the possibility that the Corinthian readers might slip into cosmic-mystical ways of thinking.

Paul holds certain ideas in common with these cosmic-mystical perspectives inasmuch as he wants to stress the idea that God's saving grace is the same for all alike and that it relates to both the whole world and every single person in his or her innermost core (ἐξ ἰσότητος). But because Hellenistic-Jewish Gnostic wisdom holds to a sweeping concept of oneness, in which the One is merged into the All and the All into the One, it tends to lose all sense of distance and all conception of any encountering the "other," whether this be God, neighbor, or community. To counter this trend, Paul found it necessary to speak of time and history—as he did in verse 14.

C. PAULINE DIALECTICS

Paul could not speak of justification without this element of the temporal. This is why he turns to Apocalyptic patterns of speech and thought. But it would be a mistake to say that Apocalyptic concepts are closer to the center of his theology than those pertaining to Hellenistic-Jewish Gnostic wisdom. Rather, Paul keeps both these approaches in a dialectically balanced relationship.[39] Both traditions are similar in that they are fundamentally concerned with the experience of salvation.[40] In terms of practice these branches of the wisdom movement have much in common,[41] but in terms of their respective goals they differ widely.[42] Obviously, Paul operates somewhere in between both these currents of thought.[43] I assume that, due to his personal origins, he was familiar with the dialectical exchange between the two schools.[44] The dialectics of Pauline speech are practically identical with the relationship between these traditions, but in this case the dialectics of language correspond to a dialectical presentation of subject matter. This has been succinctly described by the formula "Already—not yet," a maxim Paul succeeds in radicalizing to the extreme. Did the impetus for such radicalization stem from something other than his Jewish background?

One should notice that II Corinthians 8:13-15 mentions neither God nor Christ. The overall impression this passage seems to give is one of detachment. One expects to find imperatives, but there are none. Paul simply makes a statement and writes as if dealing with a process that follows a natural law of necessity. This emphasis on the lawful unfolding of things corresponds to a distinctive feature of wisdom thinking. Paul's cool matter-of-factness results from the dialectical manner in which he presents his argument. Hidden behind this soberness lies not only an awareness of the steady and inexorable flow of the events described, but also an absolute certainty about the true origin of those events. While the sudden appearance of "Thanks (*χάρις*) be to God" (verse 16) relieves the tension produced by the preceding text, it also relates to that text. Obviously, Paul weighs his words carefully when choosing the term *χάρις* (here, "thanksgiving").

The matter-of-fact statement in II Corinthians 8:14-15 refers to the present. This must be stressed, as one might be tempted to believe that the final clause refers to a time other than the present.[45] To do so is to raise inappropriate questions about the manner and timing of the reaction of the congregation at Jerusalem.[46] Neither of the two halves of the sentence contains any specifics on the "shortage" or the "plenty," presumably because Paul is dealing with "shortage" and "plenty" in general and with the balance between the two, which necessity has produced. This balance exists in the form of a mutual dependency between Jewish and Gentile Jesus believers. This, in my opinion, is the meaning of the *ἵνα* ("in order that"). There is no indication of any subjective intention, only that of the objective tendency inherent in the process at hand. How could it be otherwise? The event—equity—must correspond to the source—equity. Gustav Stählin believes that this sentence stands in contradiction to Romans 15:27, but I cannot find this to be true.[47] Paul rather seems to be dealing with two similar issues, although here in II Corinthians 8 he does so in a much broader sense. This would have been made completely clear had Paul repeated the first half of verse 14. Nonetheless, the text does demonstrate the fact that Paul wants to describe a circular movement, a fact of which II Corinthians 9 gives even clearer evidence.

CHAPTER 6

THE CIRCULAR LETTER TO THE ACHAIAN CONGREGATIONS

A. THE MOTIF OF BLESSING

In II Corinthians 9:5 the collection that the Achaian Jesus congregations had promised for some time, and which they are now called upon to complete, is called εὐλογία.[1] It "seems quite reasonable to assume that Paul has in mind a play on words when thinking of writing λογεία first, but then choosing the much richer εὐλογία."[2] This assumption, put forth by Hans Windisch, offers a credible explanation for the sudden appearance of εὐλογία, a term that carries the meanings "[human] gift" or "present" and "bountiful return," that appear nowhere else in the New Testament and rarely outside of it. Still, even in this sense, the inherent aspect of blessing asserts itself, particularly in the case of the latter meaning, "bountiful return." Paul still has a gift of blessing in mind. According to the biblical usage of the term, εὐλογία can mean not only the impartation of a gift of blessing, but also the blessing itself. For example, in Judges 5:5 (similar in Joshua 15:19) it is the gift made by the father to his departing daughter. But sometimes the gift of blessing can underline the benediction.[3] When used thus, εὐλογία stands for the confirmation or the establishment of a communal relationship, not just for a prayerful wish or thanks.

Assuming that Paul followed this biblical usage, εὐλογία in II Corinthians 9 resembles the combination of the terms λογεία and χάρις used in I Corinthians 16:1 and 3 for designating the collection. In that case, Paul must have felt that the Achaians had promised to perform an action that would confirm a communal relationship between themselves and Jerusalem—a communion that had already existed (at least latently) for some time. This confirmation would also assure Jerusalem that the Achaians truly wished the Jerusalem congregation to be blessed. This reading is particularly interesting in the light of the issues under debate in II Corinthians 9:10-15.

Just as he had played on the various meanings of *χάρις* in II Corinthians 8, so also Paul could have chosen to elucidate the true nature of the collection by using the various shades of meaning of the term *εὐλογία* in II Corinthians 9—especially in reference to the interdependence of divine and human action. But he did not do so (deliberately, it would seem), as can be seen from verse 7, in which he quotes Proverbs 22:8 (according to LXX), but replaces *εὐλογεῖ*, with its biblical meaning of "He (i.e., God) blesses," with *ἀγαπᾷ*. Similarly in verse 8, he writes *πᾶσαν χάριν περισσεῦσαι*, instead of the possible *πᾶσαν εὐλογίαν περισσεῦσαι*. Why Paul chose this alternative we cannot say.[4]

B. SAPIENTIAL REASON

In order to stress his request that they give generously and without miserliness, Paul introduces a traditional wisdom saying, originally a farmer's rule and later incorporated into Jewish wisdom proverbs: "Yet this (is a fact): a farmer who sows sparingly will harvest but sparingly, but if he sows bountifully, he will harvest bountifully."[5] Jewish wisdom transposed this farmer's rule, according to which the crop will always correspond to the seed, into the motif of "just reward."[6] The same idea still prevails in later wisdom writings,[7] down to Apocalyptic literature.[8] In the Apocalyptic context, the interrelatedness of seed and harvest corresponds to deeds done "now" and the future judgment on those deeds. It becomes a paraphrase for the absolute inexorability of the eschatological reward for deeds performed in the earthly context.[9]

In Galatians 6:7-10 Paul takes up this theme of seed and harvest and paints a colorfully Apocalyptic picture of what is meant by "just rewards." But he does no such thing in II Corinthians 9:5;

here, both the imagery and its application are presented in very sober tones. Paul simply tells us that generosity and miserliness always get their just rewards. Not even the contrast between the two (and their respective rewards) is stated in absolute terms. As in Jewish experiential wisdom, the maxim addresses itself to reason. It is characteristic of sapiential reason to show compassion and to show it generously.[10] Paul's seriousness in appealing to reason as a result of wisdom becomes evident also in verse 7: "Each one (should give) as he or she has decided in his or her heart." This statement brings together ideas from Jewish wisdom and Cynic-Stoic popular philosophy.

By the time of the second and first centuries B.C.E., Hellenistic-Jewish wisdom had adopted certain patterns of thought and speech originally characteristic of Hellenistic popular philosophy.[11] Evidently, Paul frequently borrowed such popular philosophical motifs and patterns of style from the wisdom tradition. Second Corinthians 9 reflects cynic-stoical discussions on the issue of free will. Epictetus (1.17, 21) had called out to his audience: "Humans, you have freedom of choice, unhindered and effortless by nature!" Any kind of coercion or pain obstructs that capacity and vice-versa.[12] Seen within the wider context of such philosophy, Paul's appended sentence in II Corinthians 7*a* makes sense: "Don't do either because of pain or coercion!" Everything is to be done out of *προαίρεσις* ("free choice"). Everything said in II Corinthians 8 about voluntary action and the importance of one's own free will—or similar such rationalistic statements—is said again in II Corinthians 9, only with much greater intensity.

C. GOD, REASON, AND JUSTIFICATION

Paul's "rationalist" tendency is confirmed by the following quotation from Proverbs: "For God loves a cheerful giver." Here, too, the focus is on the wise person. That generosity constitutes a characteristic feature of the wise, and that it can count upon God's love is seen also in Proverbs 8:17; 22:11; the Wisdom of Solomon 7:28; and Sirach 4:10, 14. In later wisdom, serenity and rationality go hand in hand; cheerfulness is the very trademark of the sage (Job 22:26; Test. Jos. 8:5). A serene face is a reflection of the wise person's open heart.[13] Philo is particularly insistent on the close connection between wisdom and serenity.[14] For Philo, serenity and generous kindness can merge, just as they can in other wisdom texts.[15] He only once connects ἱλαρός with charity. Yet, for neither Philo nor his Jewish tradition is the serenity of the sage a mere passing mood or simply the outcome of rationalistic deliberations. While it is certainly founded in rational thought, such rationality is itself a gift of grace. Wisdom brings serenity with her.[16]

In this context it seems unlikely that ἀγαπᾷ in II Corinthians 9:7 speaks of God's love as the reward for human charity—that is, that God's love is only a follow-up to human charitable deeds. It rather seems as if Paul merely mentions God's love to point to the "atmosphere" in which the cheerful giver is moving while engaged in the act of giving. This interpretation would explain the switch from εὐλογεῖ to ἀγαπᾷ. When Paul speaks of God's love elsewhere, he refers primarily to the kind of love that brings about salvation and was made apparent in the crucifixion.[17] Hence, God's love would have to be, not the consequence, but rather the origin—indeed, the very ground—from which human charity evolves.[18]

Verse 8, on the other hand, seems to contradict this: "God is able to grant a varied abundance of grace, so that you have everything you need at all times and even have plenty left over for much good praxis." The impression might be that Paul's thinking would be "turning back from the love of God to the reward gained through love, that is to say, to verse 6b,"[19] with the insistence, however, that it is not a question of material returns but of spiritual powers granted in exchange. Yet, the "rhetorical verve" of the sentence (to put it in Windisch's words)—namely, the alliteration on π and the five variations on πᾶς obtained through this alliteration, the double use of περισσεύειν, the "reference to God's ability,"[20] and the fact that not εὐλογία but χάρις is talked about—speaks against Windisch's theological interpretation of this sentence.

As a matter of fact, the very δυνατεῖ δὲ ὁ θεὸς at the beginning points to the direction in which the reading must be taken. Paul explains that humans in their seemingly independent praxis meet with the overwhelming fact of God's own praxis—an action always ahead of—and, thus superior to—the human one.

The givers realize that they are at the receiving end. Instead of losing, they are getting more; instead of exhausting themselves through giving, they suddenly dispose of inexhaustible treasures, allowing them to disburse with full hands. The crux of the matter is that God's action is not only superior to human action, but anterior to it as well, which is why human action is mentioned only at the end of the sentence.

While the reader would have expected *εὐλογία*, Paul writes *χάρις*, possibly because he wants to stress God's gracious, saving presence in his action. This probably explains as well Paul's choice of the singular of *χάρις*, even though proper Greek usage would have suggested—indeed required—the plural. But for Paul there is only one divine grace, no matter how varied it may appear in its visible results. For the same reason Paul avoids speaking of "(good) works" in the plural, although he is of course thinking of a continuing action. Paul here means praxis in a comprehensive sense.[21] Only when the rule of divine grace is not given recognition does Paul feel justified in speaking of "works" in the plural, for the logical reason that humans lose their true identity, their personhood, exactly when they are left to their own devices, to themselves. It is then that they become split up, diffused, and lost.

In so reasoning, Paul does not dismiss rational thought. Rather, he taps into Jewish wisdom's understanding of rationality as a charism. As we have seen, Paul had access to motifs belonging to Greek popular philosophy via this same Jewish tradition. In II Corinthians 9 he even works with two concepts that originated in popular philosophy at once; in addition to his aforementioned use of *προαίρεσις*, there is also *αὐτάρκεια* (verse 8)—a situation reminiscent of Philippians 4:11.

This appropriation of popular philosophy's concept of rationality has undergone far more change in Paul than it has in Hellenistic-Jewish wisdom. For the Jesus faith the "self" no longer constitutes the secure basis and the firm measure of intent and free decision.[22] Nor is it the place in which the self can experience freedom by means of personal frugality. For believers, freedom means liberation from self. True rationality and free decision-making become possible only subsequent to this liberation. It alone releases the self from the pressure to be self-sufficient. All the glamour that the Stoic philosophy and life-style ascribed to *αὐτάρκεια* has vanished. In II Corinthians 9:8 Paul understands *αὐτάρκεια* as sufficient livelihood.[23] God does not offer or command withdrawal into inwardness; on the contrary, God grants the possibility of and empowerment for active involvement within the community. Ideas only touched upon in II Corinthians 8:13-14 are thus given a much broader treatment in II Corinthians 9. Second Corinthians 9:8 confirms the impression that at issue in II Corinthians 8:14 is the constant interchange of taking and giving between the congregations.

As in II Corinthians 8, the essential point in II Corinthians 9:5-15 is no other than Paul's own doctrine of justification, spelled out now in its concrete dimensions. These chapters forcefully illustrate the liberty Paul takes to show the nature and consequences of the concept of justification. In so doing he does not follow a systematic scheme, but rather works out imaginative and inventive variations on this theme.[24] One such variation on the topic of justification is produced by Paul's manner of quoting from Jewish Scriptures to back up verse 8: "He has scattered abroad, he has given to the poor; his righteousness will remain for ever." Alfred Plummer draws attention to the fact that in this Pauline passage it is not possible to determine the subject of the quotation with certainty.[25] Paul does not indicate to whom "he" refers. In verse 8, by contrast, the subject is expressly named: God. While the subject of verse 10 is not clearly named, it too can only be God. Plummer concludes, therefore, that the subject of the sentence in verse 9 must be God as well. In the light of these considerations, the meaning of the passage could plausibly be rendered thus: It is God who dispenses all beneficial things; his righteousness, when turned upon the pious ones, will have no end. Such a reading would underscore the opening phrase of verse 8.

But in the psalm that Paul quotes here (also a wisdom psalm, by the way) it is not God, but the pious one, the just person, who is the subject. On the other hand, Psalm 112 should be studied in close conjunction with Psalm 111 (110), which also carries the marks of wisdom poetry and parallels Psalm 112 in many details. In Psalm 111, however, God is the subject. As is the pious person, God, too, is merciful and compassionate. He gives nourishment to those who fear him, and, as is the case of the godly person, his righteousness remains forever.

Paul and his readers both knew that in the passage quoted from the psalm the subject is the pious person—and Paul does not change that. Yet, in the light of the peculiar bond between Psalms 111 and 112, the deliberate vagueness of the way the quotation is incorporated into the Pauline context necessarily leads one to realize that God is the true origin of human compassion and that his righteousness is the true source of our righteousness. (Compare also the parallelism of verses 9 in Psalms 111 and 112, respectively.)

Thus "righteousness," in this context, denotes neither a quality nor a virtue nor correct moral behavior. It is rather that by which a person is defined, once he or she "has been integrated into the saving sphere of divine righteousness . . . [once he or she] receives help and furtherance [from that], and knows himself [or herself] to be duty bound to act in accordance with the requirements of his [or her] community in the face of God's covenant with humanity and all those encompassed by that covenant."[26] Neither the biblical texts nor (especially) Paul have in mind the deification of human beings. Quite to the contrary, viewing human actions must always entail the praise of God.

D. THE ESCHATOLOGICAL RELATIONSHIP BETWEEN JEWS AND GENTILES

The following verse is based to a degree on Jewish Scriptures as well: "He who gives seeds to the farmer and offers bread for food will portion out also (to you) your seed for growing and increase the harvest of the fruits of your righteousness." Here Paul calls on the prophets, although the statement has sapiential background as well. First he alludes to Isaiah 55:10, but what Deutero-Isaiah says there about the rain, Paul ascribes to God himself. There is some difference between the Isaianic text and Paul's version of it. Where Deutero-Isaiah's use of the metaphor likens rain to creation, Paul speaks of it as the creator. On the theological level Deutero-Isaiah talks of the irresistible effectiveness of God's word, Paul devotes the second half of his sentence to the effectiveness of God himself. At first sight the Pauline text is somewhat cryptic due to the fragmentary character of this biblical allusion. This fact must always be taken as a methodological indication that one should try to scrutinize the passage cited or alluded to in its wider context.

Certainly, Paul had made use of the seed-and-fruit imagery before, and it would be tempting to take the Deutero-Isaianic allusion for a mere catch-word association. But, as pointed out earlier, the Pauline text under discussion here is similar in content to the Deutero-Isaianic excerpt. As a matter of fact, this seems to be the case also for the contextual frame of Isaiah 55:10. The subject of that text is the miracle of Israel's returning home and the eternal covenant between God and Israel. Israel will call all other peoples, and they will come. Deutero-Isaiah is speaking of a universal return. The same idea is contained in Hosea 10:12, the other scriptural passage alluded to in II Corinthians 9:10.

Hence, if Paul saw such a connection between the motif of the eschatological pilgrimage of Jews and Gentiles to Jerusalem and the collection (and its transference to that city), he must have considered the collection itself a signal of the last times. The history of the collection until then had certainly helped to create that impression; if Paul did ascribe such significance to the collection, he must have viewed its implementation and its transfer as a sign, not only to the world in general, but to the Jews in particular as well. But in this concept, the priorities in the order of the events pertaining to the last times had been reversed. The Jews were not preceding the Gentiles (as announced by Deutero-Isaiah), but rather the Gentiles were preceding the Jews. The return, that which the Jews had rejected, was now being fulfilled by the Gentiles. Hosea 10:12, the second of Paul's scriptural allusions, is now to be applied to the Gentile Jesus believers.[27] The collection proved that there was "righteousness, the fruit of life, the light of knowledge, and search of the Lord" among the Gentile Jesus believers (see the LXX-text). Hence the promise that God would cause the fruit of their righteousness to grow was now applied to them, and not to the Jews.

Both Hans Windisch and Hans Lietzmann translate *δικαιοσύνη* in II Corinthians 9:9-10 as "charity" and "alms-giving"—the meaning the term can sometimes possess in later biblical and Jewish writings.[28] But in the Hebrew text of Hosea 10:12, as well as in the LXX, the term still means righteousness, an expression of divine action. Indeed, it stands for even more; God's righteousness, in this context, is a paraphrase of the contents of a theophany.

Paul employs the term here in an anthropological sense, as evidenced by the change of the dative object ὑμῖν into the genitive attribute ὑμῶν, and the use made of δικαιοσύνη in verse 9. But he is not as oblivious to the scriptural background as to turn "righteousness" into an independent human performance, a deed of charity or almsgiving or mere pious kindliness. The very dynamics of the sentence rule out such a possibility. Paul is still clearly concerned with divine action. From the very beginning of the sentence (σπόρος) everything is due to God's causal activity. Verse 10, therefore, reflects the same idea as verse 9, and δικαιοσύνη is identical in both verses. The sphere into which the just person (the "justified" one in Pauline theology) is placed by divine righteousness is the one in which God's blessing is at work. This is the idea behind the expression "fruits of righteousness"—an expression that points to the ever-increasing blessing inherent in communion with God. Paul believes that the covenant and the blessing are now destined for the Gentiles, and that the collection carried out for Jerusalem by the Gentile Jesus-believing congregations proves this idea.

Read in conjunction with its eschatologically interpreted biblical background, II Corinthians 9:10 means that the Creator is allowing the eschatological miracle of the pilgrimage of the peoples to Jerusalem to coincide with the collection of Pauline congregations (consisting in the majority of Gentiles) taken up for the Jesus-believing congregation at Jerusalem. The collected assets (in fact a donation from God himself) will certainly increase under the hands of the Gentile believers and produce blessings of far-reaching results even for these Gentiles themselves. Those who had been heathens have in the collection revealed that they belong to God's sphere of salvation. It is among them that God's covenant and righteousness have become a reality. They are the righteous ones; the blessing is meant for them, the forerunners of liberated humanity, the witnesses to the Jews to the presence of God's eschatological salvation—not the other way around.

Verse 11 summarizes verse 10: "You will be rich in everything with the result of simple kindness."[29] So for Paul, it all comes down to the concept of "simple kindness," which is granted, not in spite of wealth, but because of it. In verse 11 one is reminded of the rustic, self-effacing wisdom of Issachar in the Testaments of the Twelve Patriarchs: "God multiplied his goods in my hands ten thousand times; but also Jacob, my father, knew that God is cooperating with my simplicity. For in the goodness of my heart I granted everything of the goods of this earth to the poor and distressed" (Test. Iss. 3:7-8). Simplicity of the heart and goodness condition each other. In the Greek language both meanings inhere in one and the same term: ἁπλότης.

At first, the reader is surprised at Paul's lapse into this kind of language only a few months after having written the powerful defense of his apostleship (a text heavily laced with theologically significant reflections) and just a few weeks prior to the Epistle to the Romans. But at closer study one realizes that Paul deals with the same idea in all three instances; the life of the person under grace is both a life of weakness, and, in its renunciation of fame, the manifestation and instrument of divine strength.

E. SPIRITUAL WORSHIP AND HISTORY

The simple goodness demonstrated by the Achaians—indeed, by all the Pauline congregations—"causes thankfulness to God through us."[30] Paul refers here to the forthcoming prayer of thanksgiving on the part of the Jesus congregation at Jerusalem for the collection handed over to them. On the basis of what we have seen in Philippians 4, it is not surprising that Paul says nothing at all here about the gratitude the recipients at Jerusalem might feel toward their Gentile sisters and brothers, but rather that he immediately refers to the prayer of thanksgiving in God's honor.

Paul mentions in particular the part of those involved in conveying the collection to Jerusalem "through us"—that is, through Paul and his companions. No doubt Paul is primarily thinking of the representative role played by the delegation conveying the collection to Jerusalem, which consisted on the one hand of Paul, one of "the apostles to the peoples" (Rom. 1:5), the major missionary to the Gentiles, and on the other, the representatives of his congregations, of the Gentiles, and of the peoples of this earth at large.

The mention of the thanksgiving prayer introduces the subject matter of the following paragraph. Verses 12-15 provide the explanation for verse 11*b*. Paul explains why the handing over of the collection causes thanksgiving to God, and he describes the content of this thanksgiving: "Indeed, the enactment[31] of this priestly service not only covers the needs of the saints, it also leads to abundance through the great number of (ensuing) thanksgiving prayers to God." The financial donations made by the Pauline congregations are meant to remedy a genuine economic neediness on the part of the Jesus congregation at Jerusalem, a fact that Paul makes quite clear. But the distribution of the collection is also meant to produce abundance[32] in the wake of the great number of thanksgiving prayers that will follow.[33]

At first it seems unclear what kind of abundance is meant here. This is why the modern reader cannot directly detect to what extent verse 12*b* builds upon verse 12*a*. G. H. Boobyer's observations on these verses and their religio-historical environment will assist in understanding the theological themes underlying these verses.[34] Inspired by certain hints from his teacher Martin Dibelius, Boobyer succeeded in fitting these themes into a far-reaching network of concepts that he discovered in the Hellenistic world,[35] and that can also be traced elsewhere in the Pauline writings.[36]

The Pauline sentence immediately following yields the first clue: "Occasioned by this transfer (the *διακονία*), a successful (completion of a) test, they glorify God." Paul actually says two things here: First, he tells us that the handing over of the collection will lead to abundance caused through thanksgiving prayers. Then, paralleling this, he maintains that the transfer of the collection will cause the congregation at Jerusalem to glorify God. Hence, the abundance produced by the thanksgiving prayers is identical in significance with the praise that glorifies God—which is to say, with an "abundance" accumulating on God's behalf. Given this parallelism, one can say that the abundance is an increase of the *δόξα θεοῦ* (the *δοξάζοντες*).

Boobyer has shown that in the Hellenistic religio-historical environment both the glorification and the accumulation of the abundance to God's credit are understood in concrete terms; God's glory was thought to be a substance of heavenly light. But the praise and thanksgiving to God consist themselves of this light-substance, the gift of grace, because they are also of divine origin or, at least, caused by divine forces that are in turn themselves of the nature of light. Thus the Hellenistic idea of the "praise of God" and of thanksgiving is one of light rising upward, returning the light-substance, and so increasing God's luminous splendor, God's grace. The divine forces *λόγος*, *νοῦς*, *γνῶσις*, *πνεῦμα*, and so on, all of divine light-nature, enter humans only to rise up again in the form of praise or thanksgiving to God. "The praise and thanksgiving act is therefore a circle of divine light-praise."[37] *χάρις* or *δόξα* received from above, are returned as *εὐχαριστία* or as *δοξολογία*. Although one encounters this idea in varying degrees of concreteness, "there is always the thought of an effect upon God. The *εὐχαριστία* increases the glory of God, or, put differently, God is 'strengthened.' " God's position is made more secure.[38]

These phenomena mean that spiritual worship and spiritual sacrifice are parts of a process originating in and returning to God. For the mystic, this circular movement takes hold of the entire cosmos, either because the mystic joins the song of the cosmos, or because the song of the mystic effuses the cosmos, causing it to sing, too.[39] In this religious world view praise and thanksgiving are represented under charismatic, cosmological, and soteriological aspects. The soteriological element is present in that the substance of the divine light is endowed with a saving function, and because the worshiping mystic—filled with this saving power—is often able, during acts of praise and thanksgiving, to experience liberation from this fleeting world and to make a transition into the imperishable. This realistic imagery describes not only the praise of God and thanksgiving but also the space in which they happen and where salvation comes to pass, the body of Christ and its atmosphere.

As stressed repeatedly above, Paul sees the collection for Jerusalem in a worldwide perspective. The process of the collection thus becomes a worldwide worship service, set in motion by God himself and proceeding in his own honor, for the increase of his power of grace. Paul can call the collection a "priestly service" performed by the Pauline congregations through their delegates.[40] Later on, in the Epistle to the Romans, Paul would present his entire mission among the peoples under this perspective of priestly service. For Paul, the passing on of the fruit of that service and the transfer of the collection to Jerusalem is a *διακονία*.[41] The terminology here carries a somewhat different meaning than in 8:4 and 9:1. In 9:12 the meaning is "mission"/ "delegation," in the sense of the practical execution and performance of an office. The transfer of the collection to Jerusalem is that mission. The Pauline congregations are represented in this office, this *διακονία*, by their envoys. The task of the envoys constitutes their destiny; their mission establishes a firm bond between those who sent them and the Jerusalem congregation.

Paul is convinced of the successful completion of the delegation's task and, hence, that the collection itself will be a success. He is quite certain that the envoys will carry out their office blamelessly and assist the congregation of Jerusalem in praising God (v. 13).[42] For Paul, the very momentum of the affair guarantees its success. He is obviously possessed of the same certainty here as in chapter 8. Paul considered it self-evident that the envoys would succeed in manifesting to the sisters and brothers at Jerusalem the substance of the collection: obedience on the one hand, and simple goodness on the other. "They will be occasioned into praising God by the proof (consisting) in transferring (the collection) because of the obedience which consists in your confession vis à vis the Gospel of Christ and because of the simple goodness which consists in the sign of solidarity with them and (all) others."[43]

The *ὑποταγή τῆς ὁμολογίας* in this verse is to become *ὑπακοή τῆς πίστεως*, later, in the Epistle to the Romans (Rom. 1:5; see 15:18; 16:19). The *εὐαγγέλιον τοῦ Χριστοῦ* (the message about God's eschatological king) has rung out in the world of the Gentiles and has been answered by the Pauline congregations. They have said "yes" to God's action as manifested through the crucified and resurrected Jesus. They have acknowledged that in the cross and the resurrection of Jesus, God has acted in and for the world, making the divine will creatively active in history. In receiving into their hands the collection, the Jerusalem congregation will have the tangible proof that the Pauline congregations have submitted to this divine action and that God's Christ is also their Christ. It is possible that when writing *ὑποταγή*, Paul had in the back of his mind the same psalm he also quotes (although in an Apocalyptic context) in I Corinthians 15:27: "He placed everything under his [the Christ's] authority" (Ps. 8:7). This would explain why he chose ὑποταγή instead of ὑπακοή. If this is the case, II Corinthians 9 would indicate that (for Paul) the subjugation of the cosmos has already begun, of which the transfer of the collection is the visible sign. A subjugation of the Gentiles to the Jews is not in view, nor the other way round. In this much the prophecies concerning the pilgrimage of the peoples are not heeded at all.

Only after these clarifications on the "dogmatic" foundation for the forthcoming praise of God in Jerusalem does Paul return to the idea of "simple goodness," the "ethical" premise postulated in verse 11 as the causative basis for the giving of thanks.[44] The simple goodness of the Pauline congregations must be seen as a cause for thanksgiving on the part of the Jewish believers, because this goodness testifies to the Pauline congregations' willingness to enter into communion not only with the congregation at Jerusalem but also with all other churches. This broadening of the concept of solidarity is meant to express the idea that the collection of the Pauline congregations factually constitutes a self-manifestation of the Body of Christ. The parallelism of εἰς αὐτοὺς καὶ εἰς πάντας and εἰς τὸ εὐαγγέλιον Χριστοῦ speaks for itself.

The hope expressed in verse 14 further evidences Paul's focus on the concept of communion as based on and defined by the gospel of Christ: "And in prayer for you they prove their yearning for you because of the overwhelming grace of God (revealing itself) in you."[45] The act of thanksgiving performed by the congregation in Jerusalem will turn into a prayer of intercession for the givers, for the Pauline congregations, and even for the church at large.[46] This intercession will be a fitting response to the lovingkindness shown to the congregation at Jerusalem by their visitors and the congregations they represent. The solidarity of all believers will be rendered yet more evident.

Further, this intercession will manifest the causal principle behind that solidarity. Both the intercession and the lovingkindness will be brought about because the congregation at Jerusalem will notice (following the gift of the collection offered to them by the envoys for the congregations) the extent to which the latter has been moved into action through the grace of God. Thus the circular movement that had begun in God and is now returning to God by way of the congregations will be completed and the circle closed. But just as this movement passes through the congregations, it also flows back and forth between them, connecting them to one another. This idea, hinted at in II Corinthians 8:13-14 and elaborated on further in II Corinthians 9:8-11, is developed full scale in II Corinthians 9:12-14.

While passing through these descriptive phases, Paul has finally succeeded in fully historicizing the mystical theme of spiritual worship. In this spiritual service God is himself both origin and goal. He brings the congregations together in solidarity. This spiritual worship occurs within the historical development of the Christ community, and a material occurrence such as a collection of money plays a decisive part in its evolution. Cultic sacralism, already modified by Hellenistic mysticism, is now completely nullified by Paul. The history of the Christ community as a pluralistic whole constitutes its spiritual worship—a worship in the course of which that community proves to be itself the "body of Christ."[47]

F. GOD'S SOVEREIGNTY

Second Corinthians 9:15 reads as follows: "Thanks be to God for his gift (too wonderful) to be expressed in words." The transition from the preceding sentence to this statement is made by a meaningful play of words. Verse 14 ends with: *διὰ τὴν ὑπερβάλλουσαν χάριν* (effect of grace) *τοῦ θεοῦ ἐφ᾽ ὑμῖν*. Verse 15 starts with *χάρις* (thanksgiving) *τῳ θεῳ*. This play on words not only contains the entire message of chapter 9, but also touches upon certain ideas presented in chapter 8. There Paul had spoken of grace and its effects, and also of thanksgiving. In 9:15, the apostle deals with God's grace as a gift made to humans. The term *gift* (*δωρεά*) is often employed in Hellenistic texts in conjunction with *χάρις* or even used synonymously with it.[48] In the New Testament *δωρεά* is always filled with theological meaning and implicitly or explicitly bound up with the idea of *πνεῦμα* or *χάρις*. In Romans 5:15, 17—the one other New Testament text in which Paul uses the term—*δωρεά* refers to the justification granted the godless through the saving event of

Christ. It would seem that this is quite close to what he means to express in II Corinthians 9:15, where Paul directs the attention of his readers back to the true origin of the undertaking of the collection. Once more he points to the grace of God as the vast horizon of that undertaking, showing that the collection's goal and purpose can be God's glorification alone.

At this point it seems appropriate to refer to I Chronicles 29, a biblical document that contains a great number of the motifs touched upon in II Corinthians 8 and 9, and where the praise of God's sovereignty is given primary attention. Paul must have had this text in mind when composing his epistles pertaining to the collection because of its focus on the Temple as the central symbol of the Jewish community. "David donated (the necessary funds for the construction of the Temple) not only according to what he could afford (as king), but more than that" (by offering in addition his private property).[49] David encourages everyone to show as much generosity as he does himself. In the LXX, the verb used in this connection is *προθυμεῖσθαι*. The same verb occurs six more times in I Chronicles 29, but only four more times in all the other LXX texts. In the light of this fact, it is particularly interesting to note that Paul employs the term *προθυμία* four times in II Corinthians 8 and 9.

When the leaders of the people comply with his request, David offers a prayer of blessing (*εὐλογεῖν εὐλογητός*; compare the *εὐλογία* in II Cor. 9:5-6) which gives praise to the greatness and the might of the Lord (*κύριος*). He is the origin of both the riches (II Cor. 9:8, 11) and the glory (*δόξα*); his are the rulership, the power, the might. Therefore, praise is given to him (*ἐξομολογεῖσθαι*, compare *ὁμολογία* in II Cor. 9:13). The ensuing confession of human powerlessness is typical: "Who am I, and who are my people, that we should be able to give so much by our own free will?" In view of God's sovereignty, the answer must of course be "nobody"; "for everything belongs to you; we only give to you from what is yours already."

Then David continues by pointing out once more the divine origin of all human giving: "Oh Lord, our God, all this wealth (i.e., the donated assets) that I have offered you to build a temple for your holy name, (all this) originated in your hand." The parallel character of this confession to the repeated reference to God's sovereignty and creative activity in II Corinthians 8 and 9 is obvious. It follows a brief excursus on Israel's status as aliens in the world comparable to the eschatological nature of the people of God sojourning worldwide and thus organizing and receiving the collection on a worldwide scale, according to II Corinthians 8 and 9. As in II Corinthians 8 and 9, we are told in I Chronicles 29 that God in his sovereignty can reach even into the human heart: "I knew, Lord, that you are the one who scrutinizes the human heart and (the one who) loves righteousness.[50] In simplicity (ἁπλότης, a term used three times in II Cor. 8 and 9) of the heart I have shown readiness for all that, and I have seen your people, gathered here, offering joyously and willingly their readiness to you" (see also II Cor. 8:2). David's eulogy is followed by a eulogy of the people, proclaiming their submission to the κύριος.

To the extent that this text serves Paul as a model and source of inspiration, he must have found in it all he needed to strengthen his conviction that the collection is part of God's overall and supreme action of grace. At the same time, it permits him to see in the collection and its implementation an all-encompassing demonstration of the vitality of the worldwide communion of the godless ones justified by grace. On the other hand, in interpreting the chronicler's text in this way, he also contradicted entirely the intention of the chronicler, the most law-bound of all biblical writers.[51] Paul decries enthusiastic advocacy of ritualized Law abidance, the glorification of the Temple, the special status of Jerusalem as the privileged place of worship, the cult-related offices, and the pious deeds. The justification of the godless could be declared only in contradiction to the chronicler's point of view. The chronicler had been no longer in a position to write about Israel's election in history nor about God's entering into a covenant with his people. But Paul speaks of the eschatological people of God as being covenanted with Jews and Gentiles alike, the new creation. For Paul the collection constitutes the tangible expression of precisely these facts.

Hence, in the course of its own unfolding in history, the collection became something of a case study of Paul's overall theological position. It demonstrates that Pauline theology (including the doctrine of justification) is deeply concerned with the historical realm and must, therefore, be placed in equal distance from Gnostic and Apocalyptic speculation.

CHAPTER 7

CLOSURE OF THE COLLECTION AND PLANNING OF THE JOURNEY TO JERUSALEM (WINTER 55/56 C.E.)

A. CONCLUDING ACTIVITIES IN THE EAST (ROM. 16)

Paul wrote the circular letter addressed to the Achaian congregations shortly before he concluded his activities in Macedonia. From Macedonia he traveled to Greece, where he stayed three months (Acts 20:2-3)—the three winter months, to judge by the schedule detectable in the ensuing report in Acts. Here "Greece" certainly refers to Paul's congregations in Achaia and, especially, Corinth. At last the Corinthians were paid the long promised second visit, the *δευτέρα χάρις* mentioned in II Corinthians 1:15. This visit took place in an atmosphere of harmony; the congregation was fully on its founder's side again. On the basis of this positive time with the Corinthians, Paul felt that he might well consider his mission in the eastern half of the empire as firmly anchored and start preparations for a new phase of mission in the west. All this can be gathered from Paul's correspondence written during this stay in Corinth. Two fragments of this correspondence have come down to us and are combined into the canonical Epistle to the Romans: (1) an epistle to the congregation at Ephesus (a fragment of which is preserved in Rom. 16:1-20[1]) and (2) the actual epistle to the Roman congregation.

The epistle sent to the Ephesians (Rom. 16) is occasioned by a concrete situation. Phoebe, an independent wealthy woman from Cenchreae, has to travel to Ephesus on business and Paul hands her a letter of recommendation to the congregation of that city (Rom. 16:1-2). Wishing to seize the opportunity, Paul also sends greetings to the more prominent members of the congregation in which he had been active for so long. However, the lengthy catalogue of the names of those to whom the greetings are sent makes the epistle look like a letter of farewell. Evidence for this reading can be seen in two formulations: (1) "Not only myself, but all the Gentile congregations thank them for it" and (2) "All the congregations of Christ send their greetings." These are not just empty formulas. On the contrary, these words are meant to express the feeling of a community that the congregations on the Pauline mission field share, a feeling strengthened by the events of the two preceding years. The bond that had tied them together through their joint participation in the collection was now to be extended to the church at Jerusalem, the receiving and thanksgiving end of the undertaking. In fact, the awareness of the solidarity of the Pauline congregations that these formulas express encompasses not only the congregation at Jerusalem, but the entire Christ community as well.

Even though this fragment of the letter to the Ephesians contains no indication of whether this congregation was also involved in the collection (Rom. 15:26 is also silent on this point), one may assume that it was, due to the fact that the catalogue of the members of the delegation traveling for the sake of the collection (Acts 20:4) also lists representatives of the province of Asia. This listing was certainly not invented, and it is too short rather than too extensive (as one would expect if it had been invented). The conjecture that Ephesus took part in the collection is reinforced by the unsuspicious mention of the Ephesian Trophimus in Acts 21:29.[2] Assuming that this interpretation is correct, the delegation must already have been in Corinth when Romans 16 was written. Given the fragmentary nature of Romans 16, the absence of a reference either to the collection or to the delegation should not be taken as a valid argument against an Ephesian participation. It may well have been that following the greetings in 16:20, the epistle originally contained another list of names (replaced now by 16:21-23), referring to the representatives of the province of "Asia," who also sent their greetings.

But the closing section (16:17-20) also testifies, by its resemblance to the literary genre of the last will, to Paul's conviction that he had reached the end of his mission activity, and to the fact that this epistle had certainly been conceived as a letter of farewell. True, Paul sends out warnings against false teachers and their power of seduction, but these remarks do not refer to identifiable individuals who would have penetrated the Ephesian congregation already, causing confusion.[3] The notice, reminiscent of the eschatological passages in the Testaments of the Twelve Patriarchs, refers to heretical teachers who might come in the future.

B. PREPARING THE MISSION IN THE WEST (ROM. 1–15)

1. The Purpose of the Epistle to the Romans

In the course of the new round of missionary work, which Paul had been planning for a long time, he had intended to visit the largest of all Gentile cities: Rome. He had received the grace and the office of apostle in order to instill the obedience of faith in the name of Jesus Christ (Rom. 1:5) among the peoples of this earth the Romans included (Rom. 1:6). He considered it his duty to bring the gospel to all people, whether they be Greeks or of barbarian stock, whether they be wise or uneducated—in short, to the Romans along with everyone else (1:14-15). However, this program stood in opposition to another principle to which Paul had so far been equally faithful—namely, to preach the gospel only in those places where the name of Jesus Christ had not yet been heard (Rom. 15:20-21). In Rome there existed a congregation of Jesus believers already.

Paul decided to turn this situation to his advantage. As the Roman congregation lay on his way, he wanted to make its acquaintance, exchange ideas with it (see for instance the transitional switch between Rom. 1:11 and 1:12, or the apologies in Rom. 15:15), and use it as the bridgehead for his work in the west. He even requested that the Romans provide him an escort to Spain (15:23-24; compare 15:28). As prelude to the envisaged exchange, Paul introduces himself to the Roman congregation by means of a letter. So, the Epistle to the Romans, with all its wealth of theological reflection, really springs from Paul's praxis, from his pragmatic intent to go to Rome.[4]

The question arises of whether the transfer of the collection is not also meant to fulfill the same function as the Epistle to the Romans, as well as Paul's plan to visit that congregation—namely, to provide backing for Paul's western mission. The structural position of the remarks pertaining to the collection and the journey to Jerusalem within the explanatory summary at the end of the original letter (Rom. 15:14-33) seems to give the first indication that this is indeed the case. The points Paul raises in this passage, as well as the order in which he raises them, are also suggestive:

—Justification for the Epistle.
—Statements of principle on the office of an apostle to the peoples.
—Statements regarding Paul's accomplishment of this task.
—Based on these considerations, the project of a mission in Spain and the promise to visit Rome.
—Mention of the collection and its transfer.
—Request made to the Romans to pray for Paul's success in the transfer of the collection.

Although Romans 15:25-33 deals with the anticipated completion of travel projects conceived at an earlier stage, and despite the break in the train of thoughts between Romans 15:24 and 15:25, this passage does not contain mere "marginal considerations."[5] Rather, the position of verse 29 within the context of chapter 15, and, more essentially Paul's request for the intercessory prayer of the Romans for his Jerusalem visit, show Paul's eagerness to communicate to the Romans the close connection between the collection and the journey to Jerusalem and the rest of Paul's work. Paul emphasizes the importance of the collection by this passage with an explicit plea for supportive prayers. It is the last thing Paul wishes to impart to the Romans. Only a list of greetings follows (now in Rom. 16:21-23).

2. The Relationship Between the Pauline Congregations and the Congregation at Jerusalem

At first, when discussing the journey to Jerusalem and the collection, Paul employs considerable understatement. Speaking of the purpose of his journey, Paul writes: "Now I am going to Jerusalem to serve the saints." This sentence indicates nothing of the eschatological significance of the collection and its transfer. At first glance, then, it would seem that Paul wanted to go to Jerusalem simply to bring financial relief to the congregation there.[6]

Paul's emphasis on the economic aspect of the collection in this passage manifests itself in the terminology he uses to name the recipients (Rom. 15:26). They are "the poor among the saints in Jerusalem." This wording tells us that "the poor" no longer are the Jesus believers at Jerusalem as such; "the poor" are only a certain group within the Jerusalem congregation—albeit perhaps a large one. Contrary to the terminology used in the Jerusalem agreement, the term "the poor" in this particular context is no longer used in an absolute sense as in Galatians 2:10 and, therefore, does not constitute an eschatological title, but rather a sociological designation. In II Corinthians 8:14 and 9:12, the collection had already, to a degree, taken on the meaning of a measure of economic aid. The economic perspective had been included in the venture since the beginning, but originally these economic considerations were treated as almost identical with the eschatological ones.[7]

In Romans 15:25, the collection receives a theological explanation as well, but in this explanation the eschatological significance of the Jerusalem congregation is no longer part of the argument. That this new theological explanation revolves around the economic connotations expressed in the syntactical position of "the poor" is beyond dispute. Those scholars who ascertain a direct correlation between the new motivation for the collection (v. 27) and the designation "the poor" (v. 26), and who on that basis argue that this title must mean the same thing here as it does in Galatians 2:10, have remained unsuccessful in tracing the origin of this motivation to Apocalyptic thinking and, thus, to establish a theological link to the title "the poor."

When Paul composed Romans 15:25-33, neither he nor his congregations was any longer taking account of the self-understanding of the church of Jerusalem (or the Jerusalem agreement, for that matter). The congregation at Jerusalem was, of course, still important. But in the eyes of Paul and his congregations the church's importance resided, not so much in itself, as in its relationship to the worldwide missionary activity and the worldwide church.

Certain things that had happened since the Jerusalem convention must necessarily have produced a shift in perspective. Paul had engaged in independent mission work in a territory four times the size of the area that the Antiochene missionaries took twice the time to cover in the period prior to the convention. Paul had been able to penetrate deeply into the pagan world. But from his fellow Jews he had gained little more than rejection, hatred, and persecution. From Jewish Jesus believers he had found frequent misunderstanding, even enmity. All the congregations that had grown out of Paul's mission had won their independence within a very short time, had overcome serious internal difficulties, and had proven vigorous enough to survive. This fact was evidenced, among other things, by their active engagement in the collection.[8] In short, compared to other congregations, the Pauline churches had gained an increasing weight of their own.

Paul speaks in Romans 15:26-27 of this new importance on the part of his congregations in terms one might at first take for no more than an expression of his humility. But after the rather unpretentious remark that he is about to leave for Jerusalem to serve the saints, Paul explains his intentions in the following manner: "For Macedonia and Achaia have decided to offer a sign of (their) solidarity with the poor among the saints in Jerusalem." That decision had grown out of the inner commitment of these congregations. The collection and its conveyance was theirs: "Yes, indeed, they made this decision, because they feel it to be their responsibility to perform this service."[9]

Here Paul clearly describes his congregations as the ones who were truly responsible for the collection, and himself as the mere executor of their will. Although this was not entirely correct, historically speaking, this way of putting it very well describes the importance the Pauline congregations had acquired, an importance substantiated by their active participation in the collection. Paul's congregations had made his cause increasingly their own and, in the process, had identified themselves both with Paul's message and his responsibility for the gospel and the church as a whole. It had happened exactly as Paul had predicted it would in II Corinthians 8 and 9.[10]

In Romans 15:27 Paul explains why it is the duty of the congregations to carry out the collection: "For in so far as the Gentiles share their part of their [the Jerusalem congregation's] spiritual goods, they owe it to them to serve them through earthly goods." Here Paul applies a principle to the collection that in Hellenistic syncretism governed the attitude one adopted toward pneumatics[11]—with the difference, however, that in the latter case gratitude was shown through gifts and service only to individuals, not to groups.[12]

Paul quotes this Hellenistic principle also in I Corinthians 9:11: "If we [the pneumatics] have sowed spiritual goods for you, why should it be so extraordinary that we harvest earthly goods from you?" The "spiritual goods" referred to in I Corinthians 9 are the preaching of the apostles. The "spiritual goods" in Romans 15:27 are not the Jewish tradition as understood in Jerusalem, nor are they the tradition of the historical Jesus, but are rather things belonging to the new creation, which rooted in Jesus' resurrection—that is to say, primarily the message of the resurrection as that which constitutes the church.

The conclusions to be drawn from this are as follows:

1. Paul applies to the collection a principle traditionally guiding the activities of and relations to Hellenistic pneumatics. This strengthens the impression that Paul's statements in Romans 15:25-30 show a certain distance with regard to the original concept of the collection.
2. Paul applies this same principle to the gift of the church, constituting preaching of the resurrection of Jesus.
3. In so doing, the principle is not (as one would have expected) limited to the individual witnesses to the appearances of the resurrected Jesus, nor even to "the poor" among the Jerusalem Jesus believers. Instead, it is brought to bear on the entire congregation at Jerusalem.
4. Hence the obligation to demonstrate gratitude is no longer bound up with a present event, but with the past, with history. In this, too, Paul's position differs from the Hellenistic practice with respect to pneumatics, where only the currently offered gift or performance was honored through remuneration.
5. Moreover, the thanksgiving owed is freed from all local restrictions. In Hellenistic syncretism, including many Jesus believers, the obligation to pay a remuneration existed only for

> the local audience of the pneumatic. In other words, the obligation to give thanks for the pneumatic service received existed only within the vicinity of the pneumatic's residence. By contrast, Romans 15:27 refers to a similar kind of obligation, yet one widened to an ecumenical order of magnitude.

Hence, Romans 15:27 constitutes Paul's interpretation of a decision taken by his congregations—a decision that clearly reflects a significant change in outlook. At the same time, Paul also draws attention to the fact that the former heathens had freed themselves from their past introversion and ahistorical perspective—two characteristic traits that Paul blames on their pagan conditioning. Given their newly acquired understanding, they have realized that by accepting the meaning of the preaching of Jesus' resurrection from the dead, they had been led toward and integrated into a unique, worldwide community: the people of God of the new creation. And now they fulfill the obligation incumbent on this change of status. Their donation is the evidence of their will toward partnership; it constitutes the "sign of [their] communion"[13] with the poor among the saints in Jerusalem (Rom. 15:26).

3. The Provocative Nature of the Collection

As the collection organized by the Pauline congregations for the benefit of the congregation at Jerusalem took place in full view of orthodox Jewry and conservative Jesus believers, it was increasingly understood as an unmistakable—and, hence, highly provocative—demonstration of the fact that the traditional biblical and Jewish eschatological expectation was being reversed.[14] The mere fact that the Gentile Jesus believers were allowed to consider themselves equal members with the people of the covenant, without prior compliance with the requirements of proselytes, was itself a provocation.

In addition, the Pauline mission among Gentiles and the growing importance gained by the Pauline congregations simply had to be seen as evidence that the expected sequence of events in the eschatological drama was being turned upside down. The messengers of joy one encounters in Isaiah 52:7 were not preceding the Jews as they made their way home or announcing their return; on the contrary, these messengers were now heading forth into the world to announce salvation to all peoples (Rom. 10:15), without Israel's prior acceptance of eschatological salvation. That salvation, as it was now being proclaimed, had been rejected by a majority of the Jews. With great success and in open opposition to established Jewish hope, Paul endeavored not only to gain acceptance for the idea of the salvation of the Gentiles, but also to make the mission to the Gentiles more important than that to the Jews. The salvation and glorification of Israel were no longer the prerequisite or the premise for the salvation of the Gentiles; the salvation of the Gentiles had become the prerequisite for the salvation of the Jews.

A program of this kind was bound to become a provocation. To judge by Romans 11:11-24, more than being simply aware of this, Paul had made it his declared intent. He hoped that his mission among the Gentiles and their conversion to the Christ faith right in front of the Jews would have the effect of a permanent "irritation" to the Jews, and that the salvation of the latter would eventually result from that irritation. The salvation he had in mind, however, was not one of individual Jews, but one involving the whole world in one universal eschatological miracle (Rom. 11:25-36), corresponding in its nature to the collective conversion of the peoples at large, an expectation already present in certain parts of Jewish Scriptures and in certain branches of Judaism.

Paul's mission had, therefore, become a symbolic act like the symbolic acts of the biblical prophets. They, too, had often intended to disturb the security Israel derived from the traditional ideology of salvation. And as was the case with the prophets, so now Paul's provocative thoughts and actions were based heavily on Israelite and Jewish traditions, which would provide the necessary symbolic frame of reference.

One may assume that, at the time of the convention, Paul had not as yet made such a connection between the collection and the demonstrative aspect of his mission. Such thoughts are first encountered in conjunction with the collection in II Corinthians 9. In Romans 9–11, they are formulated as the basic orientation of Paul's entire missionary effort. It may well be that the idea of relating the collection to the objective of his mission had gained its full meaning during Paul's last visit to the Macedonian congregations. This mental association would be the last of a series of gradual enhancements of the theological significance of the collection, caused by the growing zeal displayed by his congregations.

There is a connection between the passage on the collection (Rom. 15:25-33) and Paul's two programmatic statements on his missionary strategy and activity (Rom. 9–11 and 15:14-24). This connection is achieved through the following:

1. The above-mentioned ideas on the mission among the Gentiles, as contained in Romans 10:14-21 and 11:11-24.
2. The detailed discussion in Romans 15:7-13 of thoughts previously dealt with in a more general way in chapters 9–11.
3. The reiteration of Paul's fear of the "disobedient ones" (Rom. 15:31), reminiscent of the statements made on the "disobedience" of the Jews in Romans 11:30-32.

In this way an intimate connection between the collection and the mission among the Gentiles had evolved, particularly in regard to the latter's eschatological significance. This eschatological character of the mission to the Gentiles was thus to attain its climax in the collection. The collection, and most important its conveyance to Jerusalem by a major delegation of non-circumcised Gentiles (a delegation composed of representatives of various pagan peoples), simply had to revive in Jewish eyes the old concept of the eschatological pilgrimage of the peoples.[15] The difference was, however, that the offering was not brought to the Jews by the Gentiles; instead, it was the Jew Paul who brought an offering consisting of representatives of the Gentile peoples (see Rom. 15:16)—another very concrete variation on the motif of spiritual worship, already bound up with the collection.

The promised pilgrimage of the peoples had begun to materialize, but without—indeed, in spite of—the majority of the Jews. The representatives of the Gentile peoples were conveying the gifts of the heathens to Jerusalem, although intended, not for the Temple, but for Jewish people; not prestigious Jews, but rather poor ones (a preference that follows biblical, particularly prophetic, patterns). Against the background of this development, "official" Jerusalem inevitably emerged in the eyes of the Jewish prophet Paul as the hub, indeed the very bastion, of unbelief, ironically, the very Jerusalem that, according to Jewish Scriptures and later Jewish expectations, was to function as the magnetic pole of salvation. The provocative nature of Paul's plan to convey the collection must have been tremendous, especially if Paul were to arrive in Jerusalem—as he had probably originally planned—during the Passover festival.[16] That Paul was well aware of all these provocative implications—indeed, that he had even built them up deliberately—is evident in his expression of concern about the unbelieving Jews in Romans 15:31. This explains how he could make the remark about the unbelieving Jews in the same breath as the expression of hope for the favorable acceptance of the collection.

Paul knew perfectly well what was at stake.[17] He knew what he was doing when, prior to referring to the collection, he mentioned (v. 30) that he might be in danger from the Jews in Jerusalem.[18] This also explains why Paul chose, in this particular context, to call the collection for Jerusalem a *διακονία εἰς Ἰερουσαλήμ*. The report given in Acts seems to contain traces of an old reminiscence, no longer understood by Luke, of Paul's intent to produce an effect on the entire city of Jerusalem—something that, in the end, he succeeded in doing. Without any previous mention of the collection, Acts 24:17 suddenly states that Paul had come to Jerusalem to offer alms and offering "for his people." It goes without saying that Paul never thought of the Temple or Jerusalem at large or even the Jewish people as the recipients of the collection. But he must have had them in mind as part of the general scenery, as those "in the stands," as it were.[19]

4. The Collection as a Confirmation and as a Promise of the Growth of the Community of Christ

The collection is Paul's foolproof method of convincing the Jerusalem church once and for all that the work of spreading the gospel in the pagan world has borne fruit: "As soon as I have completed this (work) and sealed this fruit with them [the Jerusalem congregation]. . . ."[20] The success is borne out not only by the amount of money handed over, but also—and more essentially—by the group of Gentile believers accompanying Paul. These envoys of the congregations of the Diaspora would be able to testify to the great zeal displayed by each of the congregations involved in collecting the funds, and to the vigor with which they had made the collection their business. At the same time, the donation stands as a witness to the power inherent in the Pauline preaching to constitute and join together communities.[21] Hence, Paul is full of hope that the disbursement of the collection will contribute to the success of his future work: "(As soon as I have completed this work and sealed this fruit for them), then I will come to see you on my way to Spain" (15:28). The ensuing sentence is essential: "I am sure that when I come I will come in the plenty of the Christ's blessing" (15:29).

This reminds one of II Corinthians 9, where Paul speaks of a circular movement so strong that it sweeps everyone along with it. The origin of that movement is God himself, causing it through his actions of grace and the eschatological act of salvation, the Christ event (see also the *εὐλογία Χριστοῦ* in Rom. 15:29). All the parts of Christ's body, including the apostles, are encompassed in that movement and exist in dependence on it. Paul is convinced that the outpouring of God's acts and gifts of grace, first received and passed on by the congregation in Jerusalem, is flowing back to them in the form of the collection and the thanksgiving it represents. This response will incite the Jerusalem church to gratitude and renewed giving, thus sustaining the circular movement. This is how grace is present in the blessing—present in an overwhelming measure, as Paul never tires of stressing. Paul himself will be carried forward by that movement.

Consequently, when Paul is hopeful about being able to come in the fullness of Christ's blessing, he is thinking of nothing less than that his coming will be prompted by the same force that also moves the body of Christ. In other words, his coming will be accomplished by his life in the community of Christ.

Paul's strong dependence on the language of Jewish wisdom may tempt one to describe what Paul refers to by means of partly Apocalyptic, partly Gnostic terminology—in other words, as an Apocalyptic drama or mystical process, as found in Jewish Gnosis. As Paul sees it, what sustains and determines both himself and the entire community is the driving force of the new creation called into being and maintained among God's people by God's active grace alone. Without constant, conscious reference to Christ, who brought salvation to the world through his death on the cross and his resurrection, all of this would come to naught.

CHAPTER 8

THE CONVEYANCE OF THE COLLECTION AND ITS RESULTS (FROM SPRING 56 C.E. TO PAUL'S DEATH)

✠

Paul had his delegation together no later than the end of the winter of 55/56 C.E. Luke, who did not know about the true purpose of the delegation, gives only an incomplete listing of its members (Acts 20:4).[1] According to Luke's list, the following congregations had sent their representatives to Jerusalem: Berea, Thessalonica, Derbe, and those in the province of "Asia" (that is to say, the congregations located in and around Ephesus). Luke also mentions Paul's co-worker, Timothy.

Derbe probably got into the list due to a misunderstanding; there is no mention in any of the Pauline epistles of Lycaonian or Cilician congregations having participated in the collection. Although Gaius, the name of the person allegedly representing Derbe, is Latin, Derbe was not a Roman colony. Perhaps Luke had come across a locality in his source that was not listed in the official catalog of the Pauline mission stations, and had substituted it for that reason. It is possible, therefore, that the original list had a reference to a representative of one of the Pauline congregations from the province Galatia, which, according to I Corinthians 16:1, were expected to take part in the collection. We do know of a series of colonies of Roman settlers in Galatia. The misunderstanding might have been furthered by the mention of Timothy, who was from Lystra, a town neighboring Derbe. Timothy, however, did not travel to Jerusalem as the representative of a congregation, but as Paul's co-worker.

In addition to Galatia, Philippi is also missing from Luke's list, as are Corinth and the province of Achaia.[2] It is unthinkable that Philippi, Corinth, and the other Achaian congregations should not have been among the participants in the delegation.[3] Luke does not even mention that Paul was staying at Corinth at the time. But Paul's list in Romans 16 is also incomplete, in that it makes no reference to representatives from either Asia or Galatia. This is most probably the case because they had either not shown up yet or had not made a final commitment at the time of Paul's writing. This indicates that records of various stages of the final development may have existed.

That the delegation was a rather large one (it appears that most of the participating congregations tried if possible to send two representatives) seems to be supported by the following facts:

1. When it had become necessary to travel to Troas via Macedonia, the entire delegation did not stop over in Philippi; some of its members (the seven mentioned in Luke's list?) traveled on to Troas directly (Acts 20:3-6). The delegation might have been too large, and, therefore, it might have been an imposition on the Philippians (not a very wealthy congregation) to house all of its members for as long as after the Easter holidays.[4]
2. According to Acts 20:13-14 and especially 20:16, Paul was entitled to participate in making the decision about the course their ship would take. This rather astonishing feature of the story might best be explained by the fact that the delegation was quite large and, thus, represented a high percentage of the passengers. In view of the amount of money the delegation had paid for their fare, they were in a position to ask for special favors.

The total sum gathered for the collection must have been considerable. This is obviously the case because the final efforts, involving Paul and so many delegates, would not have been worth the trouble and expense otherwise. But it is more especially because the travel fees, which were undoubtedly high due to the length of the journey and the size of the group, and which were probably paid for in part with funds from the collection, would have amounted only to a minimal percentage of the total sum. The very fact that the congregations were prepared to spend such a large sum testifies to the ideological and material value they ascribed to the collection and its conveyance.[5]

The initial plan had been for the entire group to travel by ship from Corinth directly to Syria. The departure had certainly been planned for a time well ahead of Passover—which Paul wound up spending in Philippi (Acts 20:6). The earliest possible date for a sea journey was early March. But Paul learned from rumors that some Jews were planning an attempt on his life (Acts 20:3). If Paul felt he could avoid that danger by changing the itinerary, one may assume that the plot was to be executed on the high sea. This, in turn, tells us that there must have been a considerable number of Jews on the ship; that is to say, it must have been a shipload of pilgrims.[6] Paul changed his initial plan and proceeded by land from Corinth through Attica and Thessalonica to Macedonia. In Philippi the group accompanying him separated into two parties (20:5-6). One party continued (presumably by land) to Troas and waited there for Paul. Paul himself postponed his departure from Philippi until after Easter and then sailed to Troas. From there the delegation continued (probably in several stages) to Patara, a Lycian port (20:13ff.; 21:1).[7] From here the travelers took a ship headed for Phoenicia—a vessel probably larger and more seaworthy than the previous one, for it was ready to face the open sea (21:3). Leaving Cyprus to the northeast, the ship sailed directly to Tyrus, where the delegation managed to get a ship only to Ptolemais (21:4-5). At Ptolemais they boarded another ship for Caesarea (21:6). In all these coastal cities Jesus congregations had played host to the delegation, as one did in Caesarea (21:8-14), where Paul stayed with Philippus, the missionary known from Acts 6 and 8. Finally the delegation went up to Jerusalem (21:15-17). By that time, Pentecost might have arrived (see Acts 20:16).

It seems that when Paul arrived at Jerusalem (21:15-17), he found that James had become the undisputed leader of the congregation. Peter had long departed the city. The ensuing negotiations took place with James and the elders of the community.[8] The problems and difficulties pertaining to the report on these negotiations (Acts 21:15-26) are discussed in great detail by Ernst Haenchen, whose solution to these problems appears to contain much truth.[9] Luke does not say that the collection was received with joy; as a matter of fact, apart from the short and distorted remark in Acts 24:17, Luke remains completely silent on the collection. Haenchen explains this silence by saying that Luke must have been taken aback by the lack of undivided joy on the part of the church in Jerusalem over the arrival of the delegation and the rich offering they brought with them.

One reason for the lack of welcome the author of the Epistle to the Galatians received from the Jesus believers in Jerusalem certainly lay in their fear that they too would feel the brunt of the Jews' wrath at someone as contemptuous of the Torah as Paul was reputed to be. This danger would only be heightened by the far-reaching implications Paul had ascribed to the conveyance of the collection, as described above.

The great number of non-circumcised Gentile believers was bound to exacerbate the difficulties, tensions, and risks. The unconditional acceptance of the collection would have constituted a highly compromising step in the eyes of the local Jewish congregation. However, it was impossible simply to turn down the donation; this would have been utterly humiliating and insulting to Paul, the delegates, and the congregations they stood for. Such a refusal would quite probably have led to a breach with the Pauline congregations.

As far as we can see, the two parties chose to opt for a compromise situated somewhere between Scylla and Charybdis. Paul could be persuaded to defray the expenses for the release of four destitute Nazirites. This meant also that Paul had to go to the Temple on the third and seventh days to have himself cleansed of his sins, in order to be allowed, in this state of Levitical purity, to attend the ceremony organized in the Temple for the release of the four—and, at the same time, to pay for them. This compromise was acceptable to Paul, for it did not require him to give up his principles and was in line with the objectives of his visit, in that it gave him the opportunity to prove his communion with the Jerusalem congregation and other Jewish fellow believers. The irony was that the collection, originally not intended for the Temple at all, now ended up paying for some cultic services, although to a very minor degree.

At the same time, this compromise enabled the Jerusalem Jesus congregation not only to accept the collection but to defend Paul against the accusation of enmity toward the Torah as well. Moreover this strategy had circumvented the danger of various denunciations, including that of outright venality. In the face of risks of such gravity, any kind of conspicuous publicity about the conveyance of the collection would best be avoided.

Finally, there is also the *argumentum e silentio* for the informal delivery of the collected assets. There would have been no need to suppress any subsequent memorandum concerning the celebration that accompanied the conveyance of the collection, because none existed. Had Luke learned of such an announcement, he would certainly have made the use of it. But as things turned out, the collection—which had been started with such great hopes and had grown considerably in size, in importance, and in theological significance—was received as if "on the side," accompanied by whispers; quite a blow to the delegation. Hence, Luke, the first historian of Christianity, had good reason to pass over the whole episode in silence.

Contrary to what he seems to have expected and even feared, Paul did not cause a stir among the non-believing Jews directly through the collection and its transfer to the congregation in Jerusalem. Ironically, it was the compromise solution that proved fatal for him, because it necessarily brought with it repeated visits to the Temple. When he arrived there on the seventh day for the ceremony of release, he was discovered, apparently by Diaspora Jews, who were under the impression that he had brought into the Temple Trophimus, a non-circumcised, Gentile companion whom they knew from Ephesus. In leveling this denunciation against Paul, they were accusing him of a crime punishable by the Jewish death penalty, a punishment whose validity the imperial authorities recognized even to the extent of making it applicable to trespassing Roman soldiers. It is no wonder, therefore, that this accusation aroused the crowd against Paul, and that he was in danger of being lynched. The Roman guard saved him when, hearing of the incident, they took him into the custody in which he probably remained to the end of his life.

The details of what followed remain shrouded in darkness.[10] We can only guess that Paul's arrest, originally simply protective custody, became later a pre-trial imprisonment for investigation. Paul probably appealed to the emperor during that time, and this, along with his Roman citizenship, best explains his trip to

Rome, as a Jewish accusation would hardly have accounted for it. His appeal was granted, which is why Paul was taken to Rome by boat.

Paul's visit to Jerusalem, which he had intended as a way to support and inaugurate a new stage in his missionary effort, had thus turned into a catastrophe. The collection, on which he had spent so much time and energy—and which had become the very trademark of his missionary success—had finally gained him (even though only indirectly) imprisonment. Paul came to Rome after all, but as a prisoner. The escort the Jesus congregation at Rome was to have provided for his journey to Spain would never materialize. The sword of the powers that be had seen to that. The Epistle to the Romans, intended as the opening of a new stage of Pauline mission, had unwillingly—yet literally—turned into a last will and testament, and the statements on the collection contained therein are now the last word from Paul that we have. This epistle had initially been meant to fulfill the same purpose as the collection; the two endeavors had met a similar fate. To the long catalogs of trials punctuating the apostle's life, further trials had been added. Paul had been proven right in what he had written in II Corinthians 4:7: "We have this treasure in earthen vessels." Yet, he continues: "In order that the surplus belong to the power of God and not have its origin in us." This is the answer Paul found in response to the question of the meaning and the overall purpose of his own history—and history in general. Faith would be without foundation were it to deprive Paul's answer of its propositional form.

APPENDIX 1: THE QUESTION OF CHRONOLOGY

✠

In recent years Pauline chronology has gained renewed interest. In this regard the names of Gerd Lüdemann and Robert Jewett deserve particular mention.[1] One could ask whether it is even worthwhile to attempt a treatment of this issue after such elaborate discussions have come out since the appearance of the original German version of this book. Many points in both of these approaches are subject to question, many of them relating not so much to chronology as to different perceptions of the correspondence of Paul and the wider historical setting. None of their criticisms of my own exegeses and of my chronological conclusions have convinced me.

The greatest weakness of both their approaches, different as they are in many details, and the strongest difference from my own chronology shows in their treatment of Acts 18:22. Both follow John Knox in their claim of methodological objectivity. But curiously enough they fall for a clearly tendentious textual detail of Luke's presentation of the history of Paul, as does Knox before them. All three choose Acts 18:22 as a major point of orientation for dating the Jerusalem convention. The text reads: "He [Paul] *went up* and after having greeted the congregation went down to Antioch." Luke here clearly goads his readers into supplying a "to Jerusalem" after the "he went up," as is common in biblical usage. Even the pagan Hellenistic reader might infer here a "to the capital" (See BAG, *ἀναβαίνω*). Luke wants the readers to bring this to the text because he is interested to have even the clearly independent mission of Paul to western Asia Minor, Macedonia, and Greece seen as being put under the tutelage of the Twelve and the Jerusalem church.

Knox, Lüdemann, and Jewett cannot satisfactorily reason why and how Paul and Barnabas should and could have met at that time, long after their separation, in order to go to Jerusalem; and it remains unclear why the convention was necessary then. The silence of Paul about his own missionary activity in Asia Minor and around the Aegean Sea in the account given at the end of Galatians 1 or in the report on the Jerusalem convention itself is not sufficiently explained by these authors either.

I am convinced that my chronology has not been done away with by the new hypotheses, and that my suggestions still deserve further consideration. They are intimately connected to the methodology of the study at hand, where observation of the historical situations is interconnected with an assessment and appraisal of the theological arguments made by the texts, a process that is especially necessary because of the apparent variety, if not discrepancy, of all the statements and data on the topic in question.

An essential date for the history of the collection for Jerusalem is, of course, that of the Jerusalem convention. Besides the failed attempts of Knox, Lüdemann, and others to use Acts 18:22 for the dating of the convention there have been various suggestions to interrelate Acts 11:27-30 and Galatians 2:1-10.

Ferdinand Hahn has made attempts to use Acts 11:27-30 for an early dating of the convention.[2] He suggests the winter of 43/44 as the latest possible date. To substantiate his calculations he maintains the following: (1) the convention must have been convened prior to the persecution in the year 44; (2) this is the case because the reference to the Antiochene collection (Acts 11:27-30) presupposes the convention; and (3) because the address section of the letter contained in Acts 15:23 must also be taken into account—an address in which the territories in southern Asia Minor outside of Cilicia are not yet listed.

But the information given in Acts 11:27-30 can be considered conclusive for the dating of the convention only if, compared to Luke's report, the journey to Jerusalem mentioned here is dated not only after the convention but also after the persecutions recorded in the ensuing chapter (Acts 12). But Luke connects the Jerusalem visit of chapter 11 clearly to the narrative of chapter 12—that is, to a course of events prior to chapter 15. A prior journey is reported, related to other fixed dates. Hahn dates the conveyance of the Antiochene collection of chapter 11 as late as 46/47—perhaps even 48. With this, as well as with the dislocation of Acts 13–14 and Acts 15, Hahn completely discredits the Lukan chronology. Why should the persecution reported in Acts 12 be dated after the convention? Hahn holds (quite contrary to Acts 12:2) that not only James, the son of Zebedee, but also his brother John (who, according to Gal. 2:9, was still present at the convention) was martyred.[3] The only reference we have to that double martyrdom is found in the Syrian Martyrology. But a martyrs' calendar is certainly not the best documentation to be relied on for correct dating calculations; such calendars always tend to "arrange" history for the sake of establishing fixed dates for the purpose of setting up days for celebrations of memorials according to the calendar.[4] Hahn would have done better not to refer to Peter's departure as reported in Acts 12:17, as this verse is no more than a traditional closing formula used in old legends which seems to have become an everyday expression.[5] Equally legendary is the connection Luke establishes between the stories concerning Peter and the one surrounding Herod's death: "A new connotation—namely, the idea of 'de mortibus persecutorum'—was added to the original hubris motif of this initially self-contained legend (Acts 19:23) when it was incorporated into this particular context."[6] Furthermore, as the dating of the Passover festival in Acts 12:3-4 also stands in contradiction to the connection between the persecutions of the Jesus believers and Herod's death, it would be better to disregard it in determining the precise time of the Jerusalem convention.[7]

Galatians 2:9 seems to speak against dating the martyrdom of James, Zebedee's son and John's brother, after the convention, for had he still been alive during the time of the summit, it is hardly plausible that the other James, the brother of Jesus, should have been mentioned in Paul's report without any further attribute distinguishing him from the Zebedee (different in Gal. 1:19). This improbability is heightened by the fact that James, the son of Zebedee, who enjoyed great respect within the early church and also among the Jews, appears in the Gospel tradition together with his brother, John, and Simon Peter—the same configuration of names as in Galatians 2:9![8] Besides, had James, the son of Zebedee, after the convention really been the first from among the disciples to suffer martyrdom, the chronicler would certainly have given expression to such outstanding dignity. One can hardly argue, therefore, that the narrator might have deliberately left out mentioning that disciple or, even less acceptable, that he may have substituted another man's name for the disciple's.

The objection that Paul had written about these things from a standpoint based on much later circumstances—that is, at a time where the name "James" was no longer identified with anyone else than the Lord's brother—does not hold for the simple reason that in Galatians 1:19, a passage obviously intended as historical narrative, Paul clearly states that the James he was reporting about was indeed the Lord's brother. Further, the man referred to as "James" in Galatians 2:9 can only have been the Lord's brother, as the other "James" is not mentioned here. The alternative solution—namely, that Paul had deliberately neglected to mention James, the son of Zebedee, although he had still met him at the convention, is to be refuted. During his first visit to Jerusalem Paul had not met him there. It is to be concluded, therefore, that Galatians 2:9 is best explained by assuming that by the time of the convention at Jerusalem, James, the son of Zebedee, had been dead for several years.

But Hahn's calculations as regards the dates of the convention and the persecution also seem improbable on other grounds. Had the persecution of Acts 12 (probably the first bloody one the early Aramaic-speaking church had to face) occurred after the convention, Paul and Barnabas most probably would have decided to urge, even more forcefully than initially intended, the speedy organization and execution of the collection at Antioch, since the premises on which the agreement on that collection had been based would have appeared even more pressing. Hahn (pp. 70, 78), however, maintains that three to four years must have passed before the Antiochenes actually started to act, and when they finally did, they only did so following a serious reminder from a prophet.

Not only does the entire tone of Galatians 2 utterly contradict such reading, but it is also totally unwarranted from a historical point of view. The early tradition yields nothing on Paul's (and Barnabas's) possible activities during all that time. And the longer the period of time one assumes between the convention and the Antioch incident, the less acceptable it becomes that Paul should have kept silent for such an extended period of time, during which he was engaged in a joint endeavor with Barnabas. This difficulty would increase if Luke's narrative on the missionary journey through Pamphylia, Pisidia, and Lycaonia were credited with authenticity and dated after the Antiochene collection.[9]

The longer the timespan between the convention and the incident at Antioch, the more incomprehensible it becomes that Simon Peter should have postponed his first visit to that congregation until then, for it is impossible to argue that the visit of Peter to Antioch, mentioned in Galatians 2:11-21, was not his first. Hahn bases his dating of the convention heavily on the importance he ascribes to the address found in Acts 15:23. But this argument soon turns against him, because—in so far as that address is viewed as genuine (and none of the reservations put forth against its authenticity appear to be convincing[10])—the Decree of the Apostles (also according to Hahn drafted after the Antioch incident) must necessarily be correlated with Galatians 1:22, because both texts state identical confines for the zones of mission. No mention is made, as yet, of Cyprus or of any of the areas covered in missionary activity during the so-called first missionary journey—that is, the provinces in southern Asia Minor. This abrogates Hahn's argument that Paul and Barnabas had carried out missionary work in Cyprus, Pamphylia, Pisidia, and Lacaonia prior to the crisis in Antioch.

As a consequence, the period of time unaccounted for between the Jerusalem convention (if one dates it in 43/44) and the spring of 49 turns out to be much too long.[11] It seems most appropriate, therefore, to follow the suggestion put forth by both Ernst Haenchen and Hans Conzelmann that the convention must have taken place in the year 48, which sets aside Acts 11 as a source. This case need not be reopened on the basis of Alfred Suhl's advocacy of a connection between Acts 11 and Galatians 2 as pertains to the convention. Jewett has given the arguments of Suhl thorough attention and has convincingly disproven them, pointing out that such dating has to jam far too many events and evolving phenomena into all too short a period of time.[12]

Accepting this date of 48 C.E. as a starting point for further calculations, it is also possible to arrive at more acceptable dates and periods of time at which to fix earlier events, for instance Paul's calling and Jesus' death. Indeed, since Hahn correlates the date given in Galatians 2:1 with Galatians 1:18 (p. 78), he has to assign Paul's calling to the year 29 (perhaps even 28)—that is to say, only one or two years after the year Hahn assumes for Jesus' execution[13]—hardly an acceptable computation.

This dating would be based on the premise that an overwhelming number of highly significant events had occurred in the young church and that a strong tradition would have evolved in a matter of one or two years at most. This, however, is hardly possible, even with extremely enthusiastic groups. Were this theory to be taken as a fact, the founding of the Aramaic-speaking and, later, the Greek-speaking church at Jerusalem, the mission carried out by these groups in that city, the ensuing persecutions, the mission outside Jerusalem, the setting up of countless congregations—including that of Damascus, Paul's own involvement in persecutions against Jesus people, and many other things would all have had to occur within this extremely short span of time.

Further, a far-flung and highly differentiated theological tradition would have had to develop during this rather brief period, a tradition whose christological components Hahn himself has discussed in his book on the issue of christological titles. Other traditions, no less complex, would have to be assumed as unfolding coincidentally. And finally, had Paul really been called this shortly after the Easter events, his apostleship would hardly have been questioned—indeed attacked!—on the grounds that it had its roots in a much too belated calling.

Neither is it convincing to date the death of Jesus in the year 27. The only factor speaking in favor of this possibility is the fact that in the year 14 or 15 Nissan might have fallen on a Friday. Any of the other arguments advanced by Hahn (after Gustav Hölscher[14]) are not convincing.[15] After all, the date of Jesus' death could very well be placed in the year 30.[16]

The fact remains that more than two years must be assumed for the time between Jesus' death and Paul's calling. Presupposing a lapse of five years, the entire range of events and theological developments listed above could more possibly have come to pass. In this alternative—especially if we assume that Jesus did die in the year 30—Paul's calling could have taken place in the year 35. Starting from this hypothesis, the period of time preceding the convention would have amounted to approximately thirteen years (i.e., the interval mentioned in Gal. 2:1). An even longer stretch of time between Paul's calling and the convention—fifteen years, if the dates given in Galatians 1:18 and 2:1 are added up—would mean that Paul had been engaged in missionary effort over an even longer period. A definite decision proves impossible. A valid chronology for the events leading up to the convention of the apostles at Jerusalem cannot be established. Assuming, however, that Paul had started his independent missionary work in the year 49, further possible target dates can be suggested (these computations are in agreement with the figures arrived at by Ernst Haenchen for the duration of Paul's stay in Thessalonica).[17] I date the first Epistle to the Thessalonians in the spring of the year 50.

I cannot adhere to Haenchen's conclusions, however, as regards the dating of the events from the spring of 52 on. According to Acts 20:21, Paul must have spent approximately three years in Ephesus. This seems rather a generous reckoning; "close to three years" probably means "nearly three years." On the basis of Acts 19:8-10 and Acts 19:22, however, greater dating precision seems possible. According to Acts 19:8 Paul had been preaching in the Ephesian synagogue for no more than three months when the pressure exerted by the Jewish establishment became so strong that he had to move into the lecture hall of Tyrannus, where he continued to preach for two more years.

Finally, without any further explanation, Luke reports in Acts 19:22 that Paul had remained in Asia "for some time." It is my opinion that the "some time" of a stay in Asia is to be added to the three months and two years mentioned before. For Luke the information about that additional span of time in Asia serves only as an introduction to the episode of the Demetrius rebellion (Acts 19:23-40) anyhow. But with a view to II Corinthians 1:8-11 (also Rom. 16:3, 7), it seems that this report on the Demetrius episode carries with it the remnants of reminiscences of a much more serious incident that caused Paul's arrest. The correspondence contained in the canonical Epistle to the Philippians (and also Philemon) was probably written during that imprisonment (see p. 62-63, above).

It could be that the vaguely remembered knowledge about the time Paul had to spend in prison toward the end of his stay at Ephesus had triggered Luke's remark about Paul's staying on in Asia "for some time." The fact that Luke does not explain his remark and, further, that this mention of a prolonged stay is definitely correlated somehow with the report on the Demetrius revolt, appears to support this interpretation. The sending of Timothy and Erastus (not necessarily identical with the Corinthian city treasurer mentioned in Rom. 16:23) could be identical with the phenomenon described in I Corinthians 16:10-11 (4:17).

Therefore, a good two and a half years suggest themselves for the stay of Paul in Ephesus. The dates given in Acts 20:31, on the one hand, and Acts 19:8-10, 22, on the other, would, therefore, complement each other. Against Walter Schmithals, I would also claim that the events mentioned in the Pauline correspondence, particularly that with the Corinthians, but also that with the Galatians and the Philippians, would require the length of time I have suggested.[18]

But there are still a few additional observations regarding the demarcation in the time of Paul's stay at Ephesus: It was followed by Paul's journey to Macedonia via Troas and his stay there (II Cor. 2:12-13; 7:5-6; 8:1-5; 9:2-4; compare Acts 20:1-2). It would be a mistake to assume too short a time for that particular phase of Paul's activities. At their end stood Paul's arrival at Corinth in the later part of autumn, and—as stated in Acts 20:3-4 (where "Greece" stands for Corinth)—he remained there for three months. Therefore, the beginning of that traveling period—that is, the departure from Ephesus, must be fixed in the early summer (or even spring) of the same year. Hence, Haenchen's timetable (spring 52, tour through Asia Minor to Ephesus, and from there to Macedonia in 54) does not allow enough time for the stay in Ephesus and, even less so, in Macedonia.

During the journey from Antioch through Asia Minor to Ephesus (Acts 18:23), Paul must have made his second stopover in Galatia (Gal. 4:13), which probably lasted more than just a few weeks. I want to conclude, therefore, that Paul traveled from Antioch to Ephesus in the spring and summer of 52, that he remained in Ephesus from the summer of that year until the spring of 55, and that the journey from Ephesus to Macedonia—including the time spent there—lasted from spring to the fall of 55.

If the beginning of the stay at Ephesus is dated summer of 52, the Epistle to the Galatians must have been written in the year 53 (in Ephesus itself or some place near by), and the first Epistle to the Corinthians during autumn 53 or in spring of 54.

In this hypothesis, the apology in II Corinthians 2:14–7:4 as its major part would have been written in the second half of 54—as also the "letter of tears" in II Corinthians 10–13. As to the Philippian correspondence, it would have to be dated winter 54/55—during the time of Paul's Ephesian imprisonment. The same goes for Philemon. Accordingly, Paul must have written the letter of reconciliation in II Corinthians 1:1–2:13 and 7:5-16 from Macedonia in the spring of 55, and the two letters on the collection fragmentarily preserved in II Corinthians 8 and 9 in the course of the summer and fall of the same year. The Epistle to the Ephesians (Rom. 16) and the Epistle to the Romans proper would have to be assumed for the winter of 55/56—that is to say, the time of Paul's last stay in Corinth.

All this points to the fact that the conveyance of the collection as well as Paul's arrest occurred in the year 56 (at Pentecost?). Obviously, this reckoning stands in contradiction to Ernst Haenchen's calculations based on the date of change in the office of governor from Felix to Festus, counting backward from that date to arrive at the point of Paul's arrest.[19] In Haenchen's computation, that change in office, which took place while Paul was already in prison (Acts 24:27), must be dated in the year 55. In this belief, Haenchen essentially follows Kirsopp Lake.[20] Schürer's careful discussion of the date for the switch in the prefecturial office needs to be considered.[21] His treatment of the matter appears most convincing. He suggests the years 58 or 59 for that change in governorship. Schürer saw that an early dating is canceled out primarily by Josephus's narrative, in which the major part of the events under Felix are reported as belonging to the time after Nero's succession of Claudius as Caesar in Rome.[22]

The events definitely associated with the governorship of either Felix or Festus are multifarious enough to require a sufficient period for them to happen in either case. This is especially true with the events that led up to the Jewish war.[23]

Both Lake and Haenchen have interpreted the release from office of Felix's brother Pallas as a complete and final rejection by the emperor, which would have made it impossible for Pallas to intercede with the emperor Nero in his brother's defense against the Jewish accusations.[24] But Josephus mentions precisely such intercession shortly after the investiture of Festus as governor.[25] Hence, both Lake and Haenchen dated the change in office of governor, and the subsequent difficulties threatening Felix in Rome, before Pallas's release from office (end of 55). However, Tacitus also informs us about an acquittal of Pallas after a trial at about the same time, indicating that Pallas was not entirely lost.[26] So why should he not have campaigned successfully for his brother, even after his alleged "fall"? Nero ordered Pallas's execution only in the year 62 (Tac. Ann. XIV, 65; Dio LXII, 14.3).[27]

All this shows that from the point of view of common political history there are certain features suggesting that the two years mentioned in Acts 24:27 do not pertain to Felix's term in office, but to the time of Paul's imprisonment prior to the change in office of the Roman governor—a conclusion certainly borne out by the language of the passage.[28]

As a consequence, the change from Felix to Festus in the office of Roman governor can be dated on the basis of the date of Paul's imprisonment. Supposing Paul went to prison in the year 56, the transfer of power from Felix to Festus could be assumed for the year 58. This in turn would mean that the apostle was taken to Rome in the same year. Acts 28:30 informs us that he stayed there and preached in the city, unimpeded despite his imprisonment, for two years—which takes us to the year 60. There is no reason why we should think that Luke invented those two years. As convincingly detailed by Haenchen, the Lukan narrative (especially the final chapter) clearly indicates that Luke was aware of Paul's martyr's death but did not choose to report on it. At any rate, our conclusion would be that Paul's death must have come at the end of that two-year period, that he was executed in the year 60 C.E.[29]

APPENDIX 2: PHILO'S TREATISE ON ἰσότης (RER. DIV. HER. 141–206)

The tradition reflected in this treatise more or less identifies the divine logos and ἰσότης as concepts of equal meaning. In Rer. Div. Her. 166 the capacity of the logos as λόγος τόμευς to separate and to keep in equilibrium the two most noble divine powers—the world-generating, compassionate energy (Elohim) and the world-dominating, punishing force (Yahweh)—is paraphrased as ἰσότης, thus establishing the cosmic tenor of the concept. Indeed, ἰσότης constitutes a basic cosmic principle. This explains why in an interpretation of a number of verses of Genesis 1, ἰσότης is put on an equal footing with God himself (163-164). Through its regulating activity, ἰσότης becomes the wet-nurse of δικαιοσύνη (163). In this form of δικαιοσύνη, ἰσότης causes the rebalancing of any inequity, the root of partiality, conflict, war, and other expressions of injustice. Hence, ἰσότης is credited with a soterological function: "Equity/equality gives birth to peace."

The distinguishing feature of Hellenistic-Jewish Gnostic wisdom consists in the premise that cosmic concepts are correlated with mystical ones—in fact, that both merge into each other. This is why in the didactic fragment used by Philo the cosmic significance of ἰσότης is developed further into a description of the importance of ἰσότης for spiritual sacrifice, as well as pneumatic worship (174-206). In this passage ἰσότης is identified with the divine logos (201-206), which itself creates the constellations out of which develop the requirement of sacrificial acts—that is to say, it generates precisely those tensions and opposites for whose elimination sacrifice becomes imperative (182-90). Ἰσότης regulating the offering is the very essence of the offering that brings about purification and salvation, that is, heavenly wisdom.

Exodus 16:18 is given as scriptural proof of this understanding. In 191 it is said:

> The heavenly food of the soul, wisdom, which [Moses] calls manna, is distributed by the divine logos equally to all those who wish to use it, while he, the logos, above all is consideredly intent on equality. Moses testifies to that in the following way, "He, that had much, did not have too much, and he, that had little, did not lack" [in all those instances] when they used the wonderful and precious measure of analogy.

That everyone received what he or she was entitled to shows that the gift received was not an external, material one, but an inner nourishment—namely, divine wisdom.

In an earlier passage (183) this divine wisdom is depicted in the following way: "The divine [category of wisdom] is unblended, unmixed, and, therefore, offered as libation to God, the unblended, unmixed one, who is one-ness in his solitariness." Immediately afterwards it reads:

> That part of the soul which is unblended and unmixed (like the divine wisdom) is the spirit (*νοῦς*) in its absolute integrity. It (*νοῦς*) is preserved integral and unspoiled when it is inspired from heaven, from above, with the breath (of divine wisdom), guarded from malady and injury, and is offered in form of a libation to him who has inspired and guarded it from all evil that could harm it, in appropriate fashion in its entirety and, after having been reduced into a single element (exactly like divine wisdom).

In this spiritual process, which amounts to no less than the return of divine wisdom, the sacrificial gift effects the purification of the entire person. Finally, as it does in numerous other instances in corresponding Hellenistic texts dealing with sacrifice and worship, the motif of *εὐχαριστία* also appears in this didactic tradition. In the context of Hellenistic and Jewish-Hellenistic

Gnostic wisdom, *εὐχαριστία* constitutes the very climax of spiritual offering and spiritual worship. It is not surprising that in the framework of this kind of mystical thinking, the events referred to are described as being cosmic occurrences. The cosmic and the mystical become one:

> We have also an excellent example for *ἰσότης*, in the composition of frankincense offering. . . . Each of (the) ingredients . . . must be brought in equal measure to make for the amalgamation of the whole. I believe that the four parts out of which the frankincense is constituted are symbols for the elements out of which the entire world was brought to completion. . . . The harmonious composition and blending of these substances prove to be a venerable and perfect work, truly holy—[namely] the world which, as he (Moses) believes must, by the means of frankincense-offering give thanks (*εὐχαριστεῖν*) to the Creator by means of the symbolic act of a frankincense offering, so that, while by the perfumer's art it is literally burned, in reality it is the whole world wrought by divine wisdom which is offered and consumed, morning and evening, in the sacrificial fire. It is indeed a fitting life's work for the world to give thanks to the father and maker, continuously and without interruption—and [in so doing] to well nigh evaporate and to reduce oneself into a single element to show that one does not hoard any treasure but that one is offering oneself completely as a votary gift to God, the Creator. (196-200)

What is said here about the world's self-effulgence in thanksgiving prayer, about the world reducing itself to its basic substance, was previously said about the sacrifice of the pristine spirit—that is, that divine wisdom, when turned upon humans and given to them as a gift, is returned to God through thanksgiving and spiritual offering. A little later (230-36), in order to complete the circuit of concepts in motion, a parallel is established between the human *νοῦς* and the *νοῦς* of the deity, the divine Logos. Here, too, the relationship to the cosmos is present.

AFTERWORD: IS THERE JUSTIFICATION IN MONEY? A HISTORICAL AND THEOLOGICAL MEDITATION ON THE FINANCIAL ASPECTS OF JUSTIFICATION BY CHRIST

"A fool may make money, but it takes a wise person to spend it." (English Proverb)

A. INTRODUCTION

Biblical studies, theology, and the church at large are unaware that the authentic writings of Paul contain some of the most elaborate literary reflections on the flow of money surviving from the ancient world. The important texts in this regard are, principally, the eighth and ninth chapters of II Corinthians, the other passages on the collection for Jerusalem, the reflection on financial support from the Philippians, and finally the discussions on remuneration in I and II Corinthians.

Paul's reflections on money are intimately related to central theological issues and interwoven with his life and the lives of his congregations. But the usual scholarly presentations of Paul's theology and his biography to this day discuss these financial and organizational issues only in the most abstract terms, giving them marginal status at best. This is even more the case with the use of the Pauline correspondence and its message in the contemporary church. Stewardship Sundays are the place in church life for Paul's collection texts, and there they are utilized, but only as snippets.

Despite the fact that ancient reflections on economy, and particularly on the flow of money, are very rare, social and economic historians have never dealt with the Pauline texts on money. As far as literary evidence is concerned the three ancient authors presented briefly below dominate the discussion. This is particularly true of Aristotle, whose hypothesis that money developed out of the exchange of goods prevailed until recently, with major consequences for the history of economics and also for our contemporary understanding of money.

Reworking my thesis on the collection for this translation has given me the opportunity to reconsider the relevance of these Pauline texts and to relate them to my own social-historical inquiries into the interplay of Judaism and the early church with their pagan environment. The economic crises and changes at the end of our millennium, those in my own country and in the United States not least among them, have furthered my insights and opened for me new perspectives. This afterword took shape when East Germany was simply usurped by the economic strength of West Germany under the leadership of a party that claims to be Christian. This experience has sharpened my views. The economic crises around us make it more urgent for theology and the church to remember that the frame of reference of one of their most commonly used authors, Paul, has been unnecessarily curtailed.

A renewed acknowledgment of the interrelatedness of life and theology in Paul will engender fascinating suggestions. Life here means not only Paul's personal life, but also his communal and social life, and that of others. It includes economic issues directly. This suggests that the church needs to begin to reflect on justification by Christ in its financial offices as well as in its pulpits. It further implies that lay Christians will no longer view christology as a mere matter of personal opinion but as something that has relevance for their workplaces in the various branches of the economy. It follows as well that Pauline theology cannot be left to professional theologians alone, but belongs to the praxis of the church at large, a church that is not removed from the world but rather acts as a challenging and stimulating part of the world. The letters of Paul as a textbook for schools of economics and of business administration? Why not? So long as they do not replace the other textbooks, it could only enrich the curriculum.

The recent crises of economic structures have led to intensive debates about the nature of the economy and of economics. The theory of money, its character and its function, is at present under vivid discussion. The origin and history of money are still a matter of controversy. All this makes a reflection on Paul's contribution to these discussions opportune.

Paul's ideas and suggestions appear even more relevant today because the many and various studies on money that have appeared in recent decades have gone far beyond the economic value and function of currencies. The political and social sides of money have been argued about for quite some time, as have its ethical dimensions.[1] The relationship of economy and money to the law and legal order have found increasing attention.[2] The recent deliberations on the sociology of money have also uncovered its communicative importance.[3] The psychological aspects of money have also received much attention.[4] Compared with this, the theology of money has been relatively ignored.[5] But within this concert of theories the ideas and suggestions of Paul do not look strange at all. As does the contemporary discussion, Paul's ideas on the theory and practice of money go far beyond the metallic value of coins.

As we have seen (and shall see more), the historical dimensions of economy and economics, money included, have gained renewed attention. New suggestions have been made about the origin of money, its understanding and function in the ancient world.[6] My study of these matters in the context of the history of New Testament times threw new light on the Pauline correspondence. I have integrated my research on II Corinthians and on the collection into the general picture of the ancient environment, not only with respect to the history of religion and social history but also with regard to the ancient economy. The Pauline correspondence increasingly became a primary source for my understanding of the ancient world. The following essay is intended to make these ancient thoughts relevant for today through a meditation on the theological texts of Paul within their historical context. I hope to communicate not only my thoughts, but also my fascination with this subject, so that my actual suggestions can stimulate further thinking on the part of my readers.

B. SOME GENERAL REMARKS ON THE ECONOMIC SITUATION OF PAUL'S THEOLOGICAL DISCOURSE

1. The State of the Ancient Economic Discourse

Paul's writings presuppose a monetary economy of worldwide proportions with a common (Roman) currency and an easy exchange of other currencies. This means that he was familiar with an urban society with a universal market-structure. He must have taken for granted industry, division of labor, trade, and a labor market that included slave labor. Financial institutions were present. There existed during this time a strong wisdom tradition that discussed these economic issues.[7] Since Paul invokes wisdom, it can be taken as a matter of course that he was well attuned to this tradition. While he distances himself from the Apocalyptic and Gnostic denunciations of any kind of temporal economy,[8] he does not share the positive attitude that Jewish missionary wisdom held toward a performance- and market-oriented society.[9] It is clear that while Paul presupposes an effective economy, he consciously neglects certain economic principles and elements important to his day, and to ours as well.

Outside of Paul's writings, monetary issues are touched upon by Aristotle in his discussion of economics in his *Politics,* 1.2-5, especially chapters 3–4, and also in his treatment of revolutions in 5.3-5.[10] Money plays an important role in other literary and non-literary remains as well (for instance in the studies of the Elder Cato), but never in the form of a continuous reflection. Economic deliberations are presented in the dialogue "Oeconomicus" by Xenophon, and in the treatise "Oeconomica," which comes to us under the name of Aristotle, but was most probably written during the third century B.C.E. In none of these sources does one find anything similar to modern textbooks or manuals on economics or business administration, nor (certainly) anything like an introduction to social work. The texts offer economic reflections and provide technical advice, to be sure, but these considerations are embedded in general ethical, social, and political discussions. Some passages even take a storytelling approach, and piety features rather prominently. Only Aristotle deliberates to a larger degree on the monetary side of the economy.

In Xenophon's dialogue on economics, property and profit are phenomena of social relations. Their main value is not of a financial but of an unquantified, social kind. Profit means primarily usefulness in and for human relations. It is of interest to note that Paul's strong emphasis on righteousness in his arguments for the collection finds its parallel in Xenophon's use of the terms *righteous, just, righteousness,* and *justice* in the context of economics, by which he means the management of a house, particularly an estate.

Pseudo-Aristotle claims in his treatise that the economics of a private household, a city, a province, or a kingdom are basically comparable; economics is for him literally *oiko-nomia*: the regulation of a house, despite the many variations in detail.[11] What renders these economic contexts different are such things as the procurement of funds and other economic means and their use. Risks and catastrophes are taken for granted in these economies, but the need for imagination and resourcefulness is equally taken as a matter of course.

2. Juridical Elements of the Ancient Economy, Particularly Its Monetary Structure

In the main text of this book I have shown that Paul makes an easy association between righteousness and justification on the one hand and the collection on the other. The automatic response of a Protestant theologian to this discovery of the proximity of a discussion of the flow of money to the central doctrine of the Reformation is to find it shocking, if not blasphemous. This is particularly so when one remembers that Paul did not draw this connection on the grounds of the doctrines of election and sanctification, as Max Weber claimed for Calvinist economics. Paul's association is much more direct.

My studies subsequent to the writing of the German version of this book have demonstrated to me that from its inception ancient Mediterranean urban society interrelated economic issues naturally with political, social, juridical, and religious ideas as well as ethical concerns. I present the major arguments for this claim in the following paragraphs. I shall describe the primary working principles of the Mediterranean economy during this period and the role of money, market, and religion within it. Then I shall demonstrate and interpret the selective use Paul makes of these issues.

How one understands the origin of the Greco-Roman economy of the first millennium B.C.E., particularly its monetary and market structure, has direct bearing on how one understands our own today. The old Aristotelian idea that money arose out of the barter system because guaranteed metallic value facilitated and objectified exchange has lost ground recently. It appears more convincing that the concept of private property stood at the beginning of what we now call Western Civilization—that is, Greco-Roman society—and that the social and legal order were intimately associated with it. From its start the monetary system presupposed a high degree of abstraction and numerical quantification, and this in turn rested on a basic societal shift away from an orientation that was highly mythical in character to one that was less so.

It is most plausible that abstract notions of right, measurable, and divisible performance and production, and the market as a place for the exchange of surplus production originated together with private property. It seems reasonable to suppose that a sense for quantifiable signs evolved with this objectification of business. The minted coin became the expression of this process.

Recent research has shown that, after an intermediate state of Mycenaean-type cultures and economies, the Mediterranean economies of the first millennium B.C.E. were born out of catastrophes and governed by the fear of future disasters, which later were still remembered as the chaos which threatened both the legal and economic order of society.[12] Individuals who had fled natural catastrophes congregated together and formed communities, not from a feeling of solidarity, but out of common interest. These communities began as democracies of shared penury. The persons gathered agreed upon equal shares of land as their private property, forming the basis of the new form of patriarchal economy, that of the city-state.[13]

Fear of overindebtedness and a return to poverty remained inherent threats. Gaining and maintaining stock and liquidity through labor beyond sustenance-work were the means of protecting oneself against unforseeable risks. One began with one's own labor, then that of family members, debtors, and slaves. It was beneficial and created additional security to lend one's own assets to other citizens who had bad luck. This lending against security and credit promised better liquidity in times of future adversity. It lowered the costs of maintaining stock in the form of natural goods and provided additional protection. Thus the risk of holding stock and maintaining liquidity decreased, and one gained assets through the interest one placed on debtors' returns.[14]

Catastrophe and credit, protection and promise, and many more terms to be used here intimate that for ancient culture and society the divine was consistently in the picture. Debts and contracts called for witnesses and sanctions, all divine prerogatives. Temples became involved rather early as trusted institutions. Their trust became very real in terms of testifying, depositing, crediting, and collecting interest. The priests witnessed and certified the contracting and trading of debts; they wrote and executed obligations against fees and interest. These obligations were traded beyond the original parties and provided profit to the Temple and further traders involved. Thus the Temple became a bank, and money became an abstraction, depersonalized and dematerialized.[15]

Temples usually were not private property but were jointly owned by the gods themselves and the respective cities. For these stored and traded debts and the interest growing out of them, people needed legalized and nominalized tender. Minted coinage was born, guaranteed by the gods and the cities, symbols of their power and protection and of the value they guaranteed. This value, symbolized by the coins, but represented also by the written obligations behind them, was not economic alone, but was social, political, and religious as well.

The accumulated interest called for the production and exchange of goods—that is, for commodities—and for a market in which to trade and redeem them. Performance, achievement-oriented surplus, production, division of labor, and trade that transcended local boundaries came into being, stimulated, guided, and guarded by deity and state alike.[16]

It is very significant that the political theology and the reforms of Augustus and his successors (as well as such Eastern Mediterranean philosophers and theologians as Plutarch) reemphasized Theseus, Romulus, Aeneas, and other founding figures of Greek and Roman urban societies. Virgil, who was so influential in the evolution of Roman political theology of the first centuries B.C.E. and C.E., paid increasing attention to Hesiod, an author on whom Gunnar Heinsohn has drawn heavily in his reconstruction of the origin and development of an economy based on private property. The propagandistic intention was to make the social and economic traits personified in such figures a matter of public consciousness in Paul's own world.

3. Critical Omissions of Common Economic Motifs in Paul

Paul's failure to employ certain of these elements and characteristics of the Mediterranean economy in his discussion of the collection, given their wide currency, proves to be very striking. As I have pointed out, Paul makes every effort to avoid speaking of the collection as if it were a tax. But for readers who knew of the tax Jews paid regularly to the Temple in Jerusalem, this association would have been natural. Therefore, it would have been clear to them that Paul's skirting of this issue was an intentional oversight. Paul never allowed the Jerusalem Temple to enter onto the stage, although he did play with the motif of a voluntary gift for the Temple (II Cor. 9:15). If for no other reason than it was the central edifice in the Judean capital one would have expected Paul to refer to the Temple in speaking of the Jerusalem collection; yet, he made no mention of it.

The same reticence holds true for the concept of the pilgrimage of the peoples. The biblical and Jewish expressions of this motif focus, if not on the Temple itself, at least on Mount Zion. Paul's silence on this idea, therefore, becomes telling. Paul almost appears to tease when he constantly plays with different variations on the theme of sacrifice. But it is always *spiritual* sacrifice; he keeps out the idea of real sacrifice at the Temple completely.

Given the ancient financial and economic structure described, references to debts and obligations as well as to their redemption would only be natural. The customary understanding of Paul's doctrine of justification even inserts metaphors to that effect into the Pauline language and interpretation—against the evidence of the texts.[17] In keeping with this pattern Paul does not mention how the money he wants collected is to be produced. Labor and production would normally be associated with a structure that was built on debit and credit. Contrary to its claims to bank on trust, this system was not built on confidence and faith but rather on distrust, diffidence, disbelief, debt, and obligation, behind all of which lurked anxiety and fear. Paul's message offers freedom from all of these fetters. Why then should he allow such language to enter into the argument again and to corrupt his encouraging reflections on the collection? Paul's meditations on justification, which are predominantly of a positive nature, speak more of freedom for than freedom from.

As we have seen, in speaking of the collection Paul espoused a negative attitude toward the concept of self and toward the adoration of the private, privatization, and private property. In I Corinthians 16:2, personal gain is mentioned only as something to be set aside to facilitate the collection for others. There is no mention of either calculations (as to proceeds, investment, or possible quantifiable yields) or of order or law in Paul's discussion, even though all of these terms belonged to the ancient market economy, especially in its contemporary Roman form.[18]

The many participants in Paul's collection, most of them urban people who were accustomed to the market economy and its terminology, must have noticed these omissions. The exegeses of the Jerusalem convention and of Philippians 4 have shown that Paul knew the vocabulary of business language. The end of the eighth chapter II Corinthians proves that Paul did not shy away from down-to-earth matters of organization if he were so inclined. Thus Paul's reticence to employ the language of the market economy must have had a purpose.

C. THE "TRUST" STRUCTURE OF ANCIENT ECONOMIC MOBILITY AND MONETARY CIRCULATION

1. In the Mediterranean World

There is more to the interplay of religion and economics in Paul's times than the phenomena described above. It is certain that members of the Hellenistic-Jewish Diaspora, like Paul, knew such documents as I and II Maccabees. The story of Heliodorus in chapters three and four of II Maccabees certainly supports the argument made earlier that temples were banks of deposit and served as a sort of savings and loan associations. The legend of the angel's intervention during the attempted temple robbery gives credence to the belief held worldwide that the gods would safeguard not only the temples but also the deposits held there. Not only the priests but also creditors, debtors, and traders depended on this protection.

This credibility of the temples' financial role and economic importance reached far beyond the deposits and the financial business transacted in the local temples. The temples as "credit" institutions protected commerce beyond the city precincts, and they supported and guarded the mobility of merchants, creditors, and debtors in international trade. These people did not confine themselves to the places and persons with whom they had credit. They did not stop at the boundaries of the Mediterranean, or even at the outermost reaches of the Hellenistic culture. Commerce and trade had become worldwide, with black, brown, and yellow faces appearing on Mediterranean markets, and with Mediterranean tongues being heard on sea and land routes extending deep into Asia, the northern countries, and Africa.

Who protected these people when they traveled that far? Who else but their gods, who not only sailed with them but also sailed in front of them. Mutual recognition of cults and the discovery of one's own god or goddess in a foreign deity enabled a major worldwide credit structure. Money as a mobile, circulatory agent followed this development. One soon learned that the value of the currency and circulation in the markets were mutually dependent, although occasional inflations, often state manipulated, from time to time added to that flow.

The divine protecting presence with these attempts to transcend human boundaries was possible for the ancient mind because of the vertical connection between the gods and humans. The horizontal economic circulation would remain stable only if this connection with the heavenly forces held. One of the most important forms of this interplay is described in the contractual, as well as religious, formula *do ut des*, "I give in order that you give."[19] This formula did not function in only one direction; it did not simply flow from humans to gods (as the common Christian caricature of pagan religion), or merely from god to humanity (as Christians claimed of their own religion).

Rather, it worked both ways for Christian, pagan, and Jewish religions alike.

This interchange could be described as a circle, or better yet, a cycle. It could be expressed by two Greek puns: The divine gift and grace as *χάρις* correlates with *εὐχαριστία* ("gratitude"), and the divine glory as *δόξα* with *δοξολογία* ("glorification"). The character and range of this correlation have been demonstrated in the study above.[20]

This cycle was one of mutual benefit and growth. The stronger ones, the gods, gave of their strength to the weaker ones, the humans. These returned the divine gifts through worship in the form of thanksgiving and glorification. The continuation of the strength and richness of the gods, their ability to give more and more, depended on this multiplied feedback from the human, the poorer side in this exchange.

The Hellenistic mind would associate especially the goddess Tyche with this cycle, the deity distinguished by her bountiful gifts. Tyche was more than mere chance or happenstance; she was not simply capricious. Her concerns went beyond individual luck and advantage. Tyche featured prominently as constructive ability, empowerment, promise, and guidance. She was associated with the city goddesses, each of whom was seen as her manifestation, the divine essence of the community of each city. The goddess Tyche was the positive potential of the community, the city goddess was the embodiment of the Tyche's interest in constructive welfare and chance.

2. Paul's Critical Adaptation of This "Trust" Structure in His Concept of Spiritual Worship

I have argued that Paul's concept of grace and gift in II Corinthians 8–9 is not far removed from these associations, and includes even the concept of divine growth through increased human thanksgiving and glorification. It should be remembered in this context that for the Hellenistic social mind the guidance and protection of the gods were not confined to individuals but extended to the community at large. This would certainly entail the economy of the *polis,* to the extent that Tyche would relate to the economic well-being of the city and its citizens. I have shown elsewhere that the ancient reader would associate the concept of τύχη with Paul's concept of χάρις. This is all the more the case with the collection because here financial motifs enter the picture from the outset. Successful trade and god-given gain were ascribed to Tyche and Hermes, especially in their Roman forms of Fortuna and Mercury. The latter for Hellenistic-Roman culture was the journeying god who guided and protected merchants and other travelers, among them pilgrims and missionaries.

In II Corinthians 8 and 9 the original contractual purpose of the collection for Jerusalem has receded into the background. The collection has now been transformed into a paradigm for ecumenical communal exchange in the form of a financial communication. This is all the more important because it evidences a dialogue Paul had engaged in with the society of his day and its economic structures. In these critial socioreligious reflections, continuously furthered in debates with friends and opponents, the issues of performance and power made their way even more to the fore than in Paul's earlier texts. These were issues that pertained to the competitive market economy and to the religious forces that sustained it. In the discussion which the fragments of II Corinthians represents, the Pauline understanding of christology and justification by Christ gains its final form. It is then laid out in the Epistle to the Romans, to which the information on the collection forms the conclusion. This letter was intended as a new start, but in the end became the final farewell and testament of the propagator of justification by Christ, by grace, and thus by faith alone.

In the collection, a cycle of grace occurs in which money is the expression and means of a process that moves human hearts and draws people together. Thus the mobility and ready exchange of money become a manifestation of the power and essence of the Jesus movement as a missionary phenomeon. The collection turns into a demonstration of the interplay of divine gift and human gratitude. This is not, however, abstract. Both the gift and gratitude are from and to real people, for the benefit of both. Money becomes a concrete expression of χάρις in that the personal gifts, the χαρισμάτα, of the givers move toward the χαρισμάτα, the gifts, of the recipients. χάρις and χάρισμα are not on the side of the givers alone but on that of the recipients as well, with divine grace providing a bridge back and forth. In this spirit I Corinthians 16:2 uses the concept of a graduated voluntary contribution related to one's prosperity, which assumes equity not of quantity but of quality.

Paul presupposes a material cycle that understands δόξα (glory and splendor) and χάρις (grace and gift) as substances of light. Paul uses the religious dimension of the Hellenistic economy, the vertical circulation described above, to interpret the concept of money flow in a more religious way. In this interpretation he redirects and adds the vertical cycle (god-human-god-human, etc.) to the horizontal one into which he integrates the incarnate deity, as the quote from the traditional formula in II Corinthians 8:9 proves.[21]

The collection of funds for Jerusalem in Paul's interpretation transforms the idea of an economy geared toward growth of production and profit as the Hellenistic economy already was. The Hellenistic market economy obviously used interest as a major instrument of growth. Paul instead presupposes the biblical prohibition of interest (Exod. 22:24; Lev. 25:36-27), now extended to everyone. Increase of wealth for him needs to be common wealth. The money collected for Jerusalem grows also, but into a universal divine worship. The money involved becomes a social force, a gift from community to community. It is intended to forge the vitality of the community which it is given to. Here obedience and simple kindness are blended. In this process the subjugation of the universe under the Rich One who had become poor has begun, and the unification of humanity has been initiated.

This sharing becomes a manifestation of the body of Christ, the community of the justified godless and poor ones who have become rich and who are living under the leadership of the One who has become impoverished and weak. A spiritual movement takes place from God to the churches, back and forth among them, and then back to God. In so doing the cultic and sacred are replaced by an active ecumenical partnership, which includes also economic sharing.

Spiritual worship means for Paul the multi-personal, multi-faceted, and multi-dimensional life of a community, which understands itself as a model-society contrasting and redeeming the society around it. The ideas of the circulation of money and of economic growth have been exchanged for the circulation and growth of the grace of God among people, even the growth of

Godself for the benefit of all humans. Concepts of personal potential and action, of interest and of profit and of a worldwide net of markets have been absorbed by this greatly enlarged picture.

Paul's presupposition is that creation and created life originate in and are maintained by grace. Therefore, thanksgiving, the returning of grace, is called for. The collection in II Corinthians 9:1 is termed a blessing. Blessing is understood as a bountiful yield, as working capital. Its interest and profit consist most of all in the responses, the blessings of the beneficiary party, and the enrichment of the communal relationship of givers and recipients. The gift of blessing creates, maintains, and enlarges the community.

This process is associated with love, the atmosphere of Christ's body, the global realm of Christ. In this atmosphere the persons giving are taken over by grace, which makes them realize that in giving they are in fact being given to. Rather than depleting their own stocks, their treasure boxes are filled as a result of their giving to others. In this vision, magnanimity proves to be more economical than miserliness.

D. SOCIAL ASPECTS OF ANCIENT ECONOMIC AND MONETARY RELATIONS

1. Righteousness and Its Equivalents as Accompaniment of Economic and Monetary Relations

Quite in accord with this, although not without precedent in the ancient world, Paul introduces in II Corinthians 8:14-15 the term *ἰσότης* ("equity/equality"), a concept highly esteemed in Hellenistic culture. For many Hellenistic readers this would be entirely appropriate in a discussion pertaining to finances. The adage "Money is the great equalizer" was not unknown either, although not in the same wording.[22] The tendency of Paul is to exploit the dimensions of the synonymity of equity, equality, righteousness, and justice, and to explore critically the alleged equalizing power of money. He wants to move beyond the legal and economic equality that Hellenistic culture and its market-oriented society represented. Theoretically, for Hellenistic culture equity and equality as synonyms of righteousness and justice were the basis and moving force of society. For Paul righteousness precedes equity and equality. But in keeping with his wisdom background, Paul understands righteousness as efficacious divine power. It brings about equity and equality. Ἰσότης for him is a divine force among humans, making them equal "from equity (as divine potency of efficaciousness) to equality (as human experience, legal, social, and economic reality)" as the statement in II Corinthians 8:13-14 could be abbreviated in a pointed way.

In this context money does not rob debtors of their integrity and identity. On the contrary, both haves and have-nots possess and owe something in this interaction to the other party. In this positive and constructive capacity money does not move external things alone but also the inner life of persons, and it is fed back from the beneficiary to the benefactor, not as an expression of self-humiliation but as a demonstration and experience of equality. In this process money truly becomes an equalizing agent, a democratizing instrument.

For Paul this kind of monetary momentum is not wishful thinking; he sees it happen in space and time—"at the present time"—in the actual collection activities of people he knows and to whom he relates. The collection is being undertaken for certain partners he knows well. He wants the delegates to meet them, so that personal intimacy as an integral part of a universal community can increase.

The discussion of equity and equality in Paul is much less abstract than its counterpart in Aristotle, as Paul's communities are more concrete than the philosopher's from Stagira, who was never allowed to become a citizen of Athens, the city he lived in and admired so much. Paul's arguments, activities, and suggestions stem from communal praxis and move therein. According to Paul's concept of communal equity and equality, money no longer serves as a differentiating, distinguishing, isolating, and expropriating agent. It does not segregate people from one another or separate them from their economic means, as if the latter were capable of operating independently, abstracted from human brains and hearts.

The exchange, to which money is intimately related and by means of which it has its life, is an exchange among persons as equals and peers. Redemption does not belong at the end of a creditor-debtor relationship. It is the basis of all human solidarity, where people are related in their shared poverty, that is their common godlessness. Redemption is the engagement of the rich One who became poor (II Cor. 8:9) in order to make all humans rich—namely, all those who share in the common poverty—not the believers alone but all of humanity. Universal poverty and universal redemption are presupposed by Paul. Global equalization is in view, a sweeping exchange and settlement with transpartisan, transemotional, rational, as it were objective, features—elements normally associated with coined money and its proper use.

As I wrote my study on the collection of Paul, I did not deal with the biblical passages on the sabbatical and the jubilee years as possible backgrounds to Paul's thinking while he composed II Corinthians 8 and 9.[23] Today's global discussions about large-scale settlements of debts have brought actuality and relevance to these biblical ideas. They may have been at the back of Paul's mind. An analogy to these biblical motifs of restitution, minus their financial aspects, is found in the rather concrete Roman notion of the secular cycles of 110 years or so. Paul must have experienced once under Claudius's principate the secular games that celebrated the official revolutionary restitution and renewal of the Roman Empire and its institutions. In a contemporary theological and ethical reflection on Paul's collection, these analogies have to be brought into play. They demonstrate how much general institutional renewal was thinkable in Paul's time, and they correspond well to ideas and phenomena described thus far in this study and its epilogue.

Shared penury is not only at the origin of private property. Common experience and wisdom say that each individual starts and ends life penniless. We know that relentless accumulation of money and investments merely into property and goods is deadly, suicidal, at the very least from a social point of view, but most probably also from an economic one. Staggering inequity that moves fatalistically toward the insolvency of one party without any counter moves from the other party or outsiders is humanly and politically bankrupt. This is particularly true in a democratic society. It appears also economically unwise; the end of buyers and competitors would be the end of the market.

Equalization of debts is in line with Paul's notions of divine grace, the spiritual worship he sees set in motion, and the universal equality he presupposes and finds brought about by grace. The regularity of the intervals of 7 (sabbatical year), 49 (jubilee year), or 110 years (Roman secular cycle) is more rational than infrequently and erratically arranged monetary shake-ups, currency reforms, or international debt settlements of recent vintage.

2. Utopian Dimensions of Economic and Monetary Relations

It is obvious that money in the Pauline texts on the collection possesses utopian dimensions. "Remembering the poor" refers first of all to the eschatological title and privilege the early church in Jerusalem prided itself on and for which it was respected. Also in the context of economy and money, the projection into the future, and the anticipation of it, are customary; in John Maynard Keynes's words, "Money connects with the future."[24] Money always has been associated with hopes for better times, individually and collectively. Without hopes there would be no stock market, and these hopes are very often literally speculative. To reflect upon the utopian aspects of the stock market would be as appropriate as a discussion about the eschatological dimensions of capitalism. There is always a "not yet" directly beneath the stock market's surface. An "it will definitely improve in the future" is immediately invoked as soon as structural difficulties of the market show. The messianism of the free market blows its horn the most in times of economic crisis, such as recessions or worse, more easily of course if it is somebody else's crisis.

In the Pauline texts and activities, the money to be collected for Jerusalem was viewed first as a means of "remembering the poor"—that is, the church in Jerusalem as the *avant garde* of God's new age. That meant one stood not for oneself alone but anticipated the people of the new age, who would consist of the people of God restored and all pagan peoples gathered around. The money was to be used to give the Jerusalem Jesus community financial backing in its attempt to achieve a reasonable degree of economic security for its strenuous witness, needed most of all for those members who were not yet settled and/or were unemployed.

As the collection evolved independently on Paul's own mission field it was transformed into a more general paradigm. Expressed in the traditional vocabulary of biblical scholarship and contemporary theology, as used also in my study above, Paul's concepts and terminology concerning the collection remain "eschatological." But over against the traditional and prevailing contemporary scholarly use of the term *eschatological*, it has to be stated that eschatology and eschatological issues included tangible utopian dimensions and aspects. Eschatology did not relate solely to the individual; on the contrary, biblical and Jewish eschatology developed collective social visions. This collective perception could be found also in pagan eschatology, which was very much alive in Hellenistic culture, even more in its Roman form. Eschatological awareness had increased since the time of Augustus and was particularly active in the latter part of Claudius's and during Nero's principates.

Alexander's empire had been a creation and vivid manifestation of intensive utopian thought and activity.[25] This remained the case with new variations under Alexander's successors; under Hannibal as well as his Roman enemies; the various Mithradates; and among the many revolutionaries of the third to first centuries B.C.E. and C.E. Each of these persons easily stepped into that visionary pattern and attempted to bring to life a social utopia. Jewish utopias, literary and political, have to be seen within that concert as well, both in the Diaspora and in Palestine, which was part of the Hellenistic world culture.

3. Justification of the Poor Ones as Concrete Utopian Praxis

It has been a fatal side of much of Protestant exegesis that the rational as well as utopian elements of Paul's understanding of justification have been weakened or even covered up. As Paul transforms his understanding of justification into praxis and theory of the collection, the climate of a pragmatic utopia becomes apparent. In the terminology of established Reformation theology, Paul's reflections on the collection and on money, if brought out in their full historical meaning, qualify for the verdict of "enthusiasm" as it was leveled against revolting peasants, anabaptists, and spiritualists.

In fact, any attempt to cast views and perspectives of faith directly into the vision of a real communal way of life, not governed and controlled directly or indirectly by state authorities or state-established church bodies, was counted by the Reformers among the heresy of enthusiasm. But this fear of religious enthusiasm made much of Protestantism blind to all kinds of enthusiastic ventures that quickly arose in secular disguise, capitalism among them. The churches of the Reformation failed to develop practical and theoretical instruments with which to approach critically the apparent messianism of the capitalist idea and practice as they grew in the post-Reformation period. The church's denunciation of interest as usury did not help and was given up rather quickly.

The justification of all humans as thoroughly impoverished ones is a reasonable proposition for Paul, a basis for understanding and changing the world and humanity. In II Corinthians 9 Paul stresses the proximity of justification and reason. As justification is his point of departure for structuring true community as a model society, he perceives of this new society as a more reasonable one. This rationality does not establish distance of viewers and operators from people and things. The concept of the rational for Paul coincides with the concern and engagement of God as well as the members of the community for others.

Paul argues emphatically for a God engaged in the human demise and impoverishment; Paul fights against a distant and unengaged deity. The deficiency of the pagan deities in his eyes would not be that they were too human, but that they were too little involved in the human dilemma. Justification is not important merely between God and the individual, but it comes about and manifests itself in the interrelatedness of God, the world, and all humanity.

God's righteousness is the origin of human righteousness, but the latter is allowed to reflect and represent the former in full. This righteousness mirroring God's own is not a pious possession of the individual. It is the liberty of integrated human beings, incorporated into a body of justifying grace and love. This is a free space where rights, personhood, and communal relations are given, and mutual assistance exists in accordance with God and God's self-impoverishing agent. The intent is to embrace the entire human family by this concord. The intermediate realization of this is supposed to happen in the church, the model society that is charged with a realistic anticipation of that non-voracious, mutually supportive humanity.

This justifying grace creates wise and reasonable, in a word good, praxis, in which personhood and the identity of persons is formed through relatedness and concern for others. This praxis is not to be confused with treadmill tug and drudgery or with money hunting either. It is giving instead of gaining, thanks instead of interest, confidence instead of credit, trust instead of security, community instead of market, spiritual worship instead of temple cult, charisma instead of property. This praxis avoids the power that grows out of fear and that leads to exploitation and violence. Instead, this praxis affirms the power of weakness and poverty because such power allows for authentic engagement, reliable yield, and true growth. A multiplication of thanksgivings follows from this and will engage people further in this expression of gratitude. This will create radiating strength. This praxis will instigate and invigorate truly humane, namely relational, ethical, and consciously political elements in the economy, and will make them transparent.

The self is no longer the entity that is capable of giving and securing freedom through self-liberating activity. Personal freedom is even less enhanced through acquisition, holding, and accumulation of property with the false hope of the ultimate security of the self—not only suicide but also the death of the economy. Rather, freedom is the experience of liberation from the self. The isolated individual and his or her private property are governed by the fear of indebtedness and thus of spiraling poverty, with no security left. For Paul freedom is liberty from necessity and hurt. It is the diametrical opposite of the Stoic ideal of *autarky,* self-sufficiency. Autarky means, for Paul, the simplicity of an open, trusting, and faithful heart. Only this liberation enables reasonable deliberation, free will, and free decision. Only this freedom releases the person from the necessity of being obsessed with self-concern. In this way God bestows power and freedom for an active life in a free community.

The concepts of private property and private ownership find in

Paul no place at all, nor do the accompanying notions of credit, debt, obligation, interest, dividend, profit, market, temple, or bank. Why? Because they presuppose and foster fear of catastrophes, and through fear they lead to estrangement, expropriation, and exploitation—false security indeed.

From Paul's viewpoint money does not create, but it stimulates, facilitates, and sets in motion the process of thanksgiving. It has been shown that Paul has a concept of growth, too, and that he sees money as an expression of such growth. But he views it always in the context of the return of divine grace, mediated through *charismata* and accumulated thanksgiving. Thus Paul locates growth in the context of shared righteousness, the mutual respect for equality and integrity.

4. Can Any Money Be Just?

Is there anything like money that is just?[26] The dream that there could be just money if there could be neutral money—that is, indifferent money—has been around for a long time. But every effort to bring this about has failed. Cash is never cold or indifferent; it is always involved in the heat of human exchange and gains temperature in that exchange. Attempts on the part of governments to tame and control tightly what they mint, print, and issue have not succeeded either. Money, indeed, is an intimate friend of the market. Money has regulated the market, has always even been part of the market. Money is a trading object, the market's most prominent expression. Does the solution lie in leaving money and the market to their own devices?

Does the market possess its own independent laws? There is sufficient evidence that money and market bend given laws of society if left unchecked. They become a law to themselves. However, money and the market are not only means of the econcomy, but they are also means of communication within a community and between communities that all need to be fair and just. Money and market are creations of the community and have to remain community's children if they want to survive and flourish. Behind all financial credit there has to be communal trust. And this must come from a broader base than the local community. Already the Hellenistic-Roman economy had learned that such communal trust had to occur on an international scale. The economy is bound to fail if it is dictated from any side (private, group, or state), because it will have lost its communal authenticity and force. The community and the market are not identical; the community has to remain above the market, all the more the international community above the international market.

Accordingly, money and market have to remain expressions of the community's basic right and its manifestation in communal laws. This right will dissever its righting power if it fails to remain communal. Then it is no longer everyone's right but that which belongs to some people, to some groups, or to some institutions in particular. If the creditor has a prerogative over the debtor, or vice versa, then the rights of each suffer. The laborer must not be cheated of his or her wages, nor the saver or investor of his or her savings or investments, provided that these entitlements are fair and just according to the basic right that joins all members of the community equally and in a world market that must include the farthest and lowliest as integral peers. These persons must have equal standing. Their identity and integrity must be respected by the world economy fairly and justly.

It often has been said that money is a means of social communication. But is it as yet in the authentic sense of social? Does it not reward the rich and powerful more, while continuously diappointing the poor and weak? There is doubtless more to the value of money than its nominal or market value, more to it than its buying power. The presence or absence of money increases or decreases the social value and standing of persons; it increases or decreases their social acceptability and importance. This relates also to the subjective feeling of value that people have of themselves. Thus their identity and integrity are affected. Can it be in the true interest of a community that pauperization occurs in its midst? That any one of its members loses in reality her or his personal rights and standing through loss or lack of monetary means? Can the community suffer that because of financial or economic insufficiency certain members fall short of rights and potentials others maintain? Is that just "too bad" for those persons or groups? Is it not rather "too bad" for a community that permits this to happen without immediate intervention?

There is no indifferent or cold money. But what is its true warmth? That of greed or that of caring? For Paul the answer is clear: Investment in the hope of and for the deficient ones is the truly warm money. Paul returns to the poor as the target of the collection in Romans 15. This proves that in the interim the poor ones have remained the foil of Paul's reflections on the money flow. This raises the question of whether the ability to discover and respect the dignity and integrity of the poor, their gift and witness to the society, is not for him the crucial economic issue.

5. The Poor Ones as the Heart of the Wisdom of a Just and Humane Economy

In Romans 15:26 Paul returns once again to the issue of poverty. It has been demonstrated that there the economic side of poverty is more directly emphasized than in Galatians 2:10. The collection is now meant "for the poor ones among the Saints in Jerusalem." In all probability, heavy investment in the creation and maintenance of the economic stability of the Jesus community in Jerusalem remains the direct financial objective of the collection, certainly with the distribution and use of the funds left to the discretion of the recipients. Some real estate and building projects for the meeting purposes of the Jesus community in Jerusalem and their guests may be in the picture as well, but they are certainly not the primary goal. The main focus is on the economically impoverished ones.

It would be wrong to presume that the poor are now regarded by Paul as merely deficient—social and economic debris as it were—thus at best objects of the condescending charitable activity of those better off. On the contrary, whereas the powerful monetary contribution of the Diaspora churches in Romans 15:27 is reckoned among "the fleshly things," and as such represents the weak and ephemeral matters of a passing world, the poor ones among the Jesus believers in Jerusalem are taken as representative of "the spiritual things" Jerusalem has to offer. It is primarily the poor ones who stand for these spiritual things. Paul's argument about the exchange of the fleshly against the spiritual is taken from the rules of religious competition, more precisely, from the rules of the religious market, a rather important sector in the wider Hellenistic market economy. The outcome of this critical interpretation and application of competitive market language is that Paul gives the poor ones higher market value.

On the basis of the generalizing reflections since the Epistle to the Galatians, this emphasis on the poor ones as embodying a more direct blend of an economic and theological issue makes sense. The poor in the Jesus community of Jerusalem above all stand in place for the main gift of that church to the rest of the churches. They preserve the focus of the Easter witness on the word of the cross: the rich One who had engaged himself for and among impoverished humanity (II Cor. 8:9). This is the dignity of the poor ones of Jerusalem. Since the collection and the Jerusalem church have been transformed by Paul into a general paradigm, this is true for the poor elsewhere, too. There is a gift, a witnessing quality in their lives, ideally but also practically, even economically. They point to poverty as the basis for human and societal existence; they remind the society of its constant fringe. They are a continuous reminder and a challenge to all who believe themselves to be removed from poverty, who might even have barricaded themselves into golden fortresses while boasting of their security. The witness of the poor testifies to the non-poor who want to flee their human condition with the help of money that they are no longer justified by Christ but by money and the power therein. Poor people, the disenfranchised, and all those at the margins of society give evidence against society's false pride placed in wealth and strength at the expense of others. The poor and disenfranchised, the marginal people, invoke the community's unfinished business. The poor and disenfranchised point to society's deficiencies and failures, identifying them not as mere oversights or individual failures, but as systemic weaknesses and collective sins.

But the poor testify also more than any well-stocked bank to the potential, the gift, that is in human not-having, not-possessing. There is first of all the sapiential insight that, contrary to the boast of the powerful, the ones who "can make do" with little prove more than the ones who "can do" with much. But the poor point further to the redemptive engagement of Christ to whom humanity owes its survival. They herald the chances opened by that redemption. The poor call up the not-yet of society, the new vistas awaiting a community prepared to yield more power in order to gain more future. The poor ones challenge the sterility of a rich society, give it incentives to be imaginative and innovative with respect to new material investments and with regard to new spiritual engagements.

A community that turns first and foremost to its allegedly hopeless cases, to those who appear at the end of their rope materially, physically, socially, legally, psychologically, and spiritually, is clearly the more risk conscious, the more courageous, imaginative, and inventive. It is the economically more stable and promising entity, setting up a model for the wider society to do likewise.

To discover the dignity and the charisma of the poor, the inflicted, and the disenfranchised, hearing and understanding their witness as that of individual persons and of groups, is about as difficult as understanding the scandal of the cross, which the poor resemble. Because the poor also share more intimately than others the power that is manifest in the cross of Christ, investing in the poor, empowering them, has as its consequence the true empowerment of those who seem more fortunate. The poor ones in biblical terms are not the rear guard of the past but the *avant garde* of the future. Therefore, the call to invest in the poor ones represents the central, not the peripheral, concern for a market society that wants to be truly economical, a society that really desires to invest in the future.

NOTES

(Abbreviations according to *Die Religion in Geschichte und Gegnewart*, ed. by Kurt Galling, 6 vols. [Tübingen: Mohr-Siebeck, 1957-1962])

INTRODUCTION

1. See Carl Holsten, *Das Evangelium des Paulus*, vol. I (Berlin: Reimer 1880), pp. 76, 142-52.

2. See, for instance, Adolf Schlatter, *Geschichte der ersten Christenheit* (Gütersloh: Bertelsmann, 1938), pp. 164, 243; compare also p. 138.

3. Ethelbert Stauffer, "Petrus und Jakobus in Jerusalem," in Maximilian Roesle and Oskar Cullmann, eds., *Begegnung der Christen* (Stuttgart: Evangelische Verlangsanstalt, 1960), pp. 361-72.

4. See, for instance, Rudolf Bultmann, *Theology of the New Testament* (New York: Scribner's, 1951-55), p. 60. Hereafter referred to as *Theology*.

5. Johannes Munck, *Paul and the Salvation of Mankind*, trans. Frank Clarke (Atlanta: John Knox, 1977), pp. 171ff. Hereafter referred to as *Paul*. Compare also Bultmann, *Theology*, p. 94.

6. W. M. Franklin, *Die Kollekte des Paulus* (Scottsdale, Pa.: Mennonite Publishing House, 1938). Hereafter referred to as *Die Kollekte*.

1. THE CONVENTION AT JERUSALEM (48 C.E.)

1. For the problem of chronology, see Appendix 1 and footnotes 2 and 3 below.

2. This dating applies if the time-span indicated in Gal. 2:1 also relates

to that of the calling of Paul mentioned in 1:15-16, the center of the entire passage of Gal. 1:10–2:21. That the individual dating references would relate to each other is less probable. This would not only speak against the textual momentum but also would make for a wider time-frame. This would cause the chronological difficulty that the longer period makes it harder to integrate what we know about the history of Paul and of the early church.

3. Compare Gal. 2:1-10 (Acts 15:1-29). To judge by the very definite tone of Paul's assertion, this was his second journey to Jerusalem following his calling. The first visit to the city is reported in Gal. 1:18-20 (Acts 9:26-29). Luke mentions even a third journey undertaken by Paul and Barnabas sometime between these two visits, the purpose of which was to transfer an Antiochene collection to the Jerusalem congregation (Acts 11:27-30). This, however, stands against Paul's own clear statements. On the whole the Lukan narrative in Acts 11:27-30 (in conjunction with the report on a persecution in Acts 12) hardly holds firm against closer historical scrutiny. (See Ernst Haenchen, *The Acts of the Apostles: A Commentary* (Philadelphia: Westminster, 1971), pp. 373ff.; hereafter referred to as *Acts*. This is why it has sometimes been argued in biblical research that the journey spoken of in Acts 11:27-30 must be the same as the one referred to in Acts 15:1-29 (and Gal. 2:1-10). Joachim Jeremias, for instance, was of that opinion, but he dated it after the persecution and during the famine mentioned in Acts 12 ("Sabbatjahr und neutestamentliche Chronologie," *ZNW* 27 (1928): 98-103). A similar position was taken by W. M. Franklin (*Die Kollekte*, pp. 14-15), but refuted by Haenchen (*Acts*, pp. 321-22). Haenchen also established the chronological impossibility of combining Acts 11:27-30 with Acts 15:1-29 (Gal. 2:1-10) and, hence, refuses to see in Acts 11:30 the correct basis for dating the convention of the apostles (the so-called early dating theory; pp. 57-58). The modifications made to that "early dating theory" by Ferdinand Hahn, (*Mission in the New Testament*, SBT 47 [London: SCM, 1965], pp. 77-78) are discussed in Appendix 1, pp. 129-34. Among others, Hahn based his computations on my own considerations regarding the background of the remark on the collection in Acts 11:29-30 (see pp. 44-45). Due to the significantly differing interpretation Hahn and myself arrived at for Acts 11:27-30, as well as for its contextual position, I cannot, however, share his conclusions. The same goes for Acts 12–15. C. H. Buck's theory that the collection, as well as the two mission circuits accomplished by Paul in Europe, ought to be dated prior to the Jerusalem summit, appears to be definitely erroneous. Buck even argues that both Epistles to the Corinthians, the Epistle to the Galatians, and that to the Romans were all written before 48 C.E., the accepted year of the convention. As to John Knox, see pp. 211-12, note 27.

4. Martin Dibelius, *Aufsätze zur Apostelsgeschichte* (Göttingen: Vandenhoeck und Ruprecht, 1957), p. 84ff., Das Apostelkonzil. Concerning Gal. 2 see also Klaus Wegenast, *Das Verständnis der Tradition bei Paulus und in den Deuteropaulinen* (Neukirchen-Vluyn: Neukirchener, 1961), pp. 47-49. Hereafter referred to as *Tradition.*

5. Compare Ernst Haenchen, *Acts,* pp. 440ff., esp. p. 462. Still, both Dibelius and Haenchen show that the same occurrence is meant in Acts 15 and Gal. 2.

6. Such doubts were voiced by Stauffer, "Petrus und Jakobus in Jerusalem," pp. 369-70, esp. n. 56. Stauffer sees in Paul's journey to Jerusalem a capitulation in terms of church jurisdiction. On page 365 he explains the visit reported in Gal. 1:18 as indicating a breach with the concept of "apostle" as developed in Gal. 1:15—a breach only Paul would concede. On the other hand, in terms of church policy, Stauffer believes that the action had been successful.

7. This view is generally held by the majority of exegetes.

8. Compare Haenchen, *Acts,* pp. 464ff. (405-18 of the 5th German edition).

9. See ibid., p. 446. Haenchen rightly points out that Paul and Barnabas traveled to Jerusalem as two delegates of equal standing and that both were answerable to the Antiochene congregation.

10. This has been contested by Günther Klein, "Gal. 2, 6-9 und die Geschichte der Jerusalemer Urgemeinde," *ZThK* 57 (1960): 275-95. Hereafter referred to as "Gal. 2, 6-9." According to Klein, it is precisely in Gal. 2:7-8 that we have a rendition of the original situation—indeed a quotation from the official Greek version of the minutes of the convention. Klein believes that Gal. 2:2, 6, and 9 take into account the "shifts in power" that had occurred since the convention and are, therefore, anachronistic. For Klein, it was Simon Peter who held the decision-making authority at the time of the meeting. However, Gal. 2:7 and 9 appear to support the older answer that all this was due to Peter's having meanwhile become a professional missionary. Further, these arguments do not hold because they prove incompatible with the general tendency of the Pauline texts (detected by Haenchen) toward enhancing Paul's significance to the detriment of Barnabas and to conceal the fact that both of them were delegates of Antioch; in parallel to this trend, the focus is on Peter's importance. It is, however, precisely this parallel constellation which shows that Paul did not intend his simplifying modifications as a means for self-glorification for the following reasons:

1. Because the historically incorrect description of (at least) the Antiochene delegation, as well as the literary style of the passage, speak

against viewing Gal. 2:7-8 as an excerpt of the original minutes of the conference;
2. Because verse 2:9, labeled "anachronistic" by Klein, clearly does do justice to the historical position and importance of the Antiochene delegation;
3. Because Klein does not explain why it should have been precisely the text of the agreement that was not quoted from the minutes;
4. Because it is highly probable that Simon Peter had already left Jerusalem when the Epistle to the Galatians was drafted and that his journey to Antioch, mentioned in Gal. 2:11-12 (a journey resulting from clashes with James?), had marked the end of his time in Jerusalem and the start of his missionary travels abroad;
5. And because the form of the name πέτρος in Gal. 2:7 might best be explained by Paul's wish to make this updated portrayal stand out against earlier historical reports.

This is why I also cannot share Haenchen's skepticism, when he questions the usefulness of Gal. 2:7-21 for analyzing Peter's missionary activity ("Petrusprobleme," *NTS* 7 (1960/61): 26-27). Certainly, that narrative is colored by later experiences: the focus of interest had originally been on the Jerusalem-Antioch antagonism, not on Peter and Paul; that Paul was moved into the foreground does reflect subsequent developments. But it seems only logical then that the argument holds also with respect to Paul's depiction of Peter—namely, that his apparent enhancement in the present story reflects the actual situation at the time of the composition of Galatians, clearly singling out the position Peter has gained in the meantime with respect to the mission to the Jews. At any rate, the possibility that it was a case of simple—indeed, purely stylistical—equalization of Peter and Paul is to be excluded. Why should the importance Peter had gained in the meantime have been in an area of activity other than that indicated by Paul—namely, in the ἀποστολὴ τῆς περιτομῆς (2:8)? All probability speaks for an involvement of Peter in the mission to the Jews already at the time of the convention, the existence of which at that time Haenchen concedes (*Acts*, p. 195). The listing order of the names in Gal. 2:9 was certainly not intended to counter the possible misunderstanding on the part of the reader that the James mentioned here was Zebedee's son and not the Lord's brother (against Haenchen, *Acts*, p. 193). Had Paul really tried to exclude such misunderstanding, he could simply have written "our Lord's brother," as in Gal. 1:19. But such clarification was no longer necessary, as James, the son of Zebedee, had already passed away at the time. If—according to Haenchen (*Acts*, p. 193)—the present listing order of names had served to impress upon the opponents that James (the primary spokesperson for their position) had not been the last of the three to give recognition to Paul and Barnabas, the admission would have been that at least—by the time of the Epistle to the Galatians at the latest—James's privileged position had become an issue of debate. Conversely, had the opponents really used James as a reference, it would not only have been unwise, but it would have been downright suicidal for Paul to ascribe to James such a position of prestige quite contrary to historical truth. This anachronistic promotion of James by Paul would have strengthened the position of the opponents even further. Thus it seems more probable that, in putting James first, Paul mirrors the situation actually prevailing at the convention. Paul's report appears to reflect a structural change in the first Aramaic-speaking congregation at Jerusalem, which was caused primarily by an intensified missionary activity directly involving Peter. If Peter was personally engaged in such missionary work, he was by force absent from Jerusalem more and more often and for ever-increasing periods of time. Under these circumstances it must have proven more and more difficult for Peter to maintain his leadership of the Jerusalem congregation. This difficulty would have to worsen if the turn within the congregation toward mission was supported by only a part of the membership; tensions and conflicts would have to follow, calling for a more available leadership. It is not to be excluded that the Jerusalem convention—dominated as it was by the issue of mission—gave such up-drift to the mission-minded members of the community that the more apocalyptically oriented members of the congregation felt they had to react and that the ensuing discrepancies threatened to lead to a schism. Even though this interpretation must remain a mere assumption, still the visit of Peter to Antioch and his subsequent travel call for an interpretation, of which the one given appears to have plausibility. Haenchen (*Acts*, pp. 196-97) fails to offer one. Hence, the older answer, that all this was due to Peter's having meanwhile become a professional missionary, still seems to be the most satisfactory one. Galatians 2:7 and 9 appear to support that idea.

11. See Gal. 2:4, 6, 8, and 10.

12. See, for example,. Heinrich Schlier, *Der Brief an die Galater* (Göttingen: Vandenhoeck und Ruprecht, 1989), pp. 66-67.

13. See ibid., p. 65.

14. Acts 15:1 probably gives a historically correct report of these occurrences.

15. Gal. 2:4 constitutes the beginning of a new anacoluthic sentence. For the reason why this must be so, see Hans Lietzmann, *An die Galater* (Tübingen: Mohr, 1932), pp. 10-11, and Alfred Oepke, *Der Brief des Paulus an die Galater* (Berlin: EVA, 1973), pp. 46-47.

16. As rightly seen by Schlier, *Der Brief an die Galater*, p. 71.

17. Paul seems to suggest that this was a circumstance familiar to the

Galatians. But this must not mean yet that the "false brothers and sisters" mentioned earlier and the Galatian opponents were the same biographically. On this question, also see n. 19 below.

18. There is nothing in Paul's report to suggest that these people had been acting as qualified, commissioned officials. Karl Holl, in "Der Kirchenbegriff des Paulus in seinem Verhältnis zu dem Urgemeinde," in *Ges. Aufs.* II (Tübingen: Mohr, 1928), p. 57, hereafter referred to as "Kirchenbegriff," reads far more into the text than there is to it when he interprets Paul's polemical *κατασκοπῆσαι* as ascribing to the Jerusalem delegates the factual right to *ἐπισκοπεῖν*—a right to which Paul refused to subscribe. This appears to me to be far-fetched.

19. Walter Schmithals believes that these "false brothers" were unconverted Jews ("Die Häretiker in Galatien," *ZNW* 47 (1956): 27). But what standing would they have in an assembly of Jesus believers? Would they be entitled to interfere in matters of polity and jurisdiction? Wegenast points to the fact that Paul "did not qualify non-baptized Jews as brothers, but only as 'brothers according to the flesh' " (*Tradition,* p. 47). The Jerusalem convention clearly was a policy-making assembly, not a worship service. Legal standing was, therefore, important, as it would have been for visiting Jews in a Jewish Diaspora community in matters of polity. The accumulation of disqualifying remarks used by Paul with regards to these (false) brothers and sisters resulted from Paul's own subjective judgment concerning their ideas and behavior. But that judgment is not identical with the self-assessment of these people accused by Paul. In this respect there is no difference to the other polemics of Paul in his letters. Therefore, similarities to the attacks against the opponents in Galatia should not be taken as applying to people identical with the opposition in Jerusalem during the convention. Paul does not say so, and there is no indication in Gal. 2:11-12 that the people supportive of James were the same as the previously mentioned (false) brothers and sisters. The opponents at the convention must, therefore, have been locals trying to impose their own concept of a uniformly Judaized church. Yet, while one can assume that the (false) brothers and sisters of Jerusalem were not, biographically speaking, the same as the Galatian opponents, they do seem to have been of kindred spirit as regards their nomistic outlook and their tradition-mindedness, although hardly as regards their attitude toward Gnostic wisdom. It is difficult to ascertain whether or not these groups opposing Paul had started to contact one another and whether the Jerusalem Judaizers had somehow initiated such contact.

20. Schlier (*Der Brief an die Galater,* p. 65) somehow obscures the fact that Paul and Barnabas acted for Antioch at the convention of the apostles as delegates of equal standing and were considered by everyone

(Paul included) as equals. The very fact that they acted on behalf of a congregation—indeed, an entire area of mission—clearly shows that they were not operating on their own and for a cause important only to themselves. An independent Pauline mission did not, as yet, exist.

21. As can be gathered from I Cor. 14:6*b* and 26, as well as from the report on a congregational assembly in Acts 13:1-3, the gift of the Spirit is primarily and above all granted to the congregation as a whole. On the same question, see also Haenchen, "Petrus-probleme," pp. 194-95, and Schlier, *Der Brief an die Galater,* p. 66.

22. As pointed out correctly by Oepke, *Der Brief des Paulus an die Galater,* p. 44.

23. Galatians 2:3: "And even Titus, my companion, who was a Greek, was not forced to submit to circumcision."

24. Galatians 2:4-5. See also Oepke, *Der Brief des Paulus an die Galater,* p. 45.

25. As to Gal. 2:4, see p. 23, above. Verse 5 reads as follows: "But we would not submit to them even for a moment, so that truth stayed with you always."

26. For this question, the reader is referred to the commentaries on Galatians.

27. This opinion is, however, held by most commentators, most adamantly so by Schlier (*Der Brief an die Galater,* p. 68) and Stauffer ("Petrus und Jakobus in Jerusalem," p. 369). Schlier takes the journey as evidence of Paul's recognition "that the decisive authority is represented by the earlier gospel and the earlier [type of] apostleship." Since Paul had not realized this through personal insight, but had gone to Jerusalem following a revelation, Schlier concludes that "the principle of having to connect up with the tradition (in the largest sense of the term) was in itself considered as being of revelatory nature" (*Der Brief an die Galater,* p. 66). On page 76 Schlier even asserts that—as late as during the Antioch crisis—Paul was calling upon the authority of the Jerusalem apostles in connection with all doctrinal matters in order to counter effectively the attempts made by the opponents to invoke precisely that authority in support of their own argumentation. In that case, Paul has written the first chapter of the Epistle to the Galatians for nothing!

28. Stauffer believes that Paul's journey to Jerusalem was really a "trip to Canossa," that Paul had succumbed to the jurisdictional praxis inherited by the Jerusalem congregation from the Jews and exercised under James ("Petrus und Jakobus in Jerusalem," p. 369, n. 56). According to Stauffer, "any doctrinal controversies arising in the province can only be adjudicated decisively by the Great Sanhedrin of Jerusalem. For this purpose, the dissenting teachers must, therefore, appear (in court) at Jerusalem, and by their appearance, they

acknowledged the supremacy and final jurisdictional competence of Jerusalem." Stauffer believes that in the case of the convention "the choice of the geographical location for the meeting is of fundamental importance in terms of ecclesial laws." Hence, Stauffer concludes that James succeeded in making the Antiochenes (and specifically Paul) acknowledge this jurisdictional praxis and that, through their going to Jerusalem, Paul and Barnabas had documented this acknowledgment. Therefore the conference at Jerusalem constituted "[James's] first great success," as the Antiochenes had thus, "at a particularly critical juncture," given renewed recognition to the supremacy of the Jerusalem church leadership. Moreover, at the convention, James was able "to make all Christian communities of the Ecumene subscribe, *sub titulo*, to the collection for the poor, to a church tax to be paid to the central congregation at Jerusalem," to have the decree of the apostles adopted, and to stipulate the allocation of the various areas of mission—all of these being understood as juridical acts according to church law" (Stauffer, "Petrus und Jakobus in Jerusalem," pp. 369-70). But, in addition to the above-mentioned impossibility of viewing the Pauline report in the Epistle to the Galatians as a deliberate manipulation of this kind, Stauffer's exegesis is biased through its substantial imprecision. Stauffer is unable to prove, first, that the juridical practice referred to was followed also in the Hellenistic-Jewish Diaspora congregations in New Testament times and, second, that the early church actually used that practice.

29. Schlier, *Der Brief an die Galater*, p. 66.

30. This view is predominantly held by Schlier; see ibid., pp. 66-67.

31. Lietzmann (*An die Galater*, p. 10) and Schlier (*Der Brief an die Galater*, p. 67) interpret the μή πως as an expression of concern. Schlier draws far-reaching conclusions from this. But for convincing proof that the subordinate clause is of interrogative character, see Oepke, *Der Brief des Paulus an die Galater*, pp. 44ff.

32. See Gal. 5:7-8; I Cor. 9:24-26; Phil. 2:16. Schlier related this passage much too exclusively to Paul's personal faith experience (*Der Brief an die Galater*, pp. 67-68).

33. This was evidenced already by the introductory verses of the epistles.

34. This fact was pointed out above (pp. 24-25).

35. Regarding the words *the pillars*, see Ulrich Wilkens's article στῦλος in *TDNT* VII, pp. 732ff., and Schlier, *Der Brief an die Galater*, pp. 78-79. Most probably the "pillars" were identical with the "esteemed" ones, not—as Schlier (*Der Brief an die Galater*, p. 67) maintains—just a restricted circle of the "esteemed ones."

36. This argument was suggested in a footnote by Schlier in the first edition of his commentary to the Epistle to the Galatians (*Der Brief an die Galater*, p. 42, n. 4) but deleted in the second edition, because in this revised edition he more sharply accentuated the difference between the Lukan and the Pauline reports. In the first edition the footnote had served to harmonize the two reports on the convention. But the reason offered holds good also without such harmonizing intent.

37. It had already been claimed by Carl Weizsaecker (*Das apostolische Zeitalter der christlichen Kirche* [Tübingen: Mohr, 1890], pp. 173-74) that the decree of the apostles had come about after the Antioch incident and without any involvement on Paul's part in order to allow for better coexistence in the mixed congregations. Haenchen tries to argue against this view (*Acts*, pp. 468-69). Bultmann ("Zur Frage nach den Quellen der Apostelsgeschichte," in *New Testament Essays: Studies in Memory of Thomas Walter Manson*, Angus John and Brockhurst Higgins, eds. [Manchester, England: University Press, 1959], pp. 71ff.; hereafter referred to as "Quelle.") and Conzelmann ("Geschichte, Geschichtsbild, und Geschichtsdarstellung bei Lukas," *ThLZ* 85 (1960): 247) support it.

38. At least Peter and James (the latter acting through his followers), two important figures at the Jerusalem conference, must have played a decisive part in working out the compromise solution.

39. See Schlier, *Der Brief an die Galater*, pp. 75-76.

40. God's "impartiality" is spoken of in Deut. 10:17; II Chron. 19:7; Sir. 35:13; and Jub. 5:16. It implies that God cares nothing about human qualifications. In most cases this impartiality is thought of with respect to human qualities, but always God's judging activity is in view. This allows one to substitute God's election and calling, even God's justifying action, as positive contrasts to the negation in Gal. 2:6. On this see also Schlier, *Der Brief an die Galater*, p. 75.

41. See ibid., pp. 75-76.

42. As time went by, having had a personal relationship with the historical Jesus was increasingly considered a special qualification in the Jerusalem congregation and, as this idea spread forth from Jerusalem, finally in the rest of the early church.

43. A similar Pauline statement is found in II Cor. 5:16-17, (although the addressees are not the same). Also compare Gal. 6:15-16. Klein's explanation ("Gal. 2, 6-9," p. 290) of the parenthesis—namely, that Paul had overlooked certain imperfections in the "pillars" (more precisely in James and John) and that those imperfections were still carrying weight at the time of the convention, although not any longer—strikes one as somewhat far-fetched, indeed, erroneous. Here the end indeed is justified.

44. In verses 7 and 8, Paul continues by saying: "The esteemed ones did not lay anything further on me; quite the contrary, when they saw that I was entrusted with (preaching) the Gospel to those not circumcised, just as Peter was entrusted (with preaching) to those circumcised. For the One who was efficacious for Peter with the goal of the apostolate among the circumcised was also efficacious for me with the goal of the apostolate among the Gentiles; and when they saw the grace granted me. . . ." (see below).

45. Schlier has proven that this was a case of ratification of contract. He has also demonstrated that a "handshake of partnership" is meant here (*Der Brief an die Galater,* p. 79). The mention of James's name at the beginning of the list of "pillars" suggests that by the time of the convention James had already outranked Peter. The most plausible reading still remains, therefore, that this shift in the Jerusalem authority pattern had prompted the latter to leave Jerusalem as a means simply to avoid James. But the theological differences separating the two must also have been more serious than just differing degrees of liberal thinking.

46. Haenchen (*Acts,* pp. 466-67) is wrong in refuting the "official" character of the formulation in Gal. 2:9-10. It seems to me that my argument can invalidate his objections against the historicity of the phrasing used by Paul. More important, however, Haenchen does not succeed in clearly defining the relationship between the alleged original wording of the formula and its redactional interpretation. Why should Paul have failed to mention the authorization given him for a mission among the Gentiles that was free of the law?

47. See ibid., pp. 466ff.

48. Paradigm in *BAG* for εἰς, 4g ("for"). Neither the missing elliptical formulation nor an example where εἶναι εἰς is used in the postulated meaning can be found. Still, as there might have prevailed a tendency toward an abbreviated version of the statement, this unusual construction could have come about quite naturally.

49. Munck understands the first provision of the agreement as stipulating the mutual obligations and not as defining the boundaries (*Paul,* pp. 113-14). He stops short of realizing, however, that this also necessarily implied mutual recognition and, in this much, also a "partition."

50. For methodological reasons, the analysis of this second part of the agreement remains completely contextual. I have refrained from including the later collection texts. They will be discussed in their respective historical and literary settings.

51. Ernst Bammel has looked into this issue in conjunction with Judaism ("Πτωχός", *TDNT* VI, pp. 894-95), and in connection with the Pauline literature (pp. 908-9), as well as by E. Kutsch ("Armut, I,

Biblisch," *RGG* 1, cols. 622ff.). Both authors give further literary references. Romans 15:26 ought not to be considered a firsthand reference to Gal. 2:10, however, as that verse neither contains the actual title of honor of the Jerusalem congregation (against Bammel), nor represents a veiling term, as Lietzmann (*An die Römer* [Tübingen: Mohr, 1971], pp. 122-23; hereafter referred to as *Römer*) maintains in a follow-up to Holl's ideas ("Kirchenbegriff," pp. 58-62). The expression is rather to be understood in a partitive fashion: "the poor among the holy ones." Time has elapsed since the events reported on in Gal. 2:10, and this expresses itself factually (see pp. 128-37 below). Still, the rather absolute and unexplained usage of the terms does not warrant a sociological interpretation (in contrast to Bultmann, *Theology*, p. 39). Munck has no argument against a titular reading of "the poor."

52. For literary references additional to those given in the previous note, see Dibelius, *James* (Philadelphia: Fortress Press, 1976), pp. 39-45.

53. See primarily Ps. Solom 10, 15, and 18:1-5. For the self-designation of the community of Qumran, see 1 Q p Hab. XII 3.6.10; XIV 7; 1 QM XI 9.13; XIII 14; 1 QH V 13.14.16. and 22.

54. This is especially clear from the Qumran documents mentioned above.

55. See Karl-Georg Kuhn, "Askese, III: Im Judentum; IV: Im Christentum," *RGG* 1, cols. 641-42. See also by the same author "Essener," *RGG* 2, col. 702; and "Qumran," *RGG* 5, col. 749. Also important is Hans Joachim Kandler, "Die Bedeutung der Armut im Schrifttum von Chirbet Qumran," *Judaica* 13 (1957): 193-209.

56. By this I mean the congregation in Jerusalem, which consisted of the Galilean and other Aramaic-speaking Jesus believers who remained there—apart from a few exceptions—until the time of the Jerusalem convention and were still there when Paul and his delegation brought the collection.

A discussion of the causal significance of the sharing of goods for the economic neediness of the early church will be given in what follows. It was mainly W. M. Franklin who drew attention to this causal connection (*Die Kollekte des Paulus*, pp. 25ff.). But Franklin's presentation is one-sided and short-sighted in that it concentrates heavily on that aspect of the matter, while he displays little interest in the historical and theological background of the collection.

57. For the relationship of the self-designation "the poor" of the community of Qumran to the title adopted by the early church, see Kuhn, "Qumran," col. 752.

58. Contrary to Haenchen's conclusions (*Acts*, pp. 190ff., especially pp. 231 and 236), I tend to interpret the reports on the sharing of goods in the early church (Acts 4:32–5:11), not as an embellishment of individual

cases of self-sacrificing generosity, but as remnants of reminiscence.

59. See Kuhn, "Qumran," cols. 752-53.

60. Belonging to the Jewish religious structure provided the backdrop for rather aggressive self-confidence, and the basis for the contention of being the representatives of the true Israel.

61. Hellenistic Diaspora Jews had soon joined the early church (Acts 4:36ff.; 6:1ff.). It seems possible that the pneumatic experiences typical for the Jesus-believing congregations were favorable to this trend and that such experiences initially helped to overcome differences in the background. I have argued in my article on the hymn in Phil. 2 that as the group around Stephen came from Hellenistic-Jewish Gnostic wisdom it shared also with that branch of biblical-Jewish wisdom its traditio-historical relationship, not only to Apologetic but also to Apocalyptic wisdom, the latter being the tradition by which the Aramaic-speaking part of the Jerusalem Christ community was determined ("Der vorpaulinische Hymnus Phil. 2, 6-11," in *Zeit und Geschichte: Dankesgabe an Rudolf Bultmann zum 80. Gerburtag*, Erich Dinkler and Hartwig Thyen, eds. (Tübingen: Mohr, 1964), pp. 263-93; hereafter referred to as "Phil. 2:6-11"). The traditio-historical linkage of Hellenistic-Jewish Gnostic wisdom to both Apologetic and Gnostic wisdom is evidenced among others by the Wisdom of Solomon. Soon the discrepancies between the Aramaic-speaking and the Greek-speaking elements of the Christ community in Jerusalem proved so strong that the "Hellenists"—that is, the Greek-speaking Jesus believers—founded an independent congregation with rules of its own and independent activities. Hints of that schism in the Jerusalem Jesus community are still detectable in the narration of Acts 6. The theology and activity of those "Hellenists" must have been such that they not only aggravated the "conservative"-minded Aramaic-speaking Jesus believers but also the "liberal" Hellenistic Jews in Jerusalem. They brought the accusations against Stephen, and the tribunal conducting the trial against Stephen seemed to consist of Hellenistic Jews as well. They condemned Stephen, chased his friends out of Jerusalem, and persecuted them even outside the city. Wolfgang Schrage is most probably right in assuming that the "Hellenists"—that is, the Greek-speaking Jesus believers—adopted the designation *ἐκκλησία* in order to set themselves apart from the established synagogue and to start their own missionary program and activity. The christology I extricated from Phil. 2:6-11 and the accompanying call for freedom of the law (see the accusation in Acts 6:11) would concur with this reading. This made Stephen and his friends differ from the Aramaic-speaking Jesus believers in Jerusalem (the true conflict behind Acts 6:1-6), resulting in the growth of their side through missionary expansion, which in turn led to their persecution, flight, and the

establishment of ἐκκλησίαι outside of Jerusalem, particularly in the Diaspora. It has not been possible to establish the historicity of Luke's claim that the Aramaic-speaking Jesus community already had initiated an organized effort to expand itself—that is, to institute missionary activity. On the contrary, this concept of an organized expansion fits seamlessly into Luke's editorial *Tendenz* of the control of the original development in Jerusalem and the church at large being in the hands of the "Twelve." Luke's redactional remarks prove this tendency. The exaggerations contained in these remarks challenge their trustworthiness. At the least, the speeches are Luke's own work. As to the stories on the beginnings of the church, they are highly legendary and all undated, with the exception of the Pentecost story. As Peter legends, these narratives offer merely a chronology that is relative to the life of Peter. Thus historical verification of Luke's portrayal of the early church in most instances turns out to be very difficult, if not impossible. A time-spread of at least twelve years would have to be allowed for the Peter stories—that is, for whatever authentic information they might entail. Hahn—without any serious attempt at critical argumentation—tries to develop a theory based on Acts 2–5, according to which the missionary activities displayed by the early church immediately after Pentecost constituted the follow-up of Jesus' own mission and his "missionary commission" (*Mission*, pp. 37, 40). Hahn fails to realize, however, that nowhere does Acts 1–5 mention Jesus' mission or his commission. As a matter of fact, there is no reference in Acts to Jesus' sending out his disciples to preach, and Jesus' message is dealt with only rather rudimentarily (Acts 10:36; 13:26)—all this in spite of the fact that Luke wrote a Gospel in which the sending out of the Seventy (10:1ff.) is reported.

62. See Acts 12:1-3. I Thess. 2:14-16 is a pseudo-Pauline insertion, most probably presupposing the First Jewish War of 66–70. See Birger A. Pearson, "I Thessalonians 2:13-16: A Deutero-Pauline Interpolation," *HThR* 64 (1971): 79-94.

63. In addition, there was the increasing deterioration of the economic situation of the city of Jerusalem itself (see Joachim Jeremias, *Jerusalem in the Time of Jesus: An Investigation into Economic and Social Conditions During the New Testament Period*, trans. F. H. Cave and C. H. Cave (London: SCM, 1969), vol. I, pp. 31ff.). According to Josephus (Ant. XX 101), Palestine was ravaged by a famine between 46 and 48. As to Acts 11:27-30, see n.3 p.167 above, as well as p. 44.

64. There is no doubt that the tradition was to hide the flight of the (male) disciples to Galilee, as the Gospels of Luke and John and also Acts prove. Mark 14:50-52 is certainly authentic and is to be seen in conjunction with 14:28 and 16:7.

65. This had already been seen by Wellhausen, as referred to by Holl, "Kirchenbegriff," p. 55.

66. The most impressive account of the event is found in Isaiah 60:10-22*a*—a text highly significant for the subject matter under discussion here. For the entire body of ideas and conceptions pertaining to the glorification of Jerusalem within the framework of Israel's eschatological expectation, see Gerhard von Rad, *Old Testament Theology*, trans. D. M. G. Stralker (New York: Harper & Row, 1962-65), vol. II, pp. 292ff. Paradigmatic examples of the coming of Yahweh or the Messiah on Mt. Zion and the glorification of Jerusalem are offered in the following: Paul Volz, *Die Eschatologie der jüdischen Gemeinde* (Tübingen: Mohr, 1934), pp. 225, 371-72; Paul Billerbeck and Hermann Leberecht Strack, *Kommentar zum neues Testament aus Talmud und Midrasch* (Munich: Beck, 1969), vol. IV, pp. 883-86; Albert Schweitzer, *Die Mystik des Apostels Paulus* (Tübingen: Franckl, 1931), pp. 175-200; B. Sundkler, "Jésus et les paiens," *RHPhR* 16 (1936): 485ff.; Joachim Jeremias, *Jesus' Promise to the Nations*, Franz Delitzsch Lectures for 1953, SBT 24 (London: SCM, 1958), pp. 38-39; and Georg Fohrer and Eduard Lohse, *Σιών-Ἱερουσαλήμα*, *TDNT* 7 (1964), pp. 311-15, 323-25, 332-36.

67. Since the prophecy of Deutero-Isaiah, this has been an essential figure of speech within the eschatological expectation. The corresponding paradigms in Jewish thinking are found in Paul Volz, *Die Eschatologie der jüdischen Gemeinde*, pp. 344-48, 378; and Billerbeck, *Kommentar zum neues Testament aus Talmud und Midrasch*, IV, pp. 883-84 and footnotes.

68. See Isa. 2:2-4; 25:6-9; 45:20-25; 49:22-23; 55:5-7; 60; 66:18-23 (Mic. 4:1-4); Jer. 3:17; Zeph. 3:8-9; Hag. 2:6-9; and Zech. 8:20-23. For scriptural references in Jewish thinking, see Volz, *Die Eschatologie der jüdischen Gemeinde*, pp. 171-72, 358; and Billerbeck, *Kommentar zum Neuen Testament aus Talmud und Midrasch*, IV, pp. 895-96.

69. See Isa. 60:6 ff.; Hag. 2:6ff. For early Jewish theology compare Tob. 13:11; Sib. III, 718, 772-73 (565); and the scriptural paradigm given by Billerbeck, *Kommentar zum Neuen Testament aus Talmud und Midrasch*, I, p. 84; III, pp. 149-50; and IV, pp. 937-38.

But even in those cases where the eschatological metaphors were filled with spiritual or transcendental meaning the conviction that Jerusalem, together with Mt. Zion, constituted a place of sanctity was generally not given up. The concepts of the New Heaven and of the heavenly Jerusalem remained in close relationship with the hope for a renewed and glorified earthly Zion and Jerusalem. Only in a very few cases prior to the year 70 C.E. was the motif of the heavenly Jerusalem polemically pitched against the hope of a glorified earthly Jerusalem. For further details on this issue the reader is referred to the discussion of Gal. 4:21-31 on pp. 47-48 below. Paradigms for Jewish expectations of the heavenly

Jerusalem are given by Volz, *Die Eschatologie der jüdischen Gemeinde*, pp. 371ff. Although the Hellenistic-Jewish mission had modified the conceptions of Jerusalem as the true center of the world and of the Jews as a central nation, it had not abandoned it (see my book *The Opponents of Paul in 2nd Corinthians* (Philadelphia: Fortress, 1986), pp. 88, 149. Hereafter referred to as *Opponents*.

70. It is also to be noted that in Isa. 61:1-11, the great homily of consolation, the expected glorious reconstruction of the temple of Jerusalem (see also Isa. 62) follows after the eschatological promise to the poor—a passage also quoted in the New Testament.

71. The fact that this respectful remembrance in Heb. 13:7 is meant only in retrospect is, I believe, only of minor significance.

72. Ferdinand Hahn, *Mission in the New Testament* (London: SCM, 1965), p. 81, n. 2. Hereafter referred to as *Mission*.

73. There is no clear definition in Hahn's argument of what exactly is meant here by Israel's priority in the context of history of salvation. Hahn fails to provide a precise reason as to why this priority was also extended to the Jesus believers but then limited to the Jesus congregation at Jerusalem.

74. Hahn (*Mission in the New Testament*, p. 79) not only fails to produce evidence that the πρῶτον Ἰουδαίοις—undisputed also for the Hellenistic Jewish Jesus believers—had constituted "the basis for the negotiations" at the Jerusalem convention; he also falls short of giving a textual basis for his claim that "a collection for 'the poor' in Jerusalem on the part of the Gentile Jesus-believers had been negotiated because of the priority of Israel in terms of salvation history." Hahn has not even explained why the recognition of Israel's priority in salvation history made a collection for the benefit of the Jesus community in Jerusalem necessary—nor indeed to what extent the collection could have been bound up with such a recognition.

75. There is hardly any reason to assume that Paul had been forced by the Jesus community at Jerusalem to ascribe to the idea of the pilgrimage of the peoples—an idea that was of much great weight in his later theological outlook and practice. Paul must have subscribed to the idea before that time, for he had in common with the Aramaic-speaking early church not only the Scriptures, but also the Apocalyptic tradition—although the latter was certainly not the only predominant influence in his theology.

76. The only evidence Hahn is able to produce for such localized criticism of the Temple on the part of the Hellenistic-Jewish Jesus believers at Antioch is Acts 6:13-14 (*Mission in the New Testament*, pp. 61-62). He also fails to refute the well-founded interpretation of this text

given by Haenchen (also accepted by Conzelmann) that "in relating the trial of the first martyr, Luke had the trial of Jesus in mind and used material which might have been dangerous if applied to the earlier occasion. . . . In fact Luke here followed very bold tactics, using the logion as a stepping-stone for his own polemic against the Temple (and the Temple cult)" (*Acts*, p. 274). Likewise, Conzelmann has shown that it is Luke himself who has altered Stephen's speech to make it sound like a polemical outburst against the cult of the Temple. Also Bihler (quoted by Hahn, *Mission in the New Testament*, p. 62, n.1) concludes that the view of the Temple advocated in Acts 6:13-14 is actually Luke's own. All this can only mean that even if there existed an authentic Antiochene source, Acts 6:13-14 was not part of it.

77. Since congregations of Hellenistic-Jewish Jesus believers had spread over an area stretching from Jerusalem (the original location of the Hellenistic-Jewish early church) as far as at least Antioch, and from Damascus to Cyprus, and considering the great number of individual communities, one cannot expect that it constituted a homogeneous entity. The mere fact that Hellenistic-Jewish Jesus believers were persecuted by Hellenistic Jews in Jerusalem and Damascus, but not in Antioch, speaks for different profiles of these congregations. The Antioch incident confirms such differences and disallows blaming the differing experiences of these Christ congregations simply on the differences of the respective local Hellenistic-Jewish communities.

78. As regards the attitudes taken by Hellenistic Judaism with respect to the Temple, see pp. 39-40, above. Apart from Acts 6:13-14 the only scriptural proof Hahn produces of Hellenistic-Jewish Temple criticism is John 4:19-26 and Mark 14:58. But he does not supply any truly traditio-historical analysis of these passages, nor does he provide a proper classification for them. With reference to Bultmann, Hahn concedes (*Mission in the New Testament*, p. 64, n. 2) that verses 20-26 of John 4—the decisive ones in connection with this question—had undergone redactional revision, but he omits pointing out the original or, as the case may be, the secondary formulations. (Bultmann, in *The Gospel of John: A Commentary*, trans. G. R. Beasley-Murray [Philadelphia: Westminster, 1971], p. 179, has postulated that the evangelist had replaced part of the traditional source text with what is now John 4:20-26.) Nor does Hahn come up with an exact religio-historical profile, and, finally he provides no answer to the question as to why Mark 14:58 represents a production of the Hellenistic-Jewish Jesus community. There is not even evidence on whether the redactional revision of this passage—considered by Hahn himself a Markan insertion (*Mission in the New Testament*, p. 100, n. 5)—is not to be ascribed to Mark himself instead of being taken over by him.

79. Haenchen's skepticism is not warranted here. See Bultmann, "Quellen," pp 71ff; see also chap. 2, n. 5 below.

80. This represents the generally prevailing view held by almost all exegetes.

81. See Werner Georg Kümmel, "Judenchristentum, I: Im Altertum," *RGG* 3, col. 970.

82. See Exod. 25:1-7; I Chron. 29:2, 18; II Chron. 2:15-16; and Ezra 1:4; 7:15-23; and 8:24-30.

2. THE FATE OF THE JERUSALEM CONVENTION (48–53 C.E.)

1. A detailed discussion and refutation of both of these hypotheses is found in Haenchen's *Acts*, pp. 419ff. and 615ff.; see p. 167 n. 3.

2. See Haenchen, *Acts*, pp. 373ff. and p. 167, n. 3.

3. Hahn (*Mission in the New Testament*, p. 82, esp. n. 2, and pp. 84-85) agrees with my argument on this point but adds that Luke's report on the conveyance of this Antiochene collection by Paul and Barnabas themselves might well be trustworthy, after all (see p. 70, esp. n. 4, and pp. 84-85). Hahn counters the objection that Paul makes no mention of this visit to Jerusalem with the unfounded claim that "in Gal. 1-2 Paul is only interested in narrating what has happened up to the time the convention had reached a decision of principle." It is important to realize, however, that the historical references made by Paul in connection with his polemical argument continues even beyond Gal. 2:10 and that (as rightly observed by Schlier) the ὅτε δέ gives the narrative a smooth flow "without transition." Hahn does not even realize that by crediting the Agabus tradition with basic verity, he puts himself at variance with Paul's own declaration in Gal. 2:10, not only from the point of view of the spirit and letter of this agreement, but also as regards the short Pauline note about his eager endeavor to promote the remembrance of the poor. Contrary to what is apparent from the original texts in Acts, Hahn turns the prophecy of Agabus into a prophetic demand and the worldwide famine into a Palestinian one. Such equating and expurgating of dissimilar information arouse methodological qualms. The claimed value of Luke as a source is discredited by such an approach even further.

4. See Haenchen, *Acts*, pp. 473ff. Munck (*Paul*, pp. 100ff.) maintains that Gal. 2:11-21 reports on an event prior to the convention at Jerusalem, but this stands in contradiction to the chronological order in which events are depicted in Gal. 1:13–2:21. Munck even goes so far as to assert (pp. 94-95 and 102-3) that one can read between the lines of Gal.

2:11-21 to find that during the controversy at Antioch, Peter (as well as Barnabas and other Jewish Christians) had finally agreed with Paul, simply because this had been the essential argument against the Judaizing propagandists. But this *argumentum e silentio* is easily settled by simply countering with another question: Why had Paul kept silent on precisely that declaration of consent?

5. The so-called first missionary journey of Paul, reported by Luke in Acts 13 and 14, cannot have taken place at the time indicated (i.e., prior to the convention at Jerusalem). This is evidenced by the contradiction not only of Gal. 1:21 but also of Acts 15:23 and 43. For this reason scholars have repeatedly attempted to date this journey after the Jerusalem conference (see Jeremias, "Untersuchen zum Quellenproblem der Apostelgeschichte," *ZNW* 36 (1937): 205-21; Haenchen, *Acts*, p. 439; Bornkamm, "Paulus," *RGG* 5, col. 172; and Hahn, *Mission in the New Testament*, pp. 82-83). But 13:4-13 contradicts 11:19—a contradiction not to be solved by opting in favor of 11:19, as Haenchen and after him Conzelmann have done. Why should Luke contradict with 11:19 his own report in 13:4-13, especially since the order in which Phoenicia, Cyprus, and Antioch are listed did not constitute the most natural and simplest sequence and, also, because that listing order cannot be explained by saying that it had resulted from incorporating the data given in verse 20, as in that verse Phoenicia is not mentioned. In Acts 11:19-20 only verse 19*b* is authentically Lukan. As all the authors mentioned have dated this so-called first missionary journey later than Luke did because, contrary to him, they rightly assumed that Paul had accomplished important mission work in Cilicia prior to the convention, they ought actually to come forth with an explanation of why Paul and Barnabas did not leave for Cilicia from Antioch (once the collection had been organized there) to proceed, in accordance with what had been agreed upon in Jerusalem, with a collection also in that area of his missionary activity. And, as regards the journey mentioned by Luke, it remains to be explained why Paul and Barnabas did not choose Cilicia as a headquarters from which to push forth into southern Asia Minor. This would have been not only the simplest but also the best (and quickest) itinerary—namely, to proceed via the Cilician Gate—the very itinerary, in fact, Luke indicates for Paul's so-called second missionary circuit (Acts 15:40-41). Why should Paul, who later on seemed to have preferred traveling on Roman roads, have dispensed with this well-paved and guarded military carriageway and entrust his destiny to "difficult and danger-ridden roads," when setting out from Perge "for the Pisidian Antioch, about 100 miles away" (Haenchen, *Acts*, p. 349)? Worse yet, why should he have returned by such a road as well? This seems all the more questionable as Acts shows nothing about a missionary activity of Paul

between Perge and Antioch in Pisidia back along a road, where both nature and humans presented such threats to the traveler. It would also have to be explained, of course, why the "Antiochene source" does not know anything about the organization of a collection for Jerusalem in the Pisidian Antioch, Iconium, Lystra, and Derbe.

In addition to all these considerations, there remains the fact that Paul's own narrative stands contrary to the theory of a missionary journey he and Barnabas had started together following the convention at Jerusalem. As seen earlier, Paul's report on the convention in Gal. 2:11 is immediately followed by the description of the Antiochene incident. It does not seem plausible that Paul—merely by using the short ὅτε δέ—had skipped reporting on the great number of manifold experiences contained in Acts 13 and 14. The wording in Gal. 2:10*b* and the report on the Antioch incident in 2:11-21 clearly show that Paul wished to continue with his deliberately historical account beyond the report on the conference. And as evidenced already by Gal. 2:10*b*, this concern with historicity clearly reflects the evidently considerable importance Paul ascribed to the faithful and scrupulous fulfillment of the Jerusalem agreement. Such proof must have been (either negatively or positively) a new missionary campaign, especially when it led to encounters with Jewish Diaspora congregations. Paul had to bring that campaign into relation with the convention since, according to Acts 13–14, the other Antiochene delegate, Barnabas, was part of that missionary journey. It would have been surprising, therefore, had Paul decided to keep silent in Gal. 2 on his and Barnabas's adventures in Cyprus and southern Asia Minor subsequent to the Jerusalem conference—and all this despite the report on the Antiochene incident, where Barnabas (as Paul does not neglect to mention) had shown himself in such unfavorable light. It therefore seems to me that all we can conclude from Paul's silence is simply that there was nothing on which to report. But this does not mean that Acts 13 and 14 were invented by Luke completely; rather, what we have here is the improved Lukan version of an earlier model of what had become of the traditional concept of a Pauline mission circuit (*Opponents*, p. 226 n. 539), a model worked out most probably on the basis of a list of the Jesus-believing communities in Pamphylia, Pisidia, and Lycaonia.

6. This epistle was written a few months after the founding of the congregation and shortly after Timothy's return (whom Paul had sent to Thessalonica while still in Athens). According to I Thess. 1:7-8, Paul had already been successfully active in Achaia; hence the epistle would rightly be dated in the spring of the year 50. (The date suggested by Schmithals, "Zur Abfassung und ältesten Sammlung der paulinischen Hauptbriefe," *ZNW* 51 (1950): 232), subsequent to the drafting of II Cor.

2:14–7:1 and at the time of Paul's stay in Ephesus, seems totally erroneous to me.

7. See Gal. 4:13; Acts 18:23.

8. On this, see Schlier, *Der Brief an die Galater,* pp. 223-26.

9. See Schmithals, "Die Häretiker in Galatien," passim.

10. See pp. 66-67, below.

11. See Bornkamm, "Die Häresie des Kolosserbriefes," in *Gesammelte Aufsätze,* I (Munich: Kaiser, 1966), pp. 139-56.

12. In conjunction with this issue as a whole, see Helmut Koester, "Häretiker Im Urchristentum," *RGG*[3], cols. 17-22.

13. Compare Gal. 3:19 with 4:3 and 4:9-10, on the one hand, and with 3:2-3, on the other.

14. In this connection, compare Gal. 4:8ff. with 4:3.

15. For a critical description of the self-confidence of the opponents, see Gal. 5:15, 26; 6:1, 3-4, 12.

16. In Gal. 3:27 baptism is taken as an undisputed premise; circumcision is the topic of 5:2-3 and 6:12-13.

17. For this, compare the polemics contained in Gal. 1 and 2. Paul was not accused of being dependent on Jerusalem; quite to the contrary, the accusation leveled against him was of disregarding Jewish tradition, which, in the eyes of the opponents, amounted to not having been granted the gift of the Spirit and, hence, to not being entitled to the position of apostle. Galatians 1:11-12 is not meant apologetically but polemically aggressive (this in disagreement with Schmithals, "Die Häretiker in Galatien," pp. 31-42). In this context, see also the antithesis in 4:21-31. Thus the opposition is made up of people upholding the Jewish tradition. This fact alone, even more the antinomistic polemics, would forbid one to see in chapters 1 and 2 a defense against the accusation that Paul had not been a free, but rather a dependent, apostle. Out of the entire text of the two first chapters only verses 1:15-17 could be interpreted as a genuine defense against an accusation of this kind. Schlier is of the opinion that the opposing party had accused Paul of not being equipped with the directness of the call, as for instance the "original" apostles, who, therefore, also were the true apostles (Schlier, *Der Brief an die Galater,* p. 45). But this theory is deflated already by 1:12. The comparative conjunction *οὐδὲ* clearly refers to the preceding sentence and points to the *παρὰ ἀνθρώπου* (Richard Adelbert Lipsius, *Die Briefe an die Galater, Römer, und Philipper* [Tübingen: Mohr, 1893] (ibid., p. 18) in turn taking up the *κατὰ ἄνθρωπον* in the preceding phrase and modifying it. That is to say, the *ἐγώ* does not carry any particular emphasis but, rather, "enhances the person of the carrier of the message and points to him as the one to be spoken of presently. At the same time it directs a fine critical point against the attackers:

it may be they who depend on human authority'' (Oepke, *Der Brief des Paulus an die Galater,* p. 29). Wegenast draws attention to the fact that Paul makes no reference to the original apostles in the immediate context of this sentence, only to the opponents (*Tradition,* p. 40, n. 2). Schlier (*Der Brief an die Galater*) remarks: ''The other apostles are not named, but Paul has been grappling with them continuously—or with their followers, who [indirectly] confronted him with them.'' But this information leaves a great deal to be desired, for if Gal. 1:12-14 were really concerned with such immediate reference to the earlier apostles, such allusions are not enough; what is really required is that the ''original apostles'' be named. Besides, any apologetical comparison with the ''original apostles'' would make 1:13-14 not only unneccessary, but also nonsensical. The position, held also by Schlier, that Paul's opponents prevailed themselves of the figures of authority in Jerusalem and pitched them against Paul can be maintained only insofar as it is extended to the larger problem of the attitude one takes to tradition itself. Galatians 1:13-14 becomes meaningful in conjunction with the preceding and the subsequent context, insofar as the passage is understood as representing a polemical position taken up against a concept of ''true gospel'' that sees revelation founded and legitimized by the entire complex of tradition in which also the Jerusalem ''apostles'' are integrated (See also Wegenast, *Tradition,* p. 41, n. 1). Further, the parenthesis in Gal. 2:6 points in the same direction—especially if interpreted in the same sense as the one suggested by Schlier. However, the only conclusion Schlier draws from this is that tradition does not legitimize the apostle, as his authority flows from direct relevation. In that case, however, (Schlier holds) the apostle himself becomes the bearer of tradition. This exegetical view obviously maintains Paul's position in very close proximity to the view of the opponents—a type of gospel Paul refuted. For the issue is another gospel—not just differing opinions about Paul's right to claim the title of apostle and his juridical recognition by the Jerusalem authorities. The gospel preached by the opponents was embedded in the context of tradition in the largest sense of the term, whereas in Paul's view the true gospel was to be seen as set off from both the Law and the tradition—even the Jesus tradition. From Paul's point of view, therefore, the law as well as tradition belong to the wrong side, because the true gospel is as free from tradition as it is free from the law; hence, it is free for the world, even for the Gentiles.

18. A partnership for which the Jerusalem summit gave positive evidence, and Peter's and Barnabas's behavior at Antioch, negative.

19. See Paul's polemics in Gal. 4:8-11 and especially the sarcastic ἐπιστρέφετε πάλιν κτλ in 4:9.

20. Chapters 3 and 4 are guided by precisely this *leitmotiv.*
21. See I Cor. 9:4-6.
22. Paul had not yet visited Jerusalem at this time. (In this connection see Haenchen, *Acts,* pp. 547-48). Hence, Franklin's assertion (*Die Kollekte des Paulus,* pp. 18-19) that Paul had delivered the Galatian collection at the time proves unfounded. It would, indeed, be twice as bizarre to suppose that Paul had mentioned nothing about a collection carried out by the Galatians in his Epistle to the Galatians.

3. THE COLLECTION: A NEW START AND, ONCE AGAIN, ITS IMPENDING END (53 and 54 C.E.)

1. The call for a collection, mentioned in I Cor. 16:1, occurs after the composition and delivery of the Epistle to the Galatians. It must have been conveyed to the Galatians by different means. According to I Cor. 16:1, Paul had also asked the Corinthians to participate in the collection after giving similar instructions to the Galatians.
2. It would only sidetrack us here to trace the similarities (attacked in I Cor.) that existed between the Galatian and Corinthian oppositions. But there can be no doubt that such kinship existed. Both worked with a speculative soteriology that was heavily laced with cosmology, and both developed pneumatically determined tenets of self-perfection. There is evidence of many more other parallels. But it would definitely be wrong to say that both these heresies were altogether identical; the prevailing discrepancies are too weighty for that. The most important difference lies in the attitude taken with regard to the Law. The equalization of wisdom and Law that had developed within the wisdom movement of the second century B.C.E. and, as such, had been incorporated into Gnostic wisdom, enabled these two components to be differently stressed and elaborated during the subsequent historical unfolding of Gnosticism.
3. On the traditions of baptism, see I Cor. 1:15; 10:2; 12:13; and 15:29. On the traditions of the Last Supper, see I Cor. 10:4, 16; 11:23-34; and 12:13. On the traditions of the death and resurrection of Jesus, see I Cor. 15:1-7. According to I Cor. 15:1-3, 12, respectively, the Corinthians did not refute the resurrection of Christ, but the (future) resurrection of believers. See Wegenast, *Tradition,* p. 66. In this context, compare especially the polemics in I Cor. 10 and 15 (note particularly 10:12; 15:1-2, 58; and 16:13).
4. See Hans von Soden, "Sakrament und Ethik," *Ges. Aufs.,* pp. 239-75; Ernst Käsemann, "Anliegen und Eigenar der Paulinischen Abendmahlslehre," *Ges. Aufs.,* I, pp. 17-34; Bornkamm, "Herrenmahl und Kirche bei Paulus," *Ges. Aufs.* II, pp. 138-77.

5. On this issue, see especially I Cor. 14:5-7. Schmithals (*Gnosticism in Corinth*, trans. John E. Steely [Nashville: Abingdon Press, 1971] p. 24) has consistently contested this connectedness of libertinism and asceticism—right in the face of textual evidence. For the same problem, see also Köster, "Häretiker."

6. In adding the supplementary "congregations," I follow Hans Lietzmann and Werner Georg Kümmel, *An die Korinther I II* (Tübingen: Mohr, 1969), p. 166. Hereafter referred to as *An die Korinther*. However, neither the *αὐτῶν* nor the *ἡμῶν* necessarily stresses the difference as to the founders of these communities. Rather, it seems that both of these pronouns point to an existing factual difference between the Pauline and the non-Pauline communities.

7. See Wegenast, *Tradition*, pp. 52ff., esp. pp. 61-68.

8. As, for instance, in the sense of the heterodox teaching rejected in I Tim. 2:18—a doctrine claiming that "resurrection had already taken place." See also Wegenast, *Tradition*, pp. 61-62. It seems that Paul takes up the view held by the Corinthians again in II Cor. 5:1-10, but in much more positive terms.

9. The clearest evidence concerning this is I Cor. 6:13-20. Bultmann, *Theology*, p. 193, was wrong in reversing this order.

10. On this, see especially I Cor. 15:20-23, 44-57. (Compare Rom. 5:12-21 and the prophetic saying in I Cor. 15:51-52, which is not simply an Apocalyptic-minded theologian's passing inspiration.)

11. The whole text reads as follows: "Regarding the collections for the saints: As I directed the congregations in Galatia, so you (should) do, too. Every first day of the week each one of you should put aside privately that which he or she has gathered, (that is to say,) as much as he or she is able, so that the collecting (of funds) will not begin only upon my arrival. But as soon as I arrive, I shall hand letters to those you consider qualified (for the task and) send them off to carry your grace to Jerusalem. And if it seems worthwhile for me to go there myself as well, they will travel with me."

12. For the accuracy of this translation, see *TDNT*, vol. 4, pp. 282-83.

13. See Holl, "Kirchenbegriff," p. 59. For the comparison with Rom. 15:26, see pp. 175-76, n. 51 above, and pp. 113-15 below.

14. *Λογεία* also denotes the cult-connected collections (see *TDNT*, vol. 4, pp. 282-83).

15. See Gillis P. Wetter, *Charis* (Leipzig: Hinrichs, 1913), p. 208; and *BAG*, *χάρις* 5.

16. For scriptural references, see Wetter, *Charis*, pp. 211-12. The references listed by Wetter on the meaning of "gift" (among which he also includes I Cor. 16:3 and II Cor. 8:4, 19) are much more closely linked to those he previously indicated for the meaning of "favor" than

becomes clear from Wetter's own explanations. See also *BAG*, *χάρις* 3a.

17. See *BAG*, *χάρις* 3a.

18. See Henry George Liddel and Robert Scott, *A Greek-English Lexicon* (Oxford: Clarendon Press, 1925-49), *χάρις* IIIb.

19. As commonly known, this constitutes the first mention of "Sunday" in early Christian literature.

20. I cannot be convinced that this is meant to refer to the successful outcome of a business deal, as suggested by Lietzmann and Kümmel, *An die Korinther*, p. 89; *BAG*, *εὐοδόω*, who also consider this possibility.

21. See pp. 80-92, below.

22. In those letters of recommendation, Paul probably also intends to give explanatory information on the collection.

23. This is the view held by most commentators because of the reference to the Pentecostal festival in I Cor. 16:8. When Paul writes the letter, he is still counting on a period of intensive work before his mission in Ephesus draws to its end (16:8-9). However, since the epistle was probably to be carried by boat, this end might not have been foreseeable until after the resumption of sea travel in March, and this would have left little time for intensive work before the Pentecost celebrations. This period of time would be even shorter in the event that Timothy had also come to Corinth by boat. Consequently, the drafting of the first Epistle to the Corinthians might have to be dated in the autumn of the preceding year—that is, autumn 53.

24. Bornkamm has also adopted this view (*Die Vorgeschichte des sogenannten Zweiten Korintherbriefes*, SHAW. PH 2, 1961 (Heidelberg: Winter, 1961): 9). Hereafter referred to as *Vorgeschichte*.

25. See Haenchen, *Acts*, p. 613.

26. For Paul's correspondence with Corinth subsequent to I Corinthians, its fragmentary nature, the possibility of tracing these fragments, and ordering their sequence on the basis of the canonical Second Epistle, see *Opponents*, passim. The probable chronological sequence is as follows:

Fragment A (2:14–7:4, without 6:14-7:1); the so-called "Apology."
Fragment B (chaps. 10–13); the so-called "Letter of Tears" (or sorrow).
Fragment C (1:1–2:13; 7:5-16); the so-called "Letter of Reconciliation."
Fragment D (8:1-24); a plea for the collection and letter of recommendation for Titus and others to Corinth.
Fragment E (9:1-15); a plea for the collection to the congregations of the province of Achaia outside of Corinth.

27. See II Cor. 2:1; 12:14; and 13:1

28. See II Cor. 2:1-11, esp. vv. 5-11; 7:5-16, esp. vv. 11-16.

29. See II Cor. 11:7-21; for the meaning of the remuneration for

pneumatics as discussed between Paul and his opponents, see Georgi, *Opponents*, pp. 238-42.

30. See II Cor. 12:16. Translated from Hans Lietzmann's German rendering.

31. I am referring to a fragment of the so-called "letter of reconciliation" preserved in II Cor. 1:1–2:13 and 7:5-16. The passage quoted here is 1:8-11. Translated from Hans Lietzmann's German rendering.

32. See Hans Windisch, *Der zweite Korintherbrief* (Göttingen: Vandenhoeck & Ruprecht, 1970), p. 45, is right in rejecting this possibility. Hereafter referred to as *Korinther*.

33. For evidence, see Windisch, *Korinther*, p. 46. Windisch's focus of interest, however, is primarily on Paul's mood.

34. This is Dibelius's conclusion (*Paulus*, p. 75). On Paul's Ephesian captivity, see also Wilhelm Michaelis, *Die Gefangenschaft des Paulus in Ephesus* (Gütersloh: Bertelsmann, 1925), pp. 204ff. Frequently the statement ἐθηριομαχήσα ἐν Ἐφέσῳ̂ in I Cor. 15:32 is taken to refer to this imprisonment at Ephesus (as per Michaelis). But Lietzmann and Kümmel (*An die Korinther*, p. 83) argue convincingly against such realistic reading of this remark; they also show that the preceding εἰ is not used here in the meaning of an "Irrealis."

35. Schmithals has convincingly established that Phil. 4:10-23 constitutes a fragment of Paul's letter of grateful acknowledgment for a collection of the Philippians and that this letter was written prior to Paul's other correspondence. (See Schmithals, "Die Irrlehrer des Philipperbriefes," *ZThK* 54 [1957]: 306-9; hereafter referred to as "Philipper"). He is just as convincing in proving that the rest of the Epistle to the Philippians was made up of the fragments of two further epistles Paul had addressed to the Philippians, namely epistle B (1:1–3:1 and 4:4-7) and epistle C (3:2–4:3 and 4:8-9; pp. 299 ff.). On the other hand, Schmithals's discussion of the historical background to this correspondence and his portrayal of the opposition attacked are not convincing.

36. See Martin Dibelius, *An die Thessalonicher I II, An die Philipper* (Tübingen: Mohr, 1937) pp. 96-97. Hereafter referred to as *Thessalonicher/Philipper*.

37. See pp. 116-17, below.

38. "It was a great joy for me that you were at last able to bring to flourish again your loving care, your caring thinking for me [the factitivous translation is to be preferred here]. For caring thinking you possessed, but you had no opportunity [to prove it]."

39. "Not that I spoke out of neediness, for I have learned to be self-sufficient in whatever situation."

40. Continuing his train of thought in v. 12, Paul interestingly expresses himself by means of a formula borrowed from the mysteries: "I know how to fast and I know how to live in abundance. I am an initiate to any matter and to all things: both to satiate myself and to go hungry, both to live in plenty and in want. I can do everything in the one who makes me strong."

41. "Anyway, it was okay for you to share in my affliction."

42. "But, Philippians, you also know that when first starting out on [my] mission [as correctly translated by Dibelius, *Thessalonicher/Philipper*, pp. 96ff.] [that is to say], when setting out from Macedonia, there was no other congregation to enter into a relationship of mutual accountability with me except you alone: also when I was in Thessalonica you sent me something to relieve my need, once or twice."

43. "Not that I sought the gift; but I sought the fruit in rich abundance for your benefit."

44. "I herewith sign the receipt for everything, and thus I (now) live in abundance."

45. "My hands are full now [through] receiving your gift through Epaphroditus."

46. On this theme and the following, see Ernst Lohmeyer's study *Vom göttlichen Wohlgeruch*, SHAW. PH 1919, 9 (Heidelberg: Winter, 1919).

47. Ibid., p. 29.

48. Ibid., p. 30. See also the description given a little earlier of wisdom as a form of divine revelation in Sir. 24:15 (wisdom as giving off divine fragrance).

49. For the Persian concept of the fragrance of wisdom, see Lohmeyer, *Vom göttlichen Wohlgeruch*, pp. 22ff.

50. Sir. 39:12-15 reads as follows: "I shall radiate forth the wise teachings like the full moon on the twelfth day. Oh pious ones, hear me, so you will grow like the cedar tree by the flowing waters, [so] you will smell sweetly like incense and bloom like lilies. Raise up the voice, praise unanimously, praise the Lord above all his works, extol him, give thanks with harps and strings." The detectable connection between the motifs of sacrifice and of prayer is significant for what follows.

51. Charismatic concepts are best epitomized in Wisd. Sol., the most important document of Hellenistic-Jewish Gnostic wisdom prior to Philo.

52. The Apocalyptic tradition is a branch of Jewish wisdom. See von Rad, *Old Testament Theology*, pp. 451-2.

53. Essential material on the historical development of this theology was gathered by George Henry Boobyer *"Thanksgiving" and the "Glory of God" in Paul* (Borna/Leipzig: Univ.Verl. Robert Noske, 1928). Hereafter referred to as *"Thanksgiving."* Odo Casel's book *De Philosophorum*

Graecorum Silentio Mystico (Giessen: Töpelmann, 1919), is also worth consulting on the matter. Not so satisfactory from the point of view of the history of religion is the material provided by Hans Wenschkewitz, *Die Spiritualisierung der Kultusbegriffe* (Leipzig: Pfeifer, 1932). None of his studies sufficiently recognizes the great impact biblical and Jewish wisdom had on the religious history of Jewish faith and Near Eastern syncretistic tenets. On Philo, see Appendix 2.

54. The tendency toward the non-historic is particularly strong in Wisd. Sol., where the receiving of both wisdom and righteousness are spoken of by means of metaphors borrowed from nature (esp. in 15:2-3).

55. For evidence, see Boobyer, *"Thanksgiving,"* pp. 15-34; compare also pp. 65ff. On mystical silence in neo-Pythagorean texts and in Philo, see Casel, *De Philosophorum,* pp. 51-86.

56. On the concept of spiritual sacrifice and worship, see also Richard Reitzenstein, *Die hellenistischen Mysterienreligionen* (Stuttgart: Teubner, 1927) pp. 328-29; Lietzmann, *Römer,* pp. 108-9; the extensive study by Philipp Seidensticker, *Lebendiges Opfer (Röm. 12,1)* (Münster: Aschendorff, 1954), is totally unsatisfactory from the point of view of the history of religion.

57. This is demonstrated with impressive clarity above all by Boobyer.

58. "My God will remedy your want according to his glorious riches in Jesus Christ."

59. For the titular usage of the name Χριστός in the Pauline literature, see Bornkamm, *Ges. Aufs.* I, p. 40, and pp. 105-7 and 120-21 below.

60. On this phenomenon of individual New Testament epistles not infrequently being in their entirety the interpretation of a traditional creedal formula quoted in the opening of the letter, see Bornkamm, "Das Bekenntnis im Hebräerbrief," *Ges. Aufs.* II, p. 199 n. 25.

61. Compare Schmithals, "Philipper," and especially Helmut Köster, "The Purpose of the Polemic of a Pauline Fragment (Phil. III)," *NTS* 8 (1962): 317-32.

62. This similarity has been pointed out primarily by Schmithals ("Philipper"). Schmithals gives no consideration, however, to the most important link between both adversary positions to that of Paul: nomism—whose clearest expression is to be seen in the demand for circumcision. Köster emphasized this feature by drawing up an essentially convincing picture of these opponents. Köster might have given sharper outlines to the relationship between these opponents and those in Galatians, at the expense of parallels to II Cor.—the fact being that nomism and pneumaticism are interconnected in Gal. 3–6 and Phil. 3, but not in II Cor. Moreover, if the religio-historical analysis were supplemented by a form-critical analysis of the Philippian fragment, Köster's findings would gain even more profile. For more on this, see p. 193 n. 64.

63. Against Schmithals, "Philipper," pp. 297-99 and 311-38.

64. It can be shown that Paul has cast this fragmentarily preserved letter in the genre of a last will—not, however, without characteristic updating modifications. This explains the doubling of the polemics and their occurrence in two different passages separated particularly by long biographical self-description, whose polemical coloring may not be immediately obvious but is undeniable. On the genre of the Jewish testament, see Klaus Baltzer, *Das Bundesformular* (Neukirchen-Vluyn: Neukirchener Verlag, 1964), pp. 142-67). The discrepancies between 3:2-4 and 3:18-19 are best accounted for if one assumes that in 3:18 Paul still has the real opponents in mind but, in accordance with the typical pattern of the final section of the last will genre (that is, benediction and curse, reversed in this case), provides a generalized universal warning (in this regard see esp. verse 18*a*), for which he makes use of conventional polemics from Jewish last wills and similar traditions. He may be able to keep his remarks at the general level because the opponents have yet to establish a foothold among the Philippians. Later this kind of attack became the blueprint for anti-heretical polemics in the post-Pauline and early Catholic literature, as in the Pastoral Epistles and the Epistle of Jude. The other parallel to Phil. 3:17ff. is Rom. 16:17-18 (see pp. 111-12 below; also compare the deutero-Pauline example in Col. 2:23*b* with 2:16-19; on this question see also Bornkamm, "Die Häresie des Kolosserbriefes," *Ges. Aufs.* I, pp. 151-52). When compared to Gal. 5:1-26 the generalizing traits of Phil. 3:17-19 (and Rom. 16:17-18) become particularly apparent.

65. This I conclude on the basis of the link between II Cor. 1:8-9 and 2:12-13. The entire passage from 1:8 to 2:13 is written with an itinerary from Ephesus to Macedonia in mind. Paul has to explain this to the Corinthians in 1:12 to 2:11. Second Cor. 1:10-11 draws the conclusion from 1:8-9 and has the stylistic function of rounding up the proemium. Hence, 2:12-13 actually constitutes the follow-up of 1:8-9. See also Acts 19:22 and Appendix 1, p. 135-36 below.

4. THE COLLECTION IS RESUMED FOR A SECOND TIME (SPRING AND SUMMER, 55 C.E.)

1. "Also when we arrived in Macedonia, there was no rest for our flesh, but we were harassed in all possible ways: on the outside, quarrels; on the inside, anxieties" (II Cor. 7:5).

2. Walter Bauer, *BAG* see μάχη.

3. See Windisch, *2 Korinther*, pp. 226-27. His presumption can be confirmed to a high degree.

4. Windisch draws attention to this parallelism, but fails to exploit his findings (*Korinther,* p. 224).

5. Paul achieves the same end through the surprising terminological composition of πλοῦτος τῆς ἁπλότητος. On the manifold connotations of ἁπλότης, see pp. 101-2 and 105-6 below.

6. The usage of this term (χάρις) in I Cor. 16:3 is very close in meaning to that in II Cor. 8:4, 6-7, and 19—that is, to the majority of cases in which the expression occurs in II Cor. 8 and 9. But the manner in which χάρις is bound up with God's action becomes more apparent in 8:1, and naturally even more so in 8:9—indeed, this connection is established with greater clarity in this context than in I Cor. 16. I shall come back to this peculiar oscillating terminology below.

7. Paul also uses linguistic means to indicate the factual connection that exists between the conduct of the Macedonians and the activities Titus is to initiate in the Corinthian congregation. The mention of his request that Titus go to Corinth and the comment concerning the zeal shown by the Macedonians are bound up in one and the same sentence—in one breath, as it were: "But they gave themselves above all to the Lord, and then also to us through the will of God, [thus inducing us] to request Titus to bring to an end this work of grace as he had begun [it] a year earlier, with you." (In this connection, see also vv. 16-17; compare also the next note.)

8. Verses 16-17 read as follows (according to Lietzmann's rendering): "Thanks be to God, who put the same zeal the Macedonians showed [also] in Titus' heart for you, so that he accepted our request—indeed, in his overwhelming zeal he volunteered to leave for you." (Here, Paul uses the aorist of epistolary style.)

9. Verse 18 reads as follows: "But with him we sent our brother [X], whose fame in matters of preaching the Gospel has spread through all the congregations. But he not only [excels in this], he was also elected by the congregations as our traveling companion in this work of grace taken care of by us (διακονεῖσθαι) for the honor of the Lord himself and as [evidence] of our willingness." The πρὸς τὴν αὔτου κτλ is better understood as referring to διακονουμένῃ, not to χειροτονηθείς.

10. Against Lietzmann and Kümmel, *An die Korinther,* p. 136.

11. For evidence see Windisch on this passage.

12. This question is raised and discussed in great length by Munck (*Paul,* pp. 296-97), but, understandably, without arriving at any definite results. Still, Munck eliminates the Achaian and Macedonian congregations as participants in the election.

13. Windisch could be right in supposing that this unnamed man "was an itinerant preacher or community leader of great ecumenical esteem" (*Korinther,* p. 262).

14. This view (worded in an unwieldy participial construction) on the

man's qualifications was put forward by Paul as his own opinion, not as that of the congregations. Their zeal and their trust were to sweep the Corinthians along in the same movement. Paul, however, trod more carefully: "(We) shall endeavour to prevent anyone from denigrating us in the face of the rich returns we were able to achieve (διακονεῖσθαι)." Paul backs up his prudence with a wisdom saying from the Jewish Bible (Prov. 3:4 LXX): "For we are concerned about what is worthy of praise not only in God's judgement, but also in the judgement of people." By adding *οὐ μόνον . . . ἀλλά* and the second *ἐνώπιον* to the original biblical sentence, Paul makes it clear that he is particularly concerned about the good judgment of people—an idea already hinted at in the original biblical aphorism, but all the more significant because Paul decides to give even greater emphasis to the wisdom component. He does so because he is as interested in comprehensibility and reasonableness as in spirituality. This aspect of Paul's thinking is even more obvious in chapter 9.

15. The usages of *μωμᾶσθαι* listed in *BAG*, include "to deride," "to scorn," and "to debunk."

16. Windisch draws attention to this.

17. "But together with him we sent our [other] brother [Y], whom we have tested often at many occasions as being eager, but now as even more eager, because of this great confidence in you."

18. See Günther Bornkamm, *Die Vorgeschichte des sogenannten Zweiten Korintherbriefes*, SHAW. PH 2, 1961 (Heidelberg: Winter, 1965) pp. 31-32.

19. In the following discussion I have basically relied on Windisch's findings (*Korinther*, pp. 286-88).

20. On the other hand, verse 9:1 is to be explained by verse 9:2: "For I know your willingness, which—in so far as you are concerned—I have praised before the Macedonians [by saying], Achaia has been ready for a year, and your eagerness has encouraged the majority." "[But] I am sending these brothers so that our praise of you won't be empty in this respect, so that you are made ready in the way I was saying, so that when the Macedonians come with me and find you not made ready, we—not to say 'you'—will not be put to shame in this confident state of mind."

21. There is yet another difference. In II Cor. 8, Paul speaks mostly of ἡμεῖς, while in II Cor. 9. ἐγώ is predominant.

22. On this, see Hans Windisch (*Korinther*, p. 286), who gives a listing of those details in chapter 9 that provide complementary information to chapter 8, and of data featured in chapter 8, but not in chapter 9. Windisch rightly defines chapters 8 and 9 as "two separate and self-contained conceptions of the same subject-matter" (p. 287).

23. See Windisch, *Korinther*, p. 288.

24. There is also a certain lack of smoothness in style that might be

seen as indicative of the break between II Cor. 8 and 9. Second Cor. 8:24 constitutes "a torn-off sentence" (see ibid., p. 267).

25. It seems quite impossible that Titus and his companions were carrying not only their own letter of recommendation to the Corinthians but also a circular letter for the congregations in Achaia (as opposed to Windisch, *Korinther*, p. 288).

5. THE LETTER OF RECOMMENDATION FOR TITUS AND HIS COMPANIONS (II Cor. 8)

1. As can be seen by the following survey of passages dealing with the collection:

τῶν πτωχῶν μνημονεύειν (Gal. 2:10).
ἡ λογεία ἡ εἰς τοὺς ἁγίους (I Cor. 16:1).
ἡ χάρις ὑμῶν (I Cor. 16:3).
ἡ χάρις ἡ δεδομένη (II Cor. 8:1).
τὸ πλοῦτος τῆς ἁπλότητος (8:2).
χάρις (8:4, 6, 7, 19).
κοινωνία τῆς διακονίας τῆς εἰς τοὺς ἁγίους (8:4).
προθυμία τοῦ θέλειν - ἐπιτελέσαι ἐκ τοῦ ἔχειν (8:11 ff.).
ἰσότης
περίσσευμα-ὑστέρημα
ὑστέρημα-περίσσευμα
ἰσότης (8:13f.).
ἡ χάρις
ἡ διακονουμένη ὑφ᾽ ἡμῶν πρὸς τὴν αὐτοῦ τοῦ κυρίου δόξαν καὶ προθυμίαν ἡμῶν (8:19).
ἡ ἁδρότης, ἡ διακονουμένη ὑφ᾽ ἡνῶν (8:20).
ἡ ἔνδειξις τῆς ἀγάπης ὑμῶν καὶ ἡμῶν καυχήσεως ὑπὲρ ὑμῶν (8:24).
ἡ διακονία ἡ είς τοὺς ἁγίους (9:1).
ἡ προθυμία ὑμῶν (9:2).
ἡ προεπηγγελμένη εὐλογία (9:5).
ἁπλότης (9:11).
ἡ διακονία τῆς λειτουργίας ταύτης (9:12)
ἡ δοκιμὴ τῆς διακονίας ταύτης (9:13).
ἡ ὑποταγὴ τῆς ὁμολογίας ὑμῶν είς τὸ εὐαγγέλιον τοῦ Χριστοῦ (9:13).
ἡ ἁπλότης τῆς κοινωνίας εἰς αὐτοὺς καὶ εἰς πάντας (9:13).
διακονεῖν τοῖς ἁγίοις (Rom. 15:25).
κοινωίαν ποιεῖν εἰς τοὺς πτωχοὺς τῶν ἁγίων τῶν ἐν Ἰερουσαλήμ (15:26).
ὀφείλειν-λειτουργεῖν
πνευματικά-σαρκικά (15:27).

σφραγίζεσθαι αὐτοῖς τὸν καρπὸν τοῦτον (15:28).
πλήρωμα εὐλογίας Χριστοῦ (15:29).

2. Windisch succeeds in clearly indentifying the particulars of style inherent in both these chapters; unfortunately, however, the conclusions he draws from his findings are mostly limited to mere psychological considerations.

3. See Windisch, *2 Korinther,* p. 243.

4. See pp. 69-72 above.

5. See Windisch, *2 Korinther,* p. 245.

6. See ibid., p. 247.

7. Georgi, *Opponents,* pp. 27-32.

8. In II Cor. 9:1 and Rom. 15:31 the term *διακονία* carries with it the same connotations as in II Cor. 8:4. *Κοινωνία* and *χάρις* also refer to the communal connection, although *χάρις* rather tends to stand for "work of grace"—that is to say, it points toward the incentive out of which the action is born.

9. See p. 194 n. 7 above.

10. See Windisch, *Korinther,* pp. 249-50.

11. See Friedrich Wilhelm Blaß and Albert Debrunner, *A Greek Grammar of the New Testament and Other Early Christian Literature,* trans. and rev. Robert Funk (Chicago: University of Chicago Press, 1961), § 387, 3.

12. The sentence clearly implies an exhortation.

13. "I am not speaking as if to give you an order; but I am testing the authenticity of your love by means of the eagerness of others." This sentence creates many difficulties for interpreters and is most often explained in a psychologizing fashion.

14. Paul's allusion is probably also meant to provide a hint of the reconciliation that has happened before.

15. That we are dealing here with a traditional formula can be seen from the reciprocal, even chiastic, structure and the sharp succinctness of the statement clearly standing out against the surrounding text, which, as shall be shown presently, gains its theological significance only (indeed, precisely!) because the formula is used here. But the formula is neither prepared nor developed in the surrounding text.

16. As Windisch (*Korinther,* p. 252) and Lietzmann and Kümmel (*An die Korinther,* p. 134) have seen correctly.

17. This is the view held by most scholars, even by Windisch, Lietzmann, and Kümmel, who give a correct rendering of the content of the verse. Nonetheless, they argue that the meaning and the applicability of the verse flows from the exemplifying character of the occurrence to which it refers.

18. "I [only] give you an opinion on this affair."

19. For a detailed discussion of the literary style of this passage,

compare again Windisch, *2 Korinther*, pp. 256ff. Verses 11-13 read approximately as follows: "But now, also bring to an end [your] action, so that, as with your eagerness, your completion of the task be on the basis of having. For insofar as there is eagerness, it is pleasing according to what one has, not according to what one does not have. This is not that there should be for others peace and for you affliction, but equity."

20. For the translation of verse 13, see n. 19 above. Verses 14 and 15 run as follows: "At this point in time your abundance [is added] to their want, so that also their want be added to your abundance, in order that equity occur, as it is written: 'He who had much, did not have more, and he who had little, did not have less.' "

21. This term occurs only once more in the New Testament, in Col. 4:1.

22. See Gustav's Stählin's article "ἴσος κτλ" in *TDNT*, vol. 3, pp. 343ff. For the issue under debate here, see esp. pp. 345ff.

23. Ibid., pp. 347, 354-55.

24. Ibid., p. 346.

25. This was proven by Emile Bréhier, *Les idées philosphiques et religieuses de Philon d'Alexandrie* (Paris: A. Picard, 1950) pp. 86ff., and Wilhelm Bousset, *Jüdisch-christlicher Schulbetrieb in Alexandrien und Rom* (Göttingen: Vandenhoeck & Ruprecht, 1915), pp. 23-89.

26. See von Rad, *Old Testament Theology*, pp. 446-53.

27. Ibid., pp. 382-83; see also Wisd. Sol. 1–4.

28. Particularly in chaps. 7–9.

29. See Georgi, "Phil. 2:6-11," pp. 276-78.

30. II Cor. 8:15.

31. Even in those instances where Wisd. Sol. borrows from the Exodus tradition (chaps. 11–19), it remains completely unhistoric. See Georgi, "Phil. 2:6-11," passim; *Opponents*, pp. 58; 70 n. 81; 181-82 n. 59; 202-3 nn. 288-89.

32. See Windisch, *2 Korinther*, p. 259.

33. As, for instance, ibid., p. 258.

34. See also *BAG*, ἰσότης.

35. In analogy to the γένηται in the following final clause, I complete the syntactical structure by adding the lacking finite verb γίνεται in the first half of the sentence (see Windisch, *Korinther*, p. 258) and translate (according to *BAG*) γίνεσθαι as "to come."

36. This difficulty is realized by all exegetes.

37. Hans Joachim Schoeps, *Paul* (Philadelphia: Westminster Press, 1961), pp. 95-110.

38. See also Or. Sib. 7, 149.

39. This can be gathered from the Pauline letters wherever one looks. Had Paul truly been inclined to Apocalypticism, his first Epistle to the

Thessalonians would have been drafted differently; most important, I Thess. 5:1-10 would never have been written. And as for the first Epistle to the Corinthians, it would not have amounted to more than chap. 15 and a few other phrases here and there. Nor would Paul have composed II Cor. 4–5 or Phil. 3:7-21 or Rom. 10. But Paul was never—not even before his calling—a pure Apocalypticist, as he never was a pure Gnostic.

40. A detailed picture of Israel's theological wisdom is provided by von Rad (*Theology* I. pp. 491ff.).

41. As, for instance, the equalization of Law and Wisdom, the cosmological orientation of both, and a number of other points.

42. No doubt both traditions are predominantly interested in stressing the necessity of distancing oneself from world and history in order to reach salvation. But, whereas Hellenistic-Jewish Gnostic wisdom is aiming at the dissolution of history, Apocalyptic wisdom is concerned with its momentous annihilation. In other words, in one case there is the idea of presently ongoing salvation, in the other there is the expectation of a sovereign act of divine power carrying salvation in its wake.

43. That this is so can easily be seen from the way Paul handles a whole series of theologically relevant concepts, such as christology, righteousness, knowledge, charisma, law, ethics, and so on. Given the limits of this study, these issues can be pursued only selectively, most of all in the context of the conception of worship.

44. This seems particularly plausible in light of Haenchen's theory (*Acts*, p. 298) that Paul had persecuted Jesus believers only in Damascus and never in Jerusalem. This presupposes a high-ranking position for Paul in the self-administration of the Jewish congregation in Damascus—a position that could only be arrived at in that century-old, very large (approximately 10,000 members), and renowned Diaspora congregation if one had been a resident of the city for a considerable time. At the same time, given the proximity to Palestine and the location of Damascus in one of the major areas of Hellenistic syncretism the situation was particularly favorable for head-on collisions between various trends of Jewish thought. The third branch of Jewish wisdom, missionary theology, was familiar to Paul also (see *Opponents*, passim).

45. See Windisch, *Korinther*, pp. 257-58, and Lietzmann and Kümmel, *An die Korinther*, p. 134; see also the explanations given on page 135.

46. On this, consult the authors mentioned in the previous footnote. See also Alfred Plummer, *A Critical and Exegetical Commentary on the Second Epistle of St. Paul to the Corinthians* (Edinburgh: T & T Clark, 1951), pp. 244-45. Hereafter referred to as *II Corinthians*.

47. Gustav Stählin, "*ἴσος, ἰσότης, ἰσότιμος*" *TDNT* 3, p. 348.

6. THE CIRCULAR LETTER TO THE ACHAIAN CONGREGATIONS

1. Verse 5 reads as follows: "I therefore considered it a necessity to ask the brothers and sisters to come to see you before [that time] and to prepare beforehand your promised gift, so that it be ready, as an abundant gift [should be], not like a gift painfully wrung out of miserliness."

2. See Windisch, *Korinther,* p. 276.

3. This is particularly clear from I Sam. 25:27, but also from Gen. 33:11 and II Kings 5:5. First Sam. 30:26 seems also to point in that direction.

4. In verse 6 in the adverbial expression ἐπ' εὐλογίαις, the term εὐλογία also carries the same derived, metaphorical meaning it holds, "in plenty," "in handfulls," as in verse 5.

5. See Windisch, *Korinther,* p. 276.

6. See Job 4:8; Prov. 22:8; Sir. 7:3; compare also Prov. 11:21, 24 (LXX).

7. See Test. Lev. 13:6; Philo, Deus Imm. 166; Conf. Ling. 21; 152; Mut. Nom. 269; Leg. Gaj. 293; Quest. Gen. II 52—partly in analogy to certain corresponding Greek and Hellenistic phrases; Hes. Fgm. 174; Plato, Phaedr. 260 D; Arist. Rhet. 3.3,4; Demosth., 280:27; Plut. Mor. 394 D; Cicero, De Ord. 2:65, 261.

8. Apocalyptic thinking radicalized this motif under the influence of the metaphorical language of the later prophets, as per Joel 4:12-15; Isa. 27:11-12. But compare also Hos. 6:11 and Isa. 9:2, where the metaphor of harvest is already used in the sense of eschatological judgment.

9. See Ezr. 4:28ff; S. Bar. 702; compare also Matt. 13:39; Mark 4:29; Rev. 14:15-20, and the Hellenistic parallel Plut. Mor. 182 A.

10. See Prov. 3:27-28; 10:2; 11; 17:23-26; 14:31; 19:17; 21:26; 22:2, 9; 23:10-11; 24:11-12; and Sir. 3:30. Compare also the wisdom Psalm 36:21, a preparatory step to the forerunner to wisdom in Deut. 15:10. To a considerable extent wisdom presupposes Deuteronomistic preaching patterns. See also von Rad, *Old Testament Theology,* pp. 443-44.

11. This is best evidenced by the Epistle of Aristeas; Aristobulus; Pseudo-Heraclitus; Pseudo-Menander; Pseudo-Phocylides; II, III, and (especially) IV Maccabees; Philo's apologetic writings; and Josephus. Such works of Gnostic wisdom as Wisd. Sol. and Philo's allegorical commentary clearly borrowed from the Cynic-Stoic diatribe, both in terms of rhetoric and content. This is most easily explained by the fact that Gnostic wisdom had developed out of missionary wisdom (Jewish Apologetics), its immediate forerunner.

12. For the opposition between free decision and coercion and

between pain and free decision see Epictetus 3.83 and 3.1.1-2.

13. See Sir. 13:26; 26:4.

14. See Plant. 166-67; Vit. Mos. 2:21; Spec. Leg. 1:69; 2:48; Vit. Cont. 40; 77 (that is to say, passages stemming almost exclusively from missionary wisdom).

15. See Leg. Gaj. 12; 180. For scriptural evidence of Jewish wisdom apart from Prov. 22:8, see Prov. 22:12; Job 33:26; Sir. 35:8 (32:11) together with vv. 7 and 9; Ep. Ar. 18. The same concepts were to recur afterwards in Rabbinic literature. (See Bultmann, *TDNT* 3, esp. p. 786, n. 18; ThWB, III, p. 299, here esp. n. 4).

16. A good example for this idea is, of course, the text Plant. 166-67, reflecting Gnostic wisdom, but also the Apologetical text Spec. Leg. 2:48 and its context.

17. ἀγαπᾶν: Rom. 8:37; Gal. 2:20. ἀγάπη: Rom. 5:8 (compare to 5:5); 8:35, 39; II Cor. 5:14; 13:11, 13. In II Cor. 5:14 Christ's love is paraphrased as the "space" in which the believers exist.

18. "Judaism and the Gentile world, as well as Christianity, believe that cheerfulness belongs to the inner freedom of generosity. . . . What is Christian is not the thought itself but the new motivation suggested by the context in Rom. 12:8 (cf. 12:1ff.) and II Cor. 9:7 (cf 8:9; 9:8ff.) and expressly stated in I Pet. 4:9f. Reception of the gift of God makes us cheerful and drives out γογγυσμοί." Bultmann, *TDNT* 3, p. 299.

19. As Windisch puts it, as if with regret (*Korinther*, p. 277).

20. See ibid.

21. This was correctly pointed out by Lietzmann and Kümmel (*An die Korinther*, p. 207). The same terminological particularity is found also in other Pauline texts (Rom. 2:15; I Cor. 3:13-17; 9:1; 15:58; 16:10; Gal. 6:4; Phil. 1:6, 22; 2:30; and I Thess. 1:3; compare also Rom. 14:20; 15:18; and II Cor. 10:11).

22. See Hans Jonas, *Augustin und das paulinische Freiheitsproblem* (Göttingen: Vandenhoeck & Ruprecht, 1965), pp. 6-10.

23. See Windisch, *Korinther*, p. 278.

24. Käsemann's essay on Paul's concept of divine righteousness does not make this clear. The objective of this impressive article—namely, to give a precise idea of what is meant by the sovereignty and universality of divine righteousness as aspects of the "theologia crucis"—could have been fully attained, had Käsemann paid full attention to the width of Paul's doctrine of justification in terms of its subject matter, its motifs, and its linguistic and stylistic expression. (See Ernst Käsemann, "Gottesgerechtigkeit bei Paulus," *ZThK* 58 (1961): 367-78.)

25. See Plummer, *II Corinthians*, p. 261.

26. See Friedrich Horst, "Gerechtigkeit Gottes, II, Im AT und Judentum," *RGG* 2, col. 1405.

27. See also the Hosea quotation in Rom. 9:25-6.

28. See Windisch and Lietzmann, *Korinther*; see also Bauer, *BAG*, *δικαιοσύνη*, 2a.

29. That v. 11 is the direct follow-up of v. 10 (and not of v. 8) is convincingly established by Plummer, *II Corinthians*, p. 264, and Windisch, *2 Korinther*, pp. 280-81.

30. Like most other exegetes, I relate *τῷ θεῷ* to *εὐχαριστία*.

31. Bauer, *BAG* (*διακονία* 4) translates the term "kind contribution"; he obviously agrees with Plummer (*A Critical and Exegetical Commentary on the Second Epistle of St. Paul to the Corinthians*, p. 265) and Windisch (*Korinther*, p. 281) in interpreting the genitive *τῆς λειτουργίας* as a genitivus exegeticus. But since v. 12 gives the reason for the relative clause in v. 11, it clearly refers to the concrete situation prevailing at Jerusalem at the time. Hence, the *δι' ἡμῶν* can only be meant in conjunction with the handing over of the collection (namely, the *διακονία* in v. 12; see also II Cor. 8:19-20, where the usage of *διακονεῖσθαι* already hints at the interpretation required here). There can be no doubt, therefore, about how the *δοκιμὴ τῆς διακονίας* in v. 13 is to be understood, because v. 13 clearly also comments on v. 12*b*. It must be concluded, therefore, that v. 13 can only refer to the test implied in the conveyance of the collection and that the *διά* in that v. must be translated as "induced by"; it runs parallel to the *δι' ἡμῶν* in v. 11.

32. Πολλῶν is clearly an adjectival attributive of *εὐχαριστῶν*, not a noun used in an attributive sense; hence, the meaning can only be: "the thanksgiving of the many."

33. Hence, the passage constitutes the explanation for II Cor. 8:14.

34. See Boobyer, *"Thanksgiving,"* pp. 2-3, 79ff.

35. Boobyer also studies the role played by Jewish thought within the overall conception (*"Thanksgiving,"* pp. 8ff., 16ff., 30ff., and 56ff.). Today we know that the internal Jewish development (and, in this context, especially that of Philo) had much greater impact on this development in its entirety. But also from any number of other points of view certain corrective modifications are called for as regards the general understanding of the historical unfolding of this religious movement.

36. See Rom. 15:5-13; II Cor. 1:11, 20; 4:15-6; and Phil. 2:11.

37. See Boobyer, *"Thanksgiving,"* p. 70.

38. Ibid.

39. Textual evidence for this is to be found (amongst others) in Philo. (Rer. Div. Her. 226-27, 199; this is the segment of school-tradition of Hellenistic-Jewish Gnostic wisdom already referred to above in conjunction with the concept of *ἰσότης*. In this connection, also see Appendix 2; similar passages also exist in Philo, Leg. All. 1.82). The

clearest expression of this tradition is, however, given in Corp. Herm. I, 26-27; 30ff.; and XIII, 16ff. It is my opinion that Hermetic Gnosticism and Hellenistic-Jewish Gnostic wisdom were related to each other. The findings accumulated by Boobyer are supplemented by Paul Schubert, *Form and Function of the Pauline Thanksgivings* (Berlin: Töpelmann, 1939), pp. 122-31, esp. pp. 124-25.

40. As used in this instance, Plummer (*II Corinthians,* p. 265) and Windisch (*2 Korinther,* pp. 281-82) understand λειτουργία in its classical Greek sense. Plummer writes: "[The term] λειτουργία is used here in a sense closely akin to its classical meaning of 'aids' which wealthy citizens had to render to the public in financing choruses for dramas [Plummer is referring specifically to the χορηγήσει in v. 10, which can also mean "to grant the necessary financial means to the chorus for the drama"], fitting out triremes, training gymnasts, etc. These public munera were enforced by law, but St. Paul uses the word of voluntary service." Windisch goes beyond this and argues that in this meaning of the word, the term well mirrors the idea of the collection as a manifestation of the spirit of solidarity within the church and the unity of Christ's body. But, however nicely this reading seems to fit (the church as a πόλις, although of course a πόλις of its own kind), the Greek understanding of the term implies the legal responsibility of individual citizens, and there is no proof that the term was used in a figurative sense. Furthermore, its usage in the LXX is especially weighty for the historical analysis of the term. In the LXX λειτουργός, λειτουργία, and λειτουργεῖν refer to priestly service (evidence in *BAG* and Hans Strathmann, *TDNT* 4, p. 219 (λειτουργός κτλ). For this meaning of the term a figurative usage can be shown. In Sir. 4:14 it is said of the λατρεύοντες ἀυτῇ (e.g., to wisdom) that they λειτουργήσουσιν ἁγίῳ (God). See also Wisd. Sol. 18:21; Sir. 24:10; Dan. 7:10, and Strathmann, *TDNT,* pp. 221-22, on the same question. With even greater clarity than in these LXX texts, the relatedness of this terminology to spiritual worship becomes apparent in Philo (see also Strathmann, *TDNT 4,* p. 222). All this—and this is the heart of the matter—leads directly to the theological background of II Cor. 9:11-15. I am of the opinion that Paul never implies anything else but priestly services when he speaks of λειτουργός, λειτουργία, λειτουργεῖν—except in Rom. 13:1-7, where we are dealing with a passage taken directly from tradition. But when Paul uses this terminology, he does so without the original cultic aspects. He excludes any sacrality. All Pauline references to the derivatives of λειτουργ—except Rom. 13:6—mean the λογικὴ λατρεία of Rom. 12:1-2. More on this on pp. 106-7 and 119-20, below, and in the afterword, passim.

41. See p. 202 n. 31 above.

42. There will be a δοκιμὴ τῆς διακονίας ταύτης in Jerusalem. For a concrete discussion on this, see p. 202, n. 31 above. Verse 13 gives the corresponding explanation through direct reference to the beginning of vv. 15*a* and *b*. This explains the syntactical difficulties encountered here. The participle δοξάζοντες stands totally unattached in this construction.

43. In my translation of this syntactically difficult sentence I have attempted to render the parallel character of sections 13*b* and 13*c*, e.g., the parallel position of the two constructions depending on ἐπί. The sentence starts out with a dative followed by a genitive and, finally, a turn of speech with εἰς. This parallel construction does not allow one to link εἰς εὐαγγέλιον with ὑποταγή, as εἰς αὐτούς belongs to κοινωνίας. Consequently, ὑποτγή is not a nomen actionis ("self-surrender"), but means "obedience"; τῆς ὁμλογίας is just as much a genitivus epexegeticus as τῆς κοινωνίας. The sequence ὑποταγή τῆς ὁμολογίας is parallel to ὑπακοὴ τῆς πίστεως in Rom. 1:5 (see Lietzmann and Kümmel, *An die Korinther*, p. 139; see also Bultmann, *Theology*, p. 315, as well as *TDNT* 6 (πιστεύω), pp. 205-6, 218; ὑπακοὴ τῆς πίστεως refers to obedience born from faith. Bultmann also shows that for Paul faith is the same as its confession (*Theology*, pp. 317ff.; *TDNT* 6 (πιστεύω), p. 218).

44. The antecedent of the relative pronoun ἥτις is ἁπλότης.

45. For the second half of the sentence, the translation given by Lietzmann and Kümmel is chosen (*An die Korinther*, p. 138).

46. Καὶ αὐτῶν . . . ἐπιποθούντων is a genitive absolute construction. There is no change of subject. Δεήσει is a dative of precision (here I follow Windisch, *Korinther*, p. 285).

47. For the Pauline concept of λογικὴ λατρεία, see Ernst Käsemann, "Gottesdienst im Alltag der Welt (zu Röm 12)" in *Judentum-Urchristentum-Kirche*, eds. Joachim Jeremias and Walther Eltester (Berlin: Töpelmann, 1964).

48. See *BAG*, p. 272, δωρεά.

49. Compare II Cor. 8:3—although here Paul makes no differentiation between public and private assets.

50. Compare especially II Cor. 9:7-11.

51. On the theology of the work of the chronicler, see von Rad, *Old Testament Theology*, pp. 347-54.

7. CLOSURE OF THE COLLECTION AND PLANNING OF THE JOURNEY TO JERUSALEM (WINTER 55/56 C.E.)

1. For the reasons for considering Rom. 16 a fragment of an epistle written to the Ephesians, see Michaelis, *Einleitung in das Neues Testament*

(Bern: Haller, 1961), pp. 160-64. In connection with the present study it is only of secondary importance to establish where exactly that fragment begins and where it ends. On this see also Walter Schmithals, "Die Irrlehrer von Röm. 16:17-20." *StTh* 13, 1 (1959): 52ff. Recently the inclusion of Romans 16 into the original Epistle to the Romans has been defended again, especially by Ulrich Wilckens, *Der Brief an die Römer,* Evangelisch-katholischer Kommentar zum Neuen Testament 6 (Zurich: Benziger & Neukirchen, 1978), pp. 24-27; vol. 23 (1982), pp. 131-46, and Wolf Henning Ollrog, "Die Abfassungsverhältnisse von Röm 16," in *Kirche,* eds. Dieter Lührmann and Georg Strecker (Tübingen: Mohr, 1979), pp. 221-24. Both use the present textual arrangement as their strongest argument. But despite its defense by Kurt Aland, quoted by both, the textual tradition of the last three chapters of Romans shows a more than usual uncertainty about the concluding greetings. The doxology in 16:25-27 is definitely secondary, added by a later redactor who thus testifies to his manipulation, a rearrangement which makes further intrusions into the given text, particularly compilations, possible, even probable; for why should this hand have limited itself just to the final verses? Romans 16:25-27 gives clues to the theological intentions of this editor in his working over of the document received. His hermeneutical interest is to turn the Epistle to the Romans into a foundational document of the church. Transporting all the names of people greeted in chapter 16 to Rome made Paul appear that familiar with the church in Rome that he almost could count as a member of that congregation. Thus the letter to the Roman church gained the appearance of a letter from Rome. The touches of farewell contained in the original letter to Ephesus (Rom. 16), including the polemical warnings, after transmitted into the new context of Romans, changed this document into a testament, also from a literary point of view, but now to the church at large. Given this clear editorial intention of the final redactor, who may have been identical with the compiler of the final collection of Pauline and deutero-Pauline letters—that is, also with the Pastoral Epistles—the critical arguments against the integrity of the present arrangement of Romans 16 become all the stronger.

2. See Haenchen, *Acts,* pp. 617-18.

3. Schmithals turns a blind eye to this particularity of the passage and quite mistakenly interprets it as a document dealing with concrete persons and a concrete theological outlook.

4. See Adolf Schlatter, *Die Theologie der Apostel* (Stuttgart: Calwer, 1977) pp. 209-11.

5. Against Lietzmann, *Römer,* p. 163.

6. The following observations are directed against the position taken up by Holl, "Kirchenbegriff," p. 58; Lietzmann, *Römer,* p. 122; and

Bammel, *TDNT* 6 (*πτωχός*), p. 909. Hahn (*Mission in the New Testament*, pp. 108-9) claims that *οἱ πτωχοί* in Rom. 15:26 is to be understood as a traditional title of honor (as also in Gal. 2:10). He does not explain on what grounds this argument is to be accepted, nor does he refute my objections against it. He maintains that the *τῶν ἁγίων* represents a genitivus epexegeticus, but this cannot be the case because of the occurrence of *τοῖς ἁγίοις* already in 15:25 (compare also 15:31). Hence, *οἱ ἅγιοι* constitutes the leading notion of the entire passage. Had Paul wished to make an epexegetical statement in Rom. 15:26, the appropriate formulation would have been *εἰς τοὺς ἁγίους τῶν πτωχῶν*. Contrary to I Cor. 16:1, II Cor. 8:4, and II Cor. 9:1-2, the *οἱ ἅγιοι* in Rom. 15:25-26—not quite the same as what we have in Rom. 15:31—is bound up with an indication of place (that is to say, it is not simply used in an absolute sense, which would imply the knowledge of the locality referred to). This is particularly obvious in 15:26, where the purpose cannot be a more exact description of the itinerary, as Paul had given this already by his statement in 15:25.

7. See pp. 33-34 above.

8. If nothing else, this in itself should suffice to establish as totally unfounded the frequently made statement that Paul had done nothing more than found a group of wildly moving gangs of pneumatics who, because of this fact, were bound to commit enthusiastic suicide shortly after their formation. Quite to the contrary, not only did Paul himself constitute a strong protection against enthusiastic flare-ups in his congregations, but also the congregations themselves did their best to counter all possible confusion of spirit and chaos. The most impressive example here is the congregation at Corinth. Besides, one should not forget that Paul was assisted in this work by very competent fellow workers.

9. The *καί* is to be understood exegetically.

10. Could it be that only these congregations are listed here because the Macedonian and Achaian communities were the only ones to espouse enthusiastically the project of the collection as their own responsibility?

11. See *Opponents*, pp. 98-100, 152-53, 238-42.

12. Compare I Cor. 9 with II Cor. 2:16; 11:7-8; and 12:11-18.

13. Perhaps the translation in *BAG* for *κοινωνία*—"proof of brotherly unity"—would be even more to the point if the sisters are included.

14. Munck (*Paul*, pp. 299ff.) is right in stressing that the issue dealt with in Rom. 9–11 must be seen in conjunction with the text under debate here. Munck is also correct in holding that Paul's statements in Rom. 9–11 are bound up with his own missionary experiences and, thus, possess eminently practical reference. However, he argues quite

erroneously that chapters 9–11 depict the bankruptcy of the missions of Peter and other preachers among the Jews, while stressing the success of the mission among the Gentiles. This theory fails utterly to account for the factual and theological, not to mention the biographical, difficulties and questions these chapters present.

15. As rightly observed by Munck, *Paul*, pp. 303ff.

16. See Haenchens's interpretation of Acts 20:3, *Acts*, pp. 581-83.

17. Munck's assumption (*Paul*, pp. 305ff.) that Paul had traveled to Jerusalem in the multiple roles of the one propitiating for his people, the one proclaiming the representatives of the Gentile converts as "sons of God," the one who had contemplated already his confession in front of the governing authorities, and the one incorporating the second Elias, seems absurd to me.

18. On this point, see the reservations formulated on pp. 123-24 above.

19. It would be wrong to go along with Munck (*Paul*, p. 304) in taking Acts 26:6-7 and 28:20 as evidence that Paul saw the journey and the conveyance of the collection to Jerusalem as a signal of eschatological significance.

20. With this exegesis I hope to have done justice to the difficult expression *σφραγισάμενος αὐτοῖς τὸν καρπὸν τοῦτον* ("and sealed for them this fruit of theirs"). I consider this interpretation justified in the light not only of the direct link between this expression and the preceding statement about a giving and a taking (and a returning)—all of which are implied in the notion of "fruit"—but also because "to seal" can quite naturally denote an acknowledgment.

21. Munck (*Paul*, pp. 294-95) suggests that Paul's journey to Jerusalem had given new courage to the apostles in that city, whose morale had suffered from the failure of their own mission among the Jews. Munck also feels that this journey was to inform them of the results of his third mission circuit, the balance-sheet of which is drawn up in the Epistle to the Romans. But this is pure fantasy.

8. THE CONVEYANCE OF THE COLLECTION AND ITS RESULTS (FROM SPRING 56 C.E. TO PAUL'S DEATH)

1. On this list, consult Haenchen, *Acts*, pp. 581-82; Conzelmann, *Acts of the Apostles*, trans. James Linburg et al.; Eldon Jay Epp and Chris Matthews, eds. (Philadelphia: Westminster, 1987), p. 167, hereafter referred to as *Acts*; and Munck, *Paul*, pp. 293-94.

2. All this is true only insofar as the Gaius mentioned here is identical with Paul's Macedonian travel companion, Gaius, referred to in Acts

19:29. If this were the case, this travel companion could have spoken in favor of a collection in Philippi (perhaps his own congregation), while passing through Macedonia with Paul. In the final analysis, however, such reading seems hardly justified as, in that case, the added Δερβαῖος in Acts 20:4 would become totally incomprehensible. As Haenchen (*Acts,* pp. 52-3) and Conzelmann (*Acts,* pp. 167-68) clearly have established, the version Δουβ[ε]ριος constitutes a harmonizing redactional correction with a view to Acts 19:29.

3. The same may be assumed for Titus.

4. See also Haenchen's discussion of this point in *Acts,* pp. 581-82.

5. As correctly assumed by Munck, *Paul,* p. 303.

6. See pp. 119-20 above.

7. Conzelmann's claim (*Acts,* p. 171) that the itinerary described in Acts 20:14 was "construed by the author" is not convincing, because it leaves unexplained the imbalance between v. 15 and the subsequent verses. It is more plausible to assume that Luke, having found the itinerary, had used the mention of Miletus as a basis for including Ephesus in his report in order to provide Paul with an opportunity to give, at least from Miletus, a farewell address to the one congregation to which he, Luke, had granted a dominant position among all other Pauline congregations. The itinerary in Acts 20–21 is best understood as a historically correct rendering precisely because of its "incoherence."

8. For the problems pertaining to ecclesial jurisdiction, see Conzelmann, *Acts,* pp. 179ff.

9. See Haenchen, *Acts,* pp. 606ff. The objection advanced by Klein (Review of "E. Haenchen, Die Apostelgeschichte," in *ZKG* 68 [1957]: 362ff.) and Conzelmann (*Acts,* pp. 179ff.) that the report contained in the source had been biased is not convincing, simply because Paul's arrest can only have occurred within the precincts of the Temple—which means that Paul must have had an opportunity to be in the Temple. The very fact of a Temple visit itself proves a certain faithfulness to tradition on Paul's part. Any later ecclesial reporter who might have wished to change Paul's image and who hoped to achieve his end through stressing Paul's commitment to the Law could have gotten all the evidence he needed from Paul's visit to the Temple (for instance, as a pilgrim) alone and would not have had to come up with the curious episode of the release of the Nazirites to make his point.

10. See Haenchen, *Acts,* pp. 615ff.

APPENDIX 1: THE QUESTION OF CHRONOLOGY

1. Gerd Lüdemann, *Paulus der Heidenapostel: I Studien zur Chronologie,* FRLANT 123 (Göttingen: Vandenhoeck & Ruprecht, 1980); Robert

Jewett, *A Chronology of Paul's Life* (Philadelphia: Fortress Press, 1979), hereafter referred to as *Chronology*.

2. See Ferdinand Hahn, *Mission*, pp. 77-78. This follows earlier such attempts by Julius Wellhausen, *Kritische Analyse der Apostelgeschichte* (Berlin: Weidmann, 1914), hereafter referred to as *Analyse*; Eduard Schwartz, "Zur Chronologie des Paulus," *BZNF* 15 (1971): 265-66; and others; more recently also Herbert Braun, "Christentum; I Entstehung," *RGG*[3] 1, col. 1693.

3. Also in this argument Hahn follows Schwartz. See Hahn, *Mission*, p. 77, n. 3. For more on this question, also see Wellhausen, *Analyse*, pp. 21-22; Friedrich Spitta, "Die neutestamentliche Grundlage der Ansicht von E. Schwartz über den Tod der Söhne Zebedäi"; Eduard Schwartz, "Noch einmal der Tod der Söhne Zebedäi"; and Johannes Weiss, "Zum Märtyrertod der Zebedaiden," all in *ZNW* 11 (1910): 39, 89, 167 respectively. See also Weiss, *Das Urchristentum*, ed. Rudolf Knopf (Göttingen: Vandenhoeck & Ruprecht, 1917), pp. 234, 552-53; and more recently also Günther Klein, "Gal. 2:6-9," pp. 291-2.

4. Surely, one cannot disregard Mark 10:38-39 and go along with the majority of the traditional church documents in assuming that John, the son of Zebedee, died a natural death in Ephesus at a very old age. For data on this tradition, see the evidence gathered by Walter Bauer in Hennecke 3rd ed. II, pp. 24-5. The reader is also referred to the latest findings by Klein ("Gal. 2:6-9," p. 291, n. 4), although Klein's study does not yet mention the apologetically oriented article "Johannes, der Apostel" by Gerhard Delling, in *RGG 3*, cols. 803-4. Mark 10:38-39 clearly presupposes the death of both sons of Zebedee—which means that also John must have died a martyr's death before 70 C.E.—but not necessarily at the same time as his brother. There is no hint of that in Mark 10:38-39, however.

5. See Martin Dibelius, *Aufsätze*, pp. 25-26, 85 n. 1; Hans Conzelmann, *Acts*, p. 71.

6. Conzelmann, ibid. That this link-up is of Lukan origin was already established by Dibelius, *Aufsätze*, pp. 25-26, and Haenchen, *Acts*, pp. 331-32.

7. See Haenchen, *Acts*, p. 62; also see Hahn, *Mission*, pp. 76-7.

8. As shown earlier, the problems cannot be eliminated by placing the name "James" ahead of the others—a view shared also by Haenchen, "Petrus-Probleme," *NTS* 7 (1960/61): 193.

9. See p. 45, above.

10. According to both Haenchen ("Quellenanalyse und Kompositionsanalyse in Act. 15," *Judentum-Urchristentum-Kirche*, BZNW 26, ed. Walther Eltester [Berlin: Töpelmann, 1960], pp. 160ff.) and Conzelmann

(*Acts*, p. 68) the area of mission described here was not smaller in size than the territorial expansion marked by Luke, so far. On the contrary, that territory was enlarged by two further provinces and therefore stretched beyond the area over which Antioch—the inquiring congregation—had established its influence. Regrettably, neither Haenchen nor Conzelmann is able to provide a satisfactory explanation about why none of the territories listed in Acts 13 and 14 is also mentioned here. Even if one accepts the view that, for clarifying this point, it is necessary to include in one's calculations Acts 15:41, the question that arises is why not also Acts 16:4 as well—especially since the parallel nature of Acts 15:23 and 15:41 to Gal. 1:24 cannot be easily disregarded? Besides, neither Haenchen nor Conzelmann has succeeded in establishing the text of the document mentioned here as genuinely Lukan. Hence, Rudolf Bultmann's hypothesis ("Quelle," p. 71) that Luke here uses an earlier source, has not really been proven wrong.

11. The latter date is inferrable on the basis of the Gallio inscription and counting backwards to the date of Paul's departure from Antioch and the beginning of his independent missionary work in Galatia and Europe.

12. See Jewett, *Chronology*, pp. 73-75.

13. In the wake of analogous results arrived at by previous scholars, a similar view has been worked out by Braun, "Christentum," col. 1693.

14. See Gustav Hölscher, *Die Hohenpriesterliste bei Josephus und die evangelische Chronologie* (Heidelberg: Winter, 1939/40), pp. 26-27.

15. The upheavals in Palestine during Pilate's first year in office (mentioned by Josephus) were not political in nature but related to the cult, whereas Jesus' death—at least as regards the juridical aspects of his death sentence—belonged to a political context. Conversely, none of the synoptic Gospels ever mention any controversy the Jews had with the Roman governor on the purity and invulnerability of the Temple. Hence, Josephus's report on the popular unrest yields nothing for the chronology of Jesus.

John 2:20 does not help either. The forty-six years mentioned here as the time it took to erect the Temple cannot contribute to the chronology of Jesus:

1. It is highly questionable whether such a relatively late text, which is laced with dogmatic tendency, can be viewed as preserving dependable historical data—indeed, whether this text is at all interested in historical authenticity.

2. The incident narrated here (even if we accept its historicity for a moment) does not give any clue how it relates the moment of the statement about the three days to the process of construction of the Temple, particularly its last phase, the final, the forty-sixth year. Only if

exact contemporaneity were claimed with the date of conclusion of the restoration of the Temple could the statement be of help. But that is not the case. Even worse, as the comparison with the three days clearly shows, John 2:20 in both cases looks back at a period of time completed, some time, any time after the phase mentioned, the three days as well as the forty-six years of the Temple's construction. Both had come to an end in the meantime, but there is no asserting how many years afterwards.

3. One must consider, that the narrating evangelist (see Bultmann, *The Gospel of John*, pp. 89-90) was not thinking of the year of Jesus' death, but of the time of the first of Jesus' three visits to Jerusalem.

16. See for instance, Joachim Jeremias, *The Eucharistic Words of Jesus*, trans. Arnold Ehrhardt (New York: Macmillan, 1955); German: *Die Abendmahlsworte Jesu* (Göttingen: Vandenhoeck & Ruprecht, 1960), pp. 31-32.

17. Haenchen, *Acts*, p. 449; also see p. 102, above.

18. For this the reader is referred to Georgi, *Opponents*, passim, and the discussion of Schmithals's *Gnosticism in Corinth*, pp. 90-106 (German edition), as well as Günther Bornkamm, *Vorgeschichte*, pp. 8-10.

19. See Haenchen, *Acts*, pp. 60-64.

20. See F. J. Foakes-Jackson and Kirsopp Lake, *The Acts of the Apostles: The Beginnings of Christianity* (New York: Macmillan, 1965), vol. V, pp. 464-67.

21. See Emil Schürer, *The History of the Jewish People in the Age of Jesus Christ (175 B.C–A.D. 135)*, rev. Geza Vermes, Fergus Millar, and Matthew Black, 3 vols. (Edinburgh: T & T Clark, 1987), vol. I, pp. 465-46, n. 42. Hereafter referred to as *History*.

22. See Ant. XX, 137ff., and Bell. Jud. II, 247ff.

23. According to Josephus, Bell. Jud. II. 270, a little prior; according to Ant. XXX, 182ff., shortly after that switch in office. See Schürer, *History*, pp. 579-80

24. See Tacitus, Ann. XIII, 14.

25. Ant. XX, 182.

26. Ann. XIII, 23; compare also Dio LXI, 10.2.

27. Compare also P.v. Rohden, *Art.: M. Antonius Pallas*, in *Paulys Realencyclopadir der classischen Altertumswissenschaft*, ed. Georg Wissowa, Bd I (1894) col. 2634-5.

28. See Hans Conzelmann, "Geschichte, Geschichtsbild und Geschichtsdarstellung bei Lukas," *ThLZ* 85 (1960): col. 243.

29. As can be seen from these considerations, there are no grounds, therefore, on which one could reasonably accept John Knox's radical suggestions for the chronology of Paul. Knox dates the most important phase of Paul's missionary activity—including the mission accomplished in Asia Minor and Greece—prior to the convention at Jerusalem.

In his calculations, he counts only about two years for the time between the second and third (i.e., the last) journey the apostle undertook to Jerusalem. Into this brief period of time Knox has to cram all the ups and downs discussed earlier. Knox's approach appears even less acceptable, because he dates the anti-Pauline opposition very early and relates it to the Jerusalem convention as contributory, even causal. But the conference did not help; even worse, the strife increased afterwards even more.

It has been shown above that the people opposing Paul and Barnabas in Jerusalem had no direct connection with the Galatian opponents. Even less is there evidence for a world-wide opposition against Paul. On the contrary, there must have been quite a variety, as to persons and as to methods and teachings.

Paul's polemical passages in his letters do not—with the exception of Gal. 2, and here only indirectly—relate to the Jerusalem conference, not even in the most obvious polemical passages of the Epistle to the Galatians (3–5). There are names like Peter and Barnabas, issues that could associate the discussions of Jerusalem. But no mention besides Gal. 2, not even in the other collection-passages. Therefore, Paul's silence about the convention outside of Gal. 2 is weighty.

The same is true for the Antioch incident, which must have erupted around a subject matter of the greatest importance for the Pauline mission and the organization of the church as a whole, and is definitely not explained satisfactorily by Knox. In contrast, the view pursued above that Paul carried out an independent missionary work after the convention and the Antioch incident is substantiated by the epistles themselves. In this period the surviving epistles of Paul are our main, most often only, source. Neither the relationship with the Antioch congregation nor that with other missionaries, such as Simon Peter and Barnabas, is depicted as having had any true relevance to the work of Paul.

AFTERWORD: IS THERE JUSTIFICATION IN MONEY? A HISTORICAL AND THEOLOGICAL MEDITATION ON THE FINANCIAL ASPECTS OF JUSTIFICATION BY CHRIST

1. Aristotle treated these categories in his discussion of economy and money, as will be shown further below. In their focus on the ethical dimensions of money, Christian theologians of the Middle Ages and the Reformation strongly emphasized certain issues, like interest, but very much limited themselves to a moralizing approach. Since Marx's critical

contributions to the socioeconomic debate the three categories mentioned have found considerable treatment. Georg Friedrich Knapp has stimulated much debate concerning the state's role in the issue. Concerning the social side of economy and money, Talcott Parsons has furthered the discussion, building on George Herbert Mead, Max Weber, and Emile Durkheim. See also note 3.

2. This relationship of economy/money and the legal order has been seen by Aristotle. In modern times Georg Friedrich Knapp has stressed also the legal element in his monetary theory. Naturally, the negative sides of the relationship between the monetary and the legal were permanent targets of biblical prophets, but also of ancient Greek and Roman satirists. Today, the growing complexities and intricacies of the financial and economic systems, and the white collar crimes exploiting this fact, have led to ever-increasing financial and economic legislation. The creation of related branches of the judiciary corresponds to this situation. The intimate interplay of economy, money, and legal order since the beginnings of the economy of the West, which based itself on private property, will be shown below.

3. Since Talcott Parsons' elaborate discussion of this, scholars like Klaus Heinemann have furthered this insight. Jürgen Habermas has devoted the last two chapters of the second volume of his *Theory of Communicative Action* (Boston: Beacon Press, 1984) to this issue; for his critical reflection on Parson's position on money, see pp. 199-300.

4. See, for example, Ernest Bornemann, *Psychoanalyse des Geldes* (Frankfurt: Suhrkamp, 1973).

5. Wolfgang Lienemann's collection of essays by various authors (*Die Finanzen der Kirche* [München: Kaiser, 1989]) on this subject indicates that this may be changing.

6. I shall use in particular the ideas of Gunnar Heinsohn and Otto Steiger, who themselves built heavily on the work of John Maynard Keynes and Frank H. Hahn. Heinsohn's observations are not limited to the historical origin and evolution of the economy of the first millennium B.C.E., but portray its continuing character and structure down into the first century C.E. as well. Moses Isaac Finley's minimalist hesitation against reading modern economic perspectives and criteria into ancient economic structures (*The Ancient Economy* [Berkeley: University of California Press, 1973]) too quickly and too strongly calls for some caution in the use of Heinsohn's terminology. A world market in its modern sense did not exist yet nor had independently productive capital and coinage defined what money was. But Finley has overemphasized these points. An expansive network of markets flourished, as did the equivalents of checks, and written obligations were traded. See in this

regard F. M. Heichelheim's less minimalist view on these issues, *An Ancient Economic History*, 3 vols. (Leyden: Sijthoff, 1958-70).

7. See, for example, Prov. 6:1-5; 11:1; 16:11; 20:10; Sir. 8:12-13; 10:26-27; 11:10-11, 18-19; 13:21-23; 14:3-6; 20:12; 22:26-27; 24:30-32; 26:29; 27:2; 29:10; 34:1-11; 37:11; 38:24–39:11; and 40:13-14.

8. In Apocalypticism this hostile stance showed in the tendency to associate, indeed identify, state power and wealth—that is, economic and political strength—with corruption and sinfulness (see I Enoch 62–63; 94:6–104:13). Jewish Gnostic wisdom adopted and radicalized this sweeping criticism of temporal power relations and their institutions, as did the Letter of Eugnostos and the Apocalypse of Adam.

9. For instance, the individual and collective prosperity that Philo promises in *De Praemiis et Poenis* (*On Rewards and Punishments*) to the faithful is not projecting a distant eschatological future, isolated from the present experience by something like a supernatural *parousia*, nor is it a fully realized eschatology, but rather something in between. Modern theological terminology calls it "realizing eschatology."

10. The numbering of Aristotle's *Politics* is that of the Loeb edition. The discussion of the origin and use of money takes up a relatively small portion of Aristotle's treatment of household management (*oikonomia*), whereas wealth getting and trade, as larger economic issues, occupy much of chaps. 3 and 4. Here the close relationship between economy, money, and trade with politics, law, constitution, and ethics can be seen. Aristotle's reflections on the origin of money and the character of the flow of money carry a strong moralizing tone.

11. Michael Rostovtzeff has discussed this in his treatise *The Social and Economic History of the Hellenistic World* (Oxford: Clarendon Press, 1941), vol. I, pp. 440-46.

12. Heinsohn (*Privates Grundeigentum, patriachalische Monogamie und Geldwirtschaftliche Produktion: Eine sozialtheoretische Rekonstruktion zur Antike* (Bremen: Dissertation, 1983), pp. 45-57, speaks of major natural disasters in the early centuries of the first milennium B.C.E. and their immediate social consequences for matrilinear tribes. In the words of the English abstract attached to his book (pp. 278-79): "Among archaeologists the consensus is growing that the Mycenaean tribute economy collapsed in huge natural catastrophes whose causes are disputed. At the same time they agree that the origin in the 8th century B.C.E. of civilization in the polis with individual male ownership cannot so far be explained satisfactorily. In proving that Mycenae was not destroyed in the 13th/12th centuries but in the 8th century B.C.E. we can show that serfs (of the Romulus type) successfully rebelled against their masters who had become destabilized through catastrophes and that—probably aided by tribesmen who had also become uprooted by the catastrophes,

but also by noble deserters of the Theseus type—they divided up the feudal estates amongst themselves in order to prevent people from their own ranks rising and becoming new overlords."

13. See ibid., pp. 53-100. In the words of his abstract: "This [the dividing up of the feudal estates] is the origin of private ownership, with the individual free peasant who initially can at best feed one wife and therefore has to forego polygamy, which had been the due of the chiefs and feudal lords, in favour of monogamy."

14. See ibid., pp. 113-56. He summarizes on p. 278: "The abolition of the collective security provided by tribe and estate forces the private owner who now suffers from an individualized existential risk—in a way he is his own debtor—to increase his output in order to obtain a security stock as liquidity to cover himself against unforeseeably large risks. This stock is at the same time a potential lendable asset against a premium whose size is measured according to the assessment of the existential risk when it is lent to others—or oneself, if a private owner is not successful in obtaining a liquidity stock he has to ask for credit in an emergency. This the successful stockholder is happy to grant as it relieves him from the expense incurred in caring for his reserves of animals or grain. But he does not want to lose the security for which he has after all laid in this stock." For Heinsohn, this sequence of developments accounts for the origin of debt bondage, which he describes as "the preliminary stage of interest," the latter coming about as a replacement of debt bondage after its revolutionary abolition (e.g., in Athens under Solon).

15. The idea of the cultic origin of money has been particularly emphasized and developed by Bernhard Laum. He claims that money originated as a substitute for produce and animals as sacrificial gifts. He does not see the interplay between private property, debt, security/interest/obligation and money, nor the role of temples. He leaves out the advanced Mediterranean economy of classical and Hellenistic times entirely.

16. See Heinsohn, *Privates Grundeigentum*, pp. 157-95. His summary of this reads as follows: "If now [after the abolition of debt bondage] the creditor unexpectedly requires liquidity before the expiration of the credit, he can avoid a loss of substance by passing on his claim to the liquidity premium to the new provider of liquidity. Now this contract is active money. . . . The interest claim arising from the illiquidity of the creditor stands for goods that are not yet available, which now have to be produced—via surplus production—as commodities which constitute the market when they are redeemed. For the purpose of witnessing and executing the debtors' obligations as embodied in the bills of exchange, the temples generate banks which receive considerable shares of the

interest as a basis for their granting security on behalf of the creditors who become depositors. As this income in kind in turn demands high expenditure for its maintenance the banks eventually proceed to lending their property claims against interest in the form of depersonalized and denaturalized money" (p. 279). Temples as the first banks and as ongoing banking enterprises remain in the picture even after the origin and growth of secular money institutions.

The characteristics of the Mediterranean and Near Eastern economy, together with its evolution in the first millennium B.C.E. and beyond into the first four centuries C.E., are summarized by Heinsohn under the two chapter headings "Private Property and State, Individual Existential Risk and Storage of Liquidity, Credit and Debt Bondage, Interest and the Production of a Monetary Economy, Slavery and Coinage," and "Division of Classes, Division of Labor, Population Explosion and Depopulation" (my translation).

17. The only exception is in the context of Paul's discussion of the collection in Rom. 15:27, where the Gentiles are described as debtors to the Jerusalem church. But here the usual creditor-debtor relationship is turned on its head; the rich are debtors to the poor.

18. Concerning the origin and character of the social and economic concept of order, Heinsohn has made very intriguing observations and suggestions.

19. The idiom is often attributed to Cicero, but it is much older.

20. See pp. 102-4 and 107-9.

21. Here I differ greatly with my friend Karl-Josef Kuschel, who on pp. 379-82 of *Geboren vor aller Zeit: Der Streit um Christi Ursprung* (Munich: Piper, 1990) thoroughly demythologizes II Cor. 8:9. He explains the richness of God's agent here as the spiritual riches of the historical person Jesus of Nazareth. This is in line with Kuschel's general attempt to downplay the importance, often even the existence, of mythological language in the New Testament. The very realistic context in which II Cor. 8:9 speaks of actual money flow contradicts Kuschel's attempt at spiritualization. In his interpretation of II Cor. 8:9 the cross of Christ must come necessarily into a moralizing light, which contradicts all references to the cross in Paul. I have demonstrated the fact that Paul's understanding of the spiritual has to be seen according to the ancient perspective, which does not exclude mythical ideas of substance, but rather incorporates them.

22. It is most often stated cynically, as for instance in the proverbial expression in Ovid's Amores 3.8.55: "Dat census honores" ("Income assessed by the census doles out honors"; compare Fasti 1,217). The whole poem complains that wealth establishes esteem and power across the board, without regard for differences of class, status, talent, or merit.

Petronius's *Satyricon* pokes fun at the freedman Trimalchio, who, because of his wealth, believes in his equality with the freeborn, especially the senatorial and equestrian class.

23. The sabbatical year appears in Exod. 21:1-11; 23:10-11; Lev. 25:1-7, 18-22; Deut. 15:1-18. On the sabbatical year, see Ben Zion Wacholder in *The Interpreter's Dictionary of the Bible* (Nashville: Abingdon Press, 1962), Supplement, pp. 762-63. The jubilee year appears in Lev. 25:8-17, 23-28, 47-55. On the jubilee year, see Adrianus van Selms, ibid., pp. 496-98.

24. Keynes, *A Treatise on Money* (London: Royal Economic Society, 1930), p. 3.

25. Alexander's pursuits and achievement were still seen in this way long after his death. Plutarch's various reflections on Alexander give evidence of this in the latter part of the first century C.E.

26. This question is dealt with by Wilhelm Gerloff, *Geld und Gesellschaft* (Frankfurt: Frankfurter Wissenschaftliche Beiträg; Kulturwissenschaftliche Reihe 1, 1952), pp. 214-75, esp. 214-36. Gerloff reminds us that Aristotle also dealt with this issue, although not with the same terminology.

BIBLIOGRAPHY

Allo, Ernest-Bernard. *La porté de la collecte pour Jérusalem dans le plans de St. Paul.* Rev. Bibl. 45 (1936): 523-37.

Austirn, M. M., and A. N. P. Vidal-Naquet. *Economic and Social History of Ancient Greece: An Introduction.* Berkeley: University of California, 1977.

Baltzer, Klaus, *Das Bundesformular.* Neukirchen-Vluyn: Neukirchener Verlag, 1964.

Bammel, Ernst, "Judenverfolgung und Naherwartung," *ZThK* 56 (1959): 294-315.

———. *πτωχός, πτωχεία, πτωχεύω*, ThWNT, vol. 6. Stuttgart: W. Kohlhammer, 1969, 6, pp. 888-915.

Barrett, Charles Kingsley. *A Commentary on the Second Epistle to the Corinthians.* London: Black, 1973.

Bauer, Walter, *A Greek-English Lexicon of the New Testament and Other Early Christian Literature.* Translated and edited by William F. Arndt and F. Wilbur Gingrich. Chicago: University of Chicago, 1979. German: *Griechisch-deutsches Wörterbuch zum Neuen Testament.* Berlin: Walter de Gruyter, 1988; new edition by Kurt und Barbara Aland.

Baur, Ferdinand Christian. *Paul the Apostle.* London: Williams & Norgate, 1876. German: *Paulus, der Apostel Jesu Christi.* Stuttgart: Becher & Müller, 1866.

Becker, Jürgen, "Der Brief an die Galater." In Jürgen Becker, Hans Conzelmann, and Gerhard Friedrich, *Die Briefe an die Galater, Epheser, Philipper, Kolosser, Thessalonicher und Philemon.* Göttingen: Vandenhoeck & Ruprecht, 1985, pp. 1-85.

Betlyon, John W. "Money." *HBD* (1985): 647-51.

Betz, Hans Dieter. *Galatians: A Commentary on Paul's Letter to the Churches of Galatia.* Philadelphia: Fortress, 1979.

———. *2 Corinthians 8 and 9: A Commentary on Two Administrative Letters of the Apostle Paul.* Philadelphia: Fortress, 1985.

Billerbeck, Paul, and Herrmann Leberecht Strack. *Kommentar zum Neues Testament aus Talmud und Midrasch, I-IV.* München: Beck, 1969.

Blaβ, Friedrich Wilhelm, and Albert Debrunner. *A Greek Grammar of the New Testament and Other Early Christian Literature.* Translated and revised by Robert Funk. Chicago: University of Chicago, 1961. German: *Grammatik des neutestamentlichen Griechisch.* Newly revised by F. Rehkopf. Göttingen: Vandenhoeck & Ruprecht, 1984.

Bodin, Jean, *Colloquium Heptaplomeres de verum sublimium arcanis abditis,* 1593. Edited by Ludwig Noack. Paris: Suerini Megaloburgiensium, 1857.

———. *De La Démonomanie des Sorciers,* Paris, 1580. Reprint of the German translation, *Vom ausgelassenen wütigen Teufelsheer,* by J. Fischart, 1581.

———. *The Six Books of a Commonweale.* Edited by K. D. MacRae. Cambridge, Mass.: Harvard University, 1962. French: *Les Six Livres de la République,* 1576.

Bolkestein, Hendrik. *Wohltätigkeit und Armenpflege im vorchristlichen Altertum.* Utrecht: Oosthoek, 1939.

Bonnard, Pierre. *L'Épître de St. Paul aux Galats.* Neuchâtel: Delachaux et Niestlé, 1953.

Boobyer, George Henry. *"Thanksgiving" and the "Glory of God" in Paul.* Borna-Leipzig: Univ.Verl. Robert Noske, 1928.

Bornemann, Ernest, ed. *Psychoanalyse des Geldes.* Frankfurt/Main: Suhrkamp, 1973.

Bornkamm, Günther. *Das Ende des Gesetzes. Ges. Aufs.* I. München: Kaiser, 1966. (BEvTh 16). ("Taufe und neues Leben," pp. 34-50; "Paulinische Anakoluthe im Römerbrief," pp. 76-92; "Die Häresie des Kolosserbriefes," pp. 139-56; "Christus und die Welt in der urchristlichen Botschaft," pp. 157-72.)

———. *Die Vorgeschichte des sogenannten zweiten Korintherbriefes.* Heidelberg: Winter, 1965."The Letter to the Romans as Paul's Last Will and Testament." *ABR* 11 (1963): 2-14.

———. *Paul.* Translated by M. G. Stalker. New York: Harper, 1971. German: *Paulus.* Stuttgart: Kohlhammer, 1970.

———. "Paulus." *RGG*[3] 5, cols. 166-90.

———. *Studien zu Antike und Urchristentum. Ges. Aufs.* II. München: Kaiser, 1959. (BEvTh 28). ("Glaube und Vernunft bei Paulus," pp. 119-37; "Herrenmahl und Kirche bei Paulus," pp. 138-76; "Das Bekenntnis im Hebräerbrief," pp. 188-203).

Bornkamm, Günther. "μυστήριον, μυέω," *ThWNT* 4 Stuttgart: W. Kohlhammer, 1942, pp. 809-34.

Borse, Udo, "Paulus in Jerusalem." In *Kontinuität und Einheit*, edited by P. G. Muller and W. Stenger, pp. 43-64. Freiburg: Herder, 1981.

Bousset, Wilhelm, *Jüdisch-christlicher Schulbetrieb in Alexandrien und Rom.* Göttingen: Vandenhoeck & Ruprecht, 1915.

Brandh, Rudolf. "Geld und Gnade (zu 2.Kor. 8,9)." *ThZS* 41 (1985): 264-71.

Braun, Herbert. "Christentum I, Entstehung." *RGG*[3] 1, cols. 1685-95.

Bréhier, Émile. *Les idées philosphiques et religieuses de Philon d'Alexandrie.* Paris: A. Picard, 1950.

Bruce, Frederick Fyvie. "Chronological Questions in the Acts of the Apostles." *BJRL* 68 (1986): 273-95.

Buck, Charles H. "The Collection for the Saints." *HThR* 43 (1950): 1-29.

Bultmann, Rudolf. *The Gospel of John: A Commentary.* Translated by G. R. Beasley-Murray. Philadelphia: Westminster, 1971. German: *Das Evangelium des Johannes.* Göttingen: Vandenhoeck & Ruprecht, 1986 (with supplement).

———. *Theology of the New Testament.* Translated by Kendrick Grobel. New York: Scribner's, 1955. German: *Theologie des NT.* Tübingen: Mohr, 1953; Heidelberg: Frankl, 1984.

———. "Zur Frage nach den Quellen der Apostelgeschichte." In *New Testament Essays: Studies in Memory of Thomas Walter Manson*, edited by Angus John and Brockhurst Higgins, pp. 68-80. Manchester: University Press, 1959.

———. "ἱλάρος, ἱλαρότης," *TDNT* 3, pp. 298-300.

———. "πιστεύω," *TDNT* 6, pp. 197-230.

Campenhausen, Hans von. *Der Ablauf der Osterereignisse und das leere Grab.* SHAW. PH 1952, 4. Heidelberg: Winter, 1977.

———. *Ecclesiastical Authority and Spiritual Power in the Church of the First Three Centuries.* Translated by John Baker. Stanford, Calif.: Stanford University, 1969. German: *Kirchliches Amt und geistliche Vollmacht in den ersten drei Jahrhunderten.* Tübingen: Mohr, 1963 (BHTh 14).

Casel, Odo. *De Philosophorum Graecorum Silentio Mystico.* Giessen: Töpelmann, 1919 (RVV 16,2).

———. "Die λογική θυσία der antiken Mystik in christlich-liturgischer Umdeutung." *ILW* 4 (1924): 37-47.

Conzelmann, Hans. *Acts of the Apostles.* Translated by James Limburg, A. Thomas Krabel, and Donald E. Juel. Edited by Eldon Jay Epp with Chris Matthews. Philadelphia: Fortress, 1987. German: *Die Apostelgeschichte.* Tübingen: Rohr, 1963.

———. *1 Corinthians: A Commentary on the First Epistle to the Corinthians.* Translated by James W. Leitch. Edited by George W. MacRae.

Philadelphia: Fortress, 1975. Hermeneia. German: *Der erste Brief an die Korinther.* Göttingen: Vandenhoeck & Ruprecht, 1969.

———. "Geschichte, Geschichtsbild und Geschichtsdarstellung bei Lukas." *ThLZ* 85 (1960): 241-50.

———. "Heidenchristentum," *RGG*³ 3, cols. 128-41.

———. *The Theology of St. Luke.* Translated by Geoffrey Buswell. New York: Harper & Row, 1960.

Cransfield, C. E. B. *A Critical and Exegetical Commentary on the Epistle to the Romans.* 2 vols., rev. ed. Edinburgh: T & T Clark, 1980 and 1981.

Dahl, Nils Astrup. *Studies in Paul: Theology for the Early Christian Mission.* Minneapolis: Augsburg, 1977.

Davies, William David. *Jewish and Pauline Studies.* Philadelphia: Fortress, 1984.

Deißmann, Gustav Adolf. *Light from the Ancient East.* Translated by Lionel R. M. Strachan. London: Hodder & Stoughton, 1911. German: *Licht vom Osten.* Tübingen: Mohr, 1923.

———. *Paulus.* Tübingen: Mohr, 1925.

Delling, Gerhard. "Johannes der Apostel." *RGG*³ 3, cols. 803-4.

Dibelius, Martin, *An die Thessalonicher I II, An die Philipper.* Tübingen: Mohr, 1937.

———. *Aufsätze zur Apostelgeschichte.* Göttingen: Vandenhoeck & Ruprecht, 1968.

———. *James.* Revised by Heinrich Greeven. Translated by Michael A. Williams. Edited by Helmut Koester. Philadelphia: Fortress, 1976. German: *Der Brief des Jakobus.* Göttingen: Vandenhoeck & Ruprecht, 1984.

———. *Paul.* Edited and revised by Werner Georg Kümmel. London: Longmans, 1953.

Diehl, Albrecht. *Die Goldene Regel: Eine Einführung in die Geschichte der antiken und frühchristlichen Vulgärethik.* Göttingen: Vandenhoeck & Ruprecht, 1962.

———. "Goldene Regel," *RAC* 11 (1981): 930-40.

Dinkler, Erich. "Korintherbriefe." *RGG*³ 4, cols. 17-23.

Dockx, Stanislas J. "Chronologie de la vie de Saint Paul depuis sa conversion jusqu'à son séjour à Rome." *NT* 13 (1971): 261-304.

———. "Chronologie paulinienne de l'annee de la grande collecte." *RB* 81 (1974): 183-95.

Dopsch, Alfons. *Naturalwirtschaft und Geldwirtschaft in der Weltgeschichte.* Wien: Seidel, 1930.

Eckert, Jost, "Die Kollekte des Paulus für Jerusalem." In *Kontinuität und Einheit.* Edited by F. F. Mußner, P.-G. Muller, and W. Stenger, pp. 65-80. Freiburg: Herder, 1981.

Einzig, P. *Primitive Money in Its Ethnological, Historical, and Economical Aspect*. London: Eyre & Spottiswoode, 1951.
Ellul, Jaques. *L'homme et l'argent*. Neuchâtel: Delachaux & Niestlé, 1954.
Finley, Moses I. "The Ancient City: From Fustel de Coulanges to Max Weber and Beyond." In *Comparative Studies in Society and History* 19 (1977): 305-27.
———. *The Ancient Economy*. Berkeley: University of California, 1973.
———. *Economy and Society in Ancient Greece*. Edited by B. Shaw and R. P. Saller. London: Chatto & Windus, 1981.
Fitzmyer, Joseph A. *Pauline Theology: A Brief Sketch*. The Jerome Biblical Commentary. Englewood Cliffs, N.J.: Prentice Hall, 1968.
Foakes-Jackson, F. J., Kirsopp Lake, et al., eds. *The Acts of the Apostles*. The Beginnings of Christianity, vols. 4-5. Grand Rapids: Baker Book House, 1965.
Fohrer, Georg, and Eduard Lohse. "Σίων." *TDNT* 7 (1964): 292-338.
Franklin, W. M. *Die Kollekte des Paulus*. Scottdale, Pa.: Mennonite Publishing House, 1938.
Friedrich, Gerhard. "Der Brief an die Philipper." In Jürgen Becker, Hans Conzelmann, Gerhard Friedrich, *Die Briefe an die Galater, Epheser, Philipper, Kolosser, Thessalonicher und Philemon*. Göttingen: Vandenhoeck & Ruprecht, 1985, pp. 125-75.
Furnish, Victor. *Theology and Ethics in Paul*. Nashville: Abingdon, 1968.
Gager, John Goodrich. "Functional Diversity in Paul's Use of End-Time Language." *JBL* 89 (1970): 325-37.
Georgi, Dieter. "Corinthians, First Letter to the." *IDBSup* (1976): 180-83.
———. "Corinthians, Second Letter to the." *IDBSup* (1976): 183-86.
———. "Der vorpaulinische Hymnus Phil. 2,6-11." In *Zeit und Geschichte: Dankesgabe an Rudolf Bultmann zum 80. Geburtstag*. Edited by Erich Dinkler and Hartwig Thyen, pp. 263-93. Tübingen: Mohr, 1964.
———. "Exegetische Anmerkungen zur Auseinandersetzung mit den Einwänden gegen die Thesen der Bruderschaften." *TEH NS* 70 (1959): 109-38.
———. *Leben-Jesu-Theologie/Leben-Jesu-Forschung*, *TRE* vol. 20. Berlin and New York: DeGruyter, 1990, pp. 566-75.
———. *The Opponents of Paul in Second Corinthians*. Philadelphia: Fortress, 1986. German: *Die Gegner des Paulus im Zweiten Korintherbrief*. Neukirchen-Vluyn: Neukirchener, 1964.
———. "Socioeconomic Reasons for the 'Divine man' as a Propagandistic Pattern." In Elisabeth Schüssler-Fiorenza, ed. *Aspects of Religious Propaganda in Judaism and Early Christianity*. Notre Dame and London: University of Notre Dame Press, 1976, pp. 27-42.

———. "Who Is the True Prophet?" *Harvard Theological Review* 79 (1986): 100-26.

Gerloff, Wilhelm. *Die Entstehung des Geldes und die Anfänge des Geldwesens*. Frankfurt: Klostermann, 1943.

———. *Geld und Gesellschaft*. Frankfurt: Frankfurter Wissenschaftliche Beiträge Kulturwissenschaftliche Reihe 1, 1952.

Grierson, Philip. *The Origin of Money*. London: Athlone, 1977.

Haacher, Klaus. "Die Gallio-Episode und die Paulinische Chronologie." *BZNF* (1972): 252-55.

Habermas, Jürgen. *The Theory of Communicative Action*. Boston: Beacon, 1984.

Haenchen, Ernst. *The Acts of the Apostles: A Commentary*. Translated by Bernard Noble and Gerald Shinn. Edited by Hugh Anderson and Robert McLachlan Wilson. Philadelphia: Westminster, 1971. German: *Die Apostelgeschichte*. Göttingen: Vandenhoeck & Ruprecht, 1977.

———. "Petrus-Probleme." *NTS* 7 (1960/61): 187-97.

———. "Quellenanalyse und Kompositionsanalyse in Act. 15." In *Judentum-Urchristentum-Kirche*. BZNW 26. Edited by Walther Eltester, pp. 153-64. Berlin: Töpelmann, 1960; enlarged edition 1964.

Hahn, Franz. "Geldtheorie." In *Handwörterbuch der mathematischen Wirtschaftswissenschaften*, vol. I. Edited by M. J. Beckmann, G. Menges, and R. Selten (Wirtschaftstheorie). Wiesbaden: Gabler, 1979, pp. 41-67.

Hahn, Ferdinand. *Mission in the New Testament*. SBT 47. London: SCM, 1965. German: *Das Verständnis der Mission im Neuen Testament*. Tübingen: Mohr, 1965.

———. *The Titles of Jesus in Christology: Their History in Early Christianity*. Translated by Harold Knight and George Ogg. Cleveland: World Publishing, 1969. German: *Christologische Hoheitstitel*. Göttingen: Vandenhoeck & Ruprecht, 1974.

Hamburger, Herbert. "Money, Coins." *The Interpreter's Dictionary of the Bible*, vol. 3. Nashville: Abingdon, 1962.

Hands, A. R. *Charities and Social Aid in Greece and Rome*. Ithaca, N.Y.: Cornell University, 1968.

Hart, H.St.J. "Money." In *DB(H)*. Edited by Frederic C. Grant and H. H. Rowley (1963) 669-73.

Heichelheim, F. M. *An Ancient Economic History*, 3 vols. Leyden: Sijthoff, 1958-70.

———. "Geld und Münzgeschichte." In *HDSW* 4 (1965): 273-82.

Heinemann, Klaus. *Gründzuge einer Soziologie des Geldes*. Stuttgart: Ferdinand Enke, 1969.

Heinsohn, Gunnar. *Privates Grundeigentum, Patriachalische Monogamie und Geldwirtschaftliche Produktion: Eine sozialtheoretische Rekonstruktion zur Antike*. Bremen: Dissertation, 1983.

Hennecke, Edgar, *Neutestamentliche Apokryphen*. Edited by Wilhelm Schneemelcher, Tübingen: Mohr, 1990.

Héring, Jean. *La première Épître de St. Paul aux Corinthiens*. Neuchâtel: Delachaux et Niestlé, 1959.

———. *La seconde Épître de St. Paul aux Corinthiens*. Neuchâtel: Delachaux et Niestlé, 1958.

Holl, Karl, "Der Kirchenbegriff des Paulus in seinem Verhältnis zu dem der Urgemeinde," *Ges. Aufs*. II. Tübingen: Mohr, 1928, and Darmstadt: Wissenschaftliche Buchgesellschaft, 1964, pp. 44-67.

Hölscher, Gustav. *Die Hohepriesterliste bei Josephus und die evangelische Chronologie*. Heidelberg: Winter, 1939/40.

Holsten, Carl. *Das Evangelium des Paulus*, 2 vols. Berlin: Reimer, 1880 and 1898.

Holtz, Traugott. "Der antiochenische Zwischenfall (Gal. 2,11-14)." *NTS* 32 (1986): 344-61.

Horst, Friedrich. "Gerechtigkeit Gottes, II, Im AT und Judentum." *RGG*[3] 2, cols.1403-1406.

Hummel, Reinhart. *Die Auseinandersetzung zwischen Kirche und Judentum im Matthäusevangelium*. München: Kaiser, 1966.

Hurd, John Coolidge. "Pauline Chronology and Pauline Theology." In *Christian History and Interpretation*. Edited by W. R. Farmer et al., pp. 225-48. Cambridge: Cambridge University, 1967.

Hurtado, Larry W. "The Jerusalem Collection and the Book of Galatians." *JournStud NT* 5 (1979): 46-62.

Hyldahl, Nils. "Die Frage nach der literarischen Einheit des Zweiten Korintherbriefs." *ZNW* 64 (1973): 289-306.

Hyldahl, Nils, and Otto Steiger. *Die Vernichtung der weisen Frauen: Beiträge zur Theorie und Geschichte von Bevölkerung und Kindheit*. Hemsbach: März, 1985.

Jeremias, Joachim. *Jerusalem in the Time of Jesus: An Investigation into Economic and Social Conditions During the New Testament Period*. Translated by F. H. Cave and C. H. Cave. London: SCM, 1969. German: *Jerusalem zur Zeit Jesu*. Göttingen: Vandenhoeck & Ruprecht, 1962.

———. *Jesus' Promise to the Nations*. Franz Delitzsch Lectures for 1953. SBT 24. London: SCM, 1958. German: *Jesu Verheißung fur die Völker*. Stuttgart: Kohlhammer, 1956.

———. "Sabbatjahr und neutestamentliche Chronologie." *ZNW* 27 (1928): 98-103.

———. "Untersuchungen zum Quellenproblem der Apostelgeschichte." *ZNW* 36 (1937): 205-21.

Jewett, Robert. *A Chronology of Paul's Life*. Philadelphia: Fortress, 1979.

Jonas, Hans. *Augustin und das paulinische Freiheitsproblem*. Göttingen: Vandenhoeck & Ruprecht, 1965.

Käsemann, Ernst. *An die Römer*. Tübingen: Mohr, 1974.

———. "Anliegen und Eigenart der paulinischen Abendmahlslehre." *EvTh* 7 (1947/48): 263-83.

———. "Die Anfänge christlicher Theologie." *ZThK* 57 (1960): 162-71.

———. *Der Ruf der Freiheit*. Tübingen: Mohr, 1968.

———. *Exegetische Versuche und Besinnungen* I. Göttingen: Vandenhoeck & Ruprecht, 1968.

———. "Gottesdienst im Alltag der Welt (zu Röm 12)." In *Judentum-Urchristentum-Kirche*. Edited by Joachim Jeremias and Walther Eltester, pp. 165-71. Berlin: Töpelmann, 1960.

———. "Gottesgerechtigkeit bei Paulus." *ZThK* 58 (1961): 367-78.

———. *Leib und Leib Christi: Eine Untersuchung zur paulinischen Begrifflichkeit*. Tübingen: Mohr, 1933.

———. *New Testament Questions of Today*. Philadelphia: Fortress, 1969.

———. "Paulus und der Fruhkatholizismus." *ZThK* 60 (1963): 75-89.

———. *Perspectives on Paul*. Philadelphia: Fortress, 1971. German: *Paulinische Perspektiven*. Tübingen: Mohr, 1969.

———. "Zum Thema der urchristlichen Apokalyptik." *ZThK* 59 (1962): 257-84.

Kandler, Hans-Joachim. "Die Bedeutung der Armut im Schrifttum von Chirbet Qumran." *Judaica* 13 (1957): 193-209.

Keynes, John Maynard. *The General Theory of Employment, Interest, and Money*. London: Royal Economic Society, 1936.

———. "Keynes and Ancient Currencies (1920-1926)." In *The Collected Writings of John Maynard Keynes* XXVIII: *Social, Political and Literary Writings*. Edited by Donald Moggridge. London: Royal Economic Society, 1982.

———. *A Treatise on Money*. London: Royal Economic Society, 1930.

Kittel, Gerhard. λογεία. *TDNT* 4, pp. 285-86.

Klein, Günther. *Die Zwölf Apostel*. Göttingen: Vandenhoeck & Ruprecht, 1961.

———. "Gal. 2,6-9 und die Geschichte der Jerusalemer Urgemeinde." *ZThK* 57 (1960): 275-95. Also in *Rekonstruktion und Interpretation*. München: Kaiser, 1969, pp. 99-118.

Klein, Günther. Review of "E. Haenchen, Die Apostelgeschichte." *ZKG* 68 (1957): 362-71.

Klein, Peter. "Zum Verständnis von Gal 2,1. Zugleich ein Beitrag zur Chronologie des Urchristentums." *ZNW* 70 (1979): 250-251.

Knapp, Georg Friedrich. *Staatliche Theorie des Geldes*. München: Dunker & Humbolt, 1921.

Knox, John. *Chapters in a Life of Paul*. New York: Abingdon, 1950.

Knox, Wilfred Lawrence. *St. Paul and the Church of Jerusalem*. Cambridge, England: Cambridge University, 1925.

———. *St. Paul and the Church of the Gentiles*. Cambridge, England: Cambridge University Press, 1961.

Koester, Helmut. *Introduction to the New Testament*, 2 vols. Philadelphia: Fortress, 1982.

———. "Häretiker im Urchristentum." *RGG*[3] 3, cols. 17-21.

———. "The Purpose of the Polemic of a Pauline Fragment (Phil. III)." *NTS* 8 (1962): 317-32.

Kümmel, Werner Georg, *Introduction to the New Testament*. Nashville: Abingdon, 1975. German: *Einleitung in das Neue Testament*. Heidelberg: Quelle & Meyer, 1963.

———. "Judenchristentum, I, Im Altertum." *RGG*[3] 3, cols. 967-72.

Kuhn, Karl Georg. "Askese: III, Im Judentum; IV, Im Urchristentum." *RGG*[3] 1, cols. 641-44.

———. "Essener." *RGG*[3] 2, cols. 701-3.

———. "Qumran." *RGG*[3] 3, cols. 745-54.

———. "Über den ursprünglichen Sinn des Abendmahls und sein Verhältnis zu den Gemeinschaftsmahlen der Sektenschrift." *EvTh* 10 (1950/51): 508-27.

Kuschel, Karl-Josef. *Geboren vor aller Zeit: Der Streit um Christi Ursprung*. München: Piper, 1990.

Kutsch, Ernst. "Armut: I, Biblisch." *RGG*[3] 1, cols. 622-24.

Lanczkowski, Günther, and Martin Honecker. "Geld: I, Religionsgeschichtlich, II, Historisch und ethisch." *TRE* 12 (1984): 276-98.

Lang, Friedrich. *Die Briefe an die Korinther*. Göttingen: Vandenhoeck & Ruprecht, 1986.

Laum, Bernhard, *Die Banken im Altertum*. In Handwörterbuch der Staatswissenschaften II, pp. 165-68. Jena: Fischer, 1924.

———. *Heiliges Geld. Historische Untersuchungen über den sakralen Ursprung des Geldes*. Tübingen: Mohr, 1924.

Lauterbach, A. *Man, Motives, Money*. Ithaca, N.Y.: Cornell University, 1955.

Leenhardt, Franz J. *L'Épître de St. Paul aux Romains*. Neuchâtel: Delachaux et Niestlé, 1957.

Leuba, Jean-Louis. *Institution und Ereignis*. Göttingen: Vandenhoeck & Ruprecht, 1957.

Liddell, Henry George, and Robert Scott. *A Greek-English Lexicon*. Newly edited by Henry Stuart Jones and R. McKenzie. Oxford: Clarendon, 1949, reprint 1953. Supplement edited by E. A. Barber, 1968.

Lienemann, Wolfgang, ed. *Die Finanzen der Kirche*. München: Kaiser, 1989.

Lietzmann, Hans. *An die Galater*. Tübingen: Mohr, 1971.

———. *An die Korinther I II*. Tübingen: Mohr, 1969. Revised by Werner Georg Kümmel, *HNT* 9.

———. *An die Römer*. Tübingen: Mohr, 1971 (*HNT* 8).

Lohmeyer, Ernst. *Die Briefe an die Philipper, an die Kolosser und Philemon*. Göttingen: Vandenhoeck & Ruprecht, 1964.

———. *Vom göttlichen Wohlgeruch*. Heidelberg: Winter, 1919.

Lüdemann, Gerd. *Paulus, der Heidenapostel*, vol. 1: *Studien zur Chronologie*. Göttingen: Vandenhoeck & Ruprecht, 1980.

———. *Paulus, der Heidenapostel*, vol. 2: *Antipaulinismus im fruhen Christentum*. Göttingen: Vandenhoeck & Ruprecht, 1983.

Lührmann, Dieter. *Der Brief an die Galater*. Züricher Bibel-Komentare zum NT 7. Zürich: Theologischer, 1978.

Luz, Ulrich. *Das Geschichtsverständnis des Paulus*. München: Kaiser, 1968.

Manson, Thomas Walter. "St. Paul's Letter to the Romans and Others." *BJRL* 31 (1948): 224-40.

Marrow, Stanley. *Paul: His Letters and His Theology: An Introduction to Paul's Epistles*. New York: Paulist, 1986.

Merton, R. K. *Social Theory and Social Structure*. Glencoe, N.Y.: Free Press Paperback, 1957.

Michaelis, Wilhelm. *Die Datierung des Philipperbriefes*. Gütersloh: Bertelsmann, 1933.

———. *Die Gefangenschaft des Paulus in Ephesus*. Gütersloh: Bertelsmann, 1925.

———. *Einleitung in das NT*. Bern: Haller, 1961.

Michel, Otto. *Der Brief an die Römer*. Göttingen: Vandenhoeck & Ruprecht, 1978.

Minsky, Hyman P. *John Maynard Keynes*. New York: Columbia University Press, 1975.

Moggridge, D. E., ed. *Collected Writings of John Maynard Keynes*, XIV: *The General Theory and After*, pt. 2: *Defense and Development*. London: Royal Economic Society, 1973.

Mott, Stephen Charles. "The Power of Giving and Receiving: Reciprocity in Hellenistic Benevolence." In *Current Issues in Biblical and Patristic Interpretation*. Edited by G. F. Hawthorne. Grand Rapids: Eerdmans, 1975.

Munck, Johannes. *Paul and the Salvation of Mankind*. Translated by Frank Clarke. Atlanta: John Knox, 1977. German: *Paulus und die Heilsgeschichte*. Aarhus: Universitetsforlaget, 1954.

Murphy-O'Connor, Jerome. "Pauline Missions Before the Jerusalem Conference." *RB* 89 (1982): 71-91.

Mußner, Franz. *Der Galaterbrief.* Freiburg: Herder, 1977.

Nickle, Keith F. *Collection: A Study in Paul's Strategy.* Geneva, Ala.: Allenson, 1966.

Oepke, Albrecht. *Der Brief des Paulus an die Galater.* Berlin: EVA, 1973 (ThHK 9). The 1957 edition is quoted.

Ogg, George. *The Chronology of the Life of Paul.* London: Epworth, 1986.

Ollrog, Wolf Henning. "Die Abfassungsverhältnisse von Röm 16." In *Kirche.* Edited by Dieter Lührmann and Georg Strecker, pp. 221-44. Tübingen: Mohr, 1980.

———. *Paulus und seine Mitarbeiter. Untersuchungen zu Theorie und Praxis der paulinischen Mission.* Neukirchen-Vluyn: Neukirchener, 1979.

Parsons, Talcott. *Essays in Sociological Theory,* rev. ed. Glencoe, N.Y.: Free Press, 1949.

———. *The Social System.* Glencoe, N.Y.: Free Press, 1951.

———. *Social Systems and the Evolution of Action Theory.* New York: Macmillan, 1977. See especially "On Building Social Systems: A Personal History," pp. 22-76.

Parsons, Talcott, K. Shills, et al. *Theories of Society.* Glencoe, N.Y.: Free Press Paperback, 1984.

Parsons, Talcott, and N. J. Smelser. *Economy and Society.* London, New York: Routlege & Regan, 1956.

———. *Sociological Theory and Modern Society.* Glencoe, NY: Free Press Paperback, 1967. See especially "An Outline of the Social System," pp. 297-354.

Patinkin, D. *Money, Interest and Prices.* Evanston, Ill.: Row, Peterson & Co, 1965.

Pearson, Birger A. "1 Thessalonians 2:13-16: A Deutero-Pauline Interpolation." *HThR* 64 (1971): 79-94.

Pfleiderer, Otto. *Der Paulinismus.* Leipzig: Fues 1873; Leipzig: Reisland, 1890.

Plummer, Alfred. *A Critical and Exegetical Commentary on the Second Epistle of St. Paul to the Corinthians.* Edinburgh: T & T Clark, 1951 (ICC 34).

Pradl, Walter. "Das 'Apostelkonzil' und seine Nachgeschicht, dargestellt am Weg des Barnabas." *ThQ* 162 (1982): 45-61.

Pyror, F. L. *The Origins of the Economy.* New York: Academic Press,1977.

Rad, Gerhard von. *Old Testament Theology.* Translated by D. M. G. Stralker. New York: Harper & Row, 1965. German: *Theologie des AT,* 2 vols. München: Kaiser, 1987.

Reitzenstein, Richard. *The Hellenistic Mystery-Religions: Their Basic Ideas and Significance.* Translated by John E. Steely. Pittsburgh Theological Monographs 15. Pittsburgh: Pickwick, 1978. German: *Die hellenistischen Mysterienreligionen.* Darmstadt: Wissenschaftliche Buchgesellschaft, 1980.

Reumann, John. *"Righteousness" in the New Testament: "Justification" in the United States Lutheran-Roman Catholic Dialogue.* Joseph A. Fitzmyer and Jerome Quinn responding. Philadelphia: Fortress, 1982.

Robinson, James M., and Helmut Koester. *Trajectories Through Early Christianity.* Philadelphia: Fortress Press, 1971.

Roesle, Maximilian, and Oskar Cullmann. *Begegnung der Christen.* Evangelische Verlagswerk, Stuttgart, 1960.

Rohden, P. von. "Antonius Felix," *PRE* 1 (1894): 2634-2635.

Rostovtzeff, Michail I. *The Social and Economic History of the Hellenistic World,* 3 vols. Oxford: Clarendon, 1941.

———. *The Social and Economic History of the Roman Empire.* Oxford: Clarendon, 1957.

Schlatter, Adolf. *Die Geschichte der ersten Christenheit.* Gütersloh: Bertelsmann, 1938.

———. *Die Theologie der Apostel.* Stuttgart: Calver, 1977.

———. *Paulus, der Bote Jesu.* Stuttgart: Calver, 1985.

Schlier, Heinrich. *Der Brief an die Galater.* Göttingen: Vandenhoeck & Ruprecht, 1989.

Schmithals, Walter. *Das Kirchliche Apostelamt.* Göttingen: Vandenhoeck & Ruprecht, 1961.

———. "Die Häretiker in Galatien." *ZNW* 46 (1956): 25-67.

———. "Die Irrlehrer des Philipperbriefes." *ZThK* 54 (1957): 297-341.

———. "Die Irrlehrer von Röm. 16,17-20." *StTh* 13,1 (1959): 52ff.

———. "Die Korintherbriefe als Briefsammlung." *ZNW* 64 (1973): 263-88.

———. *Gnosticism in Corinth.* Translated by John E. Steely. Nashville: Abingdon, 1971. German: *Die Gnosis in Korinth.* Göttingen: Vandenhoeck & Ruprecht, 1969.

———. *Jesus Christus in der Verkundigung der Kirche.* Neukirchen-Vluyn, Neukirchener Verlag, 1972. See especially "Das Bekenntnis zu Jesus Christus," pp. 60-79.

———. *Paul and the Gnostics.* Translated by John E. Steely. Nashville: Abingdon, 1972. See especially "On the Composition and Earliest Collection of the Major Epistles of Paul," pp. 239-45. German: *Paulus und die Gnostiker. Untersuchungen zu den kleineren Paulusbriefen.* Hamburg-Bergstedt: Evangelischer, 1965.

———. *Paulus und Jakobus.* Göttingen: Vandenhoeck & Ruprecht, 1963.

———. "Review of Dieter Georgi, *Die Geschichte der Kollekte.*" *ThLZ* 92 (1967): 668-72.

———. "Zur Abfassung und ältesten Sammlung der paulinischen Hauptbriefe." *ZNW* 51 (1950): 225-45.

Schottroff, Luise. "Frauen in der Nachfolge Jesu in neutestamentlicher Zeit." In *Traditionen der Befreiung.* Edited by Willy Schottroff and

Wolfgang Stegemann, pp. 91-133. München, Gelnhausen: Kaiser, Burckhardthaus, Laetare, 1980.
———. "Wie berechtigt ist die feministische Kritik an Paulus? Paulus und die Frauen in den ersten christlichen Gemeinden im Römischen Reich." In *Einwurfe*. Edited by Friedrich-Wilhelm Marquardt et al., pp. 94-111. München: Kaiser, 1985.
Schottroff, Luise, and Willy Schottroff. *Die Macht der Auferstehung: Sozialgeschichtliche Bibelauslegungen*. München: Kaiser, 1988.
Schrage, Wolfgang. "Ekklesia und Synagoge." *ZThK* 60 (1963): 178-202.
Schubert, Paul. *Form and Function of the Pauline Thanksgivings*. Berlin: Töpelmann, 1939.
Schürer, Emil. *The History of the Jewish People in the Age of Jesus Christ (175 B.C.–A.D. 135)*. 3 volumes. Revised by Geza Vermes, Fergus Millar, and Matthew Black. Edinburgh: T & T Clark, 1987.
Schüssler-Fiorenza, Elisabeth. *In Memory of Her: A Feminist Theological Reconstruction of Christian Origins*. New York: Crossroad, 1983.
Schwank, Benedikt. "Der sogenannte Brief an Gallio und die Datierung des 1.Thess." *BZNF* 15 (1971): 265-66.
Schwartz, Eduard, "Noch einmal der Tod der Söhne Zebedäi." *ZNW* 11 (1910): 89-104.
———. "Zur Chronologie des Paulus." *BZNF* 15 (1971).
Schweitzer, Albert. *The Mysticism of Paul the Apostle*. New York: Holt, 1931. German: *Die Mystik des Apostels Paulus*. Tübingen: Franckl, 1981.
———. *Paul and His Interpreters: A Critical History*. New York: Macmillan, 1951.
Schweizer, Eduard. *Church Order in the New Testament*. London: SCM, 1961. German: *Gemeinde und Gemeindeordnung im Neuen Testament*. Zürich: Zwingli, 1962.
Seidensticker, Philipp. *Lebendiges Opfer. (Röm. 12,1)*. Münster: Aschendorff, 1954
Shaw, Graham. *The Cost of Authority: Manipulation and Freedom in the NT*. Philadelphia: Fortress, 1983.
Simmel, Georg. *Philosophie des Geldes*. Berlin: Dunker & Humbolt, 1958.
Smelser, N. J. *The Sociology of Economic Life*. Englewood Cliffs, N.J.: Prentice Hall, 1965.
Smith, Adam. *An Inquiry into the Nature and the Causes of the Wealth of the Nations (1776)*, 2 vols. Edited by R. A. Seligman. New York: Dutton, 1910.
———. *Lectures on Justice, Police, Revenue, and Arms*. (Lectures of 1763). Oxford: Clarendon, 1896.
———. *The Theory of Moral Sentiments*, 2 vols. (1739), new ed. Oxford, Clarendon, 1976.

Soden, Hans von. *Urchristentum und Geschichte I.* Tübingen: Mohr, 1951. See especially "Sakrament und Ethik bei Paulus," pp. 239-75.
Spitta, Friedrich. "Die neutestamentliche Grundlage der Ansicht von E. Schwartz über den Tod der Söhne Zebedäi." *ZNW* 11 (1910): 39-58.
Stählin, Gustav. "*ἴσος, ἰσότης, ἰσοτίμος*," *TDNT* 3, pp. 343-56.
Stauffer, Ethelbert. "Petrus und Jakobus in Jerusalem." In *Begegnung der Christen* (F. O. Karrer). Edited by M. Roesle and O. Cullmann, pp. 361-72. Stuttgart: Evangelische Verlangsanstalt, 1960.
Stendahl, Krister. *Paul Among Jews and Gentiles.* Philadelphia: Fortress, 1976.
Strathmann, Hermann. "*λειτουργέω*," *TDNT* 4, pp. 221-38.
Strobel, August. "Das Aposteldekret in Galatien: Zur Situation von Gal 1 und 2," *NTS* 20 (1974): 177-90.
Strecker, Georg. "Christentum und Judentum in den ersten beiden Jahrhunderten." *EvTh* 16 (1956): 458-77.
———. "Die sogenannte zweite Jerusalemreise des Paulus (Act. 11,27-30)." *ZNW* 53 (1962): 67-77.
———. *Eschaton und Historie.* Göttingen: Vandenhoeck & Ruprecht, 1979.
Stuhlmacher, Peter. *Der Brief an die Römer.* Göttingen: Vandenhoeck & Ruprecht, 1989.
Suggs, M. Jack. "Concerning the Date of Paul's Macedonian Ministry." *NT* 4 (1960): 60-68.
Suhl, Alfred. *Paulus und seine Briefe: Ein Beitrag zur paulinischen Chronologie.* Gütersloh: Mohn, 1975.
Sundkler, B. "Jésus et les païens." *RHPhR* 16 (1936): 462-99.
Talbert, Charles H. "Again: Paul's Visits to Jerusalem." *NT* 9 (1967): 26-40.
Theissen, Gerd. *The Social Setting of Pauline Christianity.* Philadelphia: Fortress, 1982.
Theobald, Michael. "Die überströmende Gnade: Studien zu einem paulinischen Motivfeld." Dissertation. Bonn: Rheinische Friedrich Wilhelm Universität, 1980.
Thraede, Klaus. "Gleichheit." *RAC* 10 (1979): 122-64.
Volz, Paul. *Die Eschatologie der judischen Gemeinde.* Tübingen: Mohr, 1934.
Wedderburn, A. J. M. "Keeping up with Recent Studies: VII. Some Recent Pauline Chronologies." *ET* 92 (1981): 103-8.
Wegenast, Klaus. *Das Verständnis der Tradition bei Paulus und in den Deuteropaulinen.* Neukirchen-Vluyn: Neukirchener, 1962.
Weiss, Johannes. *Das Urchristentum.* Edited by Rudolf Knopf. Göttingen: Vandenhoeck & Ruprecht, 1917.
———. *Der erste Korintherbrief.* Göttingen: Vandenhoeck & Ruprecht, 1970.

Weiss, Johannes. *The History of Primitive Christianity.* Translated by Frederick C. Grant. New York: Wilson & Erickson, 1937. Republished as *Earliest Christianity,* 2 vols. Edited by Frederick C. Grant. New York: Harper, 1959.

———. "Zum Märtyrertod der Zebedaiden." *ZNW* 11 (1910): 167.

Weizsäcker, Carl. *Das apostolische Zeitalter der christlichen Kirche.* Tübingen: Mohr, 1902.

Wellhausen, Julius. *Kritische Analyse der Apostelgeschichte.* Berlin: Weidmann, 1914.

Wenschkewitz, Hans. *Die Spiritualisierung der Kultusbegriffe.* Leipzig: Pfeifer, 1932.

Wetter, Gillis P. *Charis.* Leipzig: Hinrichs, 1913.

Wetter, Ulrich. *Griechische Ostraka.* Leipzig and Berlin: Giesecte & Devrient, 1895.

Wilckens, Ulrich. *Der Brief an die Römer,* 3 vols. Köln, Neukirchen-Vluyn: Benziger, Neukirchener, 1978-1982.

Windisch, Hans. *Der zweite Korintherbrief.* Göttingen: Vandenhoeck & Ruprecht, 1970

Zetterberg, H. L. *Social Theory and Social Practice.* New York: Bedminster, 1962.